The Resources of Critique

In Memoriam

Paul Foot
(1937–2004)

The Resources of Critique

Alex Callinicos

polity

First published in 2006 by Polity Press

Polity Press
65 Bridge Street
Cambridge CB2 1UR, UK

Polity Press
350 Main Street
Malden, MA 02148, USA

ISBN: 0-7456-3160-6
ISBN: 0-7456-3161-4 (pb)

A catalogue record for this book is available from the British Library.

Typeset in 11 on 13pt Sabon
by SNP Best-set Typesetter Ltd, Hong Kong
Printed and bound in India by Replika Press

The publisher has used its best endeavours to ensure that the URLs for external websites referred to in this book are correct and active at the time of going to press. However, the publisher has no responsibility for the websites and can make no guarantee that a site will remain live or that the content is or will remain appropriate.

Every effort has been made to trace all copyright holders, but if any have been inadvertently overlooked the publishers will be pleased to include any necessary credits in any subsequent reprint or edition.

For further information on Polity, visit our website: www.polity.co.uk

Contents

Preface and
Acknowledgements

I conceived *The Resources of Critique* in the summer before the attacks on New York and Washington. Distractions caused by the political backwash from 11 September 2001 were the main reason why the writing, and hence the publication, of this book were somewhat delayed. But this proved to be, on the whole, a useful postponement. The aim of *The Resources of Critique* is to explore the philosophical presuppositions of social critique in the political and intellectual conjuncture defined by the revival of resistance to global capitalism since the protests at Seattle in November 1999. This enterprise has, I think, been helped rather than hindered by the focus imposed by having to live in the shadow of the global state of exception into which, after the era of good feelings in the 1990s, the world was plunged on 11 September. I write these words in the days following the London bombings of 7 July 2005. This attack on the city where I have made my home for nearly thirty years is, like 9/11 itself and the destruction of Falluja by American forces in November 2004, yet another reminder of the price that this emergency is extracting from the innocent.

The Brazilian Marxist Emir Sader pointed out to me that the title of this book echoes that of Raymond Williams's *Resources of Hope*. This wasn't intended – though Williams's work is one with which any sane practitioner of social critique would be happy to be associated, but it illustrates the deep channels through which influences flow. No doubt many have contributed to my thinking in this book. One important contribution of which I am aware is that of a network of co-thinkers and friends centred both intellectually and, to a large degree, geographically on Paris – among them Daniel Bensaïd, Sebastian Budgen, Stathis Kouvelakis, Peter Thomas, and Christine Vivier. I'm sure that many of the hares that run through *The Resources of Critique* were set off by some shouting match with these dramatis personae in a Paris bistro.

I have also benefited from being able to try out some of the arguments of this book on a variety of occasions – notably the Marx International Congresses held at Nanterre in September 2001 and October 2004, the Returns to Marx conferences organized by the European Forum for Philosophy at the Tate Modern in London in June 2002 and the Collège Internationale de Philosophie in Paris in February 2003, lectures given while Benjamin Meaker Visiting Professor of Sociology at the University of Bristol in February and March 2003, and the Political Theory Workshop at the University of York in February 2005. I am particularly grateful to Jean-Jacques Lecercle for his philosophical guidance and hospitality at the 2004 Marx Congress, to Tom Baldwin and Sue Mendus for their responses to the paper I gave in York, and to Anindya Bhattacharyya and two anonymous referees for Polity Press for their comments on *The Resources of Critique* in draft. It goes without saying that only I am responsible for the use I have made of all this help.

As usual, Polity itself has been both patient and professional in all the dealings I have had with them over this book. I would like especially to thank David Held, Rachel Kerr, Ellen McKinlay, and Caroline Richmond.

Sam Ashman has been remarkably forbearing while I wrote *The Resources of Critique*. She herself has been as absorbed in her own writing, so we have had a non-aggression pact that has sometimes even extended to mutual support.

This is the last book I wrote while teaching politics at the University of York. I would like to thank all my friends and colleagues there not simply for allowing me the time to work on this book, but for all the kindness, support, and stimulation they provided in the nearly twenty-four years I was at York.

The worst thing I have so far discovered about getting old is the tendency of the people one loves to start dying. The latest is Paul Foot, whose sudden death in the summer of 2004 was the occasion of a great outpouring of grief across the British left. Paul was a wonderful man, who managed to embody in his own life and work the trajectory of revolutionary democracy from the Levellers to Marxism. While finishing *The Resources of Critique* I happened to read Paul's last, very personal book, *The Vote*. I was very touched to find some of my own books cited there. So I am repaying the compliment by dedicating *The Resources of Critique* to him. At a time when empires constantly invoke the language of freedom and democracy to legitimize conquest and domination it is good to remember someone who recalled these words to something closer to their original meanings.

I did not yet know what view I had of all this. It still wasn't clear to me whether I should be for or against it. But how does anybody form a decision to be against and persist against? When does he choose and when is he chosen instead?

Saul Bellow, *The Adventures of Augie March*

Introduction

My starting point is what might be thought of as a Kantian question: how is transcendence possible? I do not mean here 'transcendence' in the sense in which it is used, for example, in orthodox Christian theology, where transcendence is an attribute of a God distinct from and superior to his creation.[1] Rather 'transcendence' is understood here in the more basic sense that derives from its Latin root word *'transcendere'*, to climb over or beyond or to surmount; thus the oldest meanings given to 'transcend' in the *OED* involve passing or going beyond some physical or immaterial limit. Transcendence in the sense in which I am interested in it embraces in particular innovation in the social, political, and intellectual realms. How are we able to go beyond the limits set by existing practices and beliefs and produce something new?

It is not hard to find answers in the prevailing culture that trivialize the problem by privileging innovation. Thus the reigning ideology of neo-liberalism asserts that the institutions of liberal capitalism are uniquely suited to release distinctively human powers, in particular those of creativity. So – once the right institutions and policies are in place, as specified by the structural adjustment programmes favoured by the International Monetary Fund and the World Bank and by the codes of 'good governance' drafted by these and kindred international institutions – there should predictably follow a welter of innovations (and a rise in productivity and in the rate of output growth) reflecting the liberation of human creativity. The fact that more than twenty years of the application of such remedies to the global South should have produced economic stagnation, with the signal exception of the notably illiberal variant of capitalism that has developed in China, is the kind of empirical anomaly that exponents of such ideologies are usually able to ignore, since what sustains them is less the disinterested search for the truth than the prevailing relations of domination.[2]

A similar trivialization of transcendence is to be found in neo-liberalism's junior partner in the contemporary intellectual scene, the kind of vulgar postmodernism that became institutionally embedded in the Anglophone academy in the last two decades of the twentieth century. Jean-François Lyotard, for example, in the founding text of postmodernism, argues that modernity has been surpassed as a result of the ' "atomization" of the social relation into flexible networks of language games' whose comprehension requires 'agonistics as a founding principle', since 'to speak is to fight, in the sense of playing'. The relationship between language games is thus conflictual; hence Lyotard rejects Jürgen Habermas's theory of communicative action, according to which understanding presupposes an implicit orientation towards agreement: 'Such consensus does violence to the heterogeneity of language games. And invention is always born of dissension.'[3] Lyotard famously defines postmodernity as the collapse of the grand narratives of the Enlightenment, Hegel, and Marx: in place of these totalizing interpretations of the whole course of human history, we have the proliferation of 'little narratives' (*petits récits*), fragmentary discourses that instantiate the inherent heterogeneity and conflictuality of language games. Transcendence is thus here an immanent potentiality of language itself, and one moreover that is liberated by the fragmented, mobile social structure of postmodernity.

There are, of course, major differences between neo-liberalism and postmodernism. Most obviously, the former treats the subject as a dynamic unity: it is the creativity inherent in the individual human person that is liberated under capitalism. Postmodernists tend, by contrast, to draw on the critique of the sovereign, coherent subject developed in French '1968 thought', notably by Louis Althusser, Gilles Deleuze, Jacques Derrida, and Michel Foucault. But there are, nevertheless, interesting parallels between the two modes of thought. First, innovation (Lyotard prefers the term 'invention') is dependent on conflict among individuals, whether this be conceptualized as market competition, as it is in liberal capitalist ideology, or as the more abstract 'agonistic' play that Lyotard argues is inherent in and between language games. Secondly, contemporary social structures are conceived as systematically promoting innovation, either because this is held to be a property of liberal-capitalist institutions or because of the alleged shift to postmodern uncertainty and fragmentation.

In my view both these approaches trivialize transcendence by normalizing it. Treating innovation as a routine consequence of prevailing social relations has the effect of equating transcendence with the kinds of changes that are indeed a chronic feature of our societies – the improvement or (much more rarely) invention of techniques and variations in lifestyle that are, in turn, materially supported by modifications in the range of goods and services on the market. Our life-experience is undeniably altered by such changes, but they leave in place not simply the distribution of social and economic power, but also the broader styles of thought and forms of sensibility prevailing in our societies. There is then a striking contrast between widespread and frequent superficial variations that are the subject of endless but ephemeral media hype and deep-seated underlying stability, if not stasis.

This contrast presents a problem for neither neo-liberals nor postmodernists. For the former, technological modifications and lifestyle changes just are what innovation is in societies whose institutional structures broadly correspond to the requirements of human nature – societies, that is, that have reached the End of History that Francis Fukuyama claimed the triumph of liberal capitalism would bring. For postmodernists too, micro-variations are precisely what we should expect once what Lyotard calls 'the heteromorphous nature of language games' is properly recognized and given social expression; they mark our escape from the terrorist and totalitarian consequences of the grand narratives that, in pursuing total transformation, sought to corral the variety of existence into a coerced uniformity.[4] Coherent though both these positions seem to be, they are unlikely to satisfy those sensitive to, and eager to go beyond, the limits set by prevailing socio-economic structures – those of (predominantly) liberal capitalism, a totality whose presence as the horizon of the plurality and invention celebrated by Lyotard he ignores.

As this indicates, the problem of transcendence is political as well as philosophical. One sub-theme of postmodernism is that social critique – which depends on the possibility of transcendence, since it thematizes the limitations of existing social relations and therefore if only implicitly adverts to the necessity of surpassing these relations – is no longer possible. Thus Jean Baudrillard argues that in a society constituted by simulation, where the prevalence of images marks the abolition of the distinction between representations and the real, the concept of alienation no longer has any pertinence. In the tradition of Hegel and Marx, a subject is alienated when she loses some or all of her essential powers. To diagnose alienation is to draw a contrast between the present situation, where the subject may be misled by appearances into failing to recognize her loss, and a counterfactual condition of authenticity where she has all the powers proper to her. But such a contrast ceases to be meaningful once the distinction between representation and the real, appearance and essence, has been abolished. Consequently, Baudrillard argues, '[a]ll our problems today as civilized beings originate . . . not in an excess of alienation, but a disappearance of alienation in favour of a maximum transparency between subjects.' Instead of alienation giving rise to critique and revolt, we have universal indifference: 'It is no longer a question of believing or not believing in the images which pass before our eyes. We refract reality and signs without believing in them.' This metaphysical indifference subtends 'the more general problem of the indifference of institutions or of the political, etc., to themselves.'[5]

Pace Baudrillard, the turn of the millennium was marked not by a further descent into the black hole of indifference, but by the emergence of new international movements of mass resistance to capitalist globalization and (after 9/11) imperial war. Moreover, social critique enjoyed a remarkable renaissance as such figures as Walden Bello, Pierre Bourdieu, Noam Chomsky, Susan George, Michael Hardt, Naomi Klein, George Monbiot, Toni Negri, John Pilger, and Arundhati Roy found mass readerships for their diagnoses of what Bourdieu memorably called *la misère du monde* – the wretchedness of existence to which the victims of neoliberalism and Anglo-American militarism are condemned. Nor have these movements represented a simple repetition of past radicalizations. On the one hand, the ideological influence of

Marxism and of the classical left was far weaker than it had been perhaps since the Revolutions of 1848. On the other hand, new unprecedented forms of international mobilization and coordination developed, through protests such as those at Seattle (1999) and Genoa (2001) and the extraordinary venues for debate and mutual contamination offered by the World Social Forum and spin-offs such as the European Social Forum.[6]

What Luc Boltanski and Eve Chiapello call, with respect to France, the 'renewal of social critique' in response to the neo-liberal offensive forms the context in which I wish to address the problem of transcendence.[7] This book is not a general treatise on the conditions of innovation – a massive, perhaps impossible, conceivably insane undertaking. My concern is more specific: I seek to address the conditions under which social critique – understood as a theoretical genre that both thematizes and seeks to surpass the limits set by prevailing social relations – is possible today. 'Today' refers to a specific historical conjuncture – the world after the end of the Cold War, in which the global dominance of liberal capitalism and the unchallenged hegemony of the United States have produced new crises and new forms of contestation. 'Today' also denotes a specific intellectual constellation, in which new styles of social critique have emerged – styles that go beyond exposés of specific institutions or policies to offer, among other things, what amount to philosophical justifications of their own existence.

Consequently part I of this book is devoted to a critical assessment of what seem to me the most important of these styles. In chapter 1 I discuss formalist theories of modernity, of which the most influential contemporary version has been developed by Jürgen Habermas, though I also consider the interesting variant developed by Jacques Bidet. Chapter 2 is devoted to French critical sociology – not only the work of Pierre Bourdieu, but also the more relativist version developed by Luc Boltanski and Eve Chiapello. In chapter 3 I discuss two contemporary philosophers of the event, Alain Badiou and Slavoj Žižek. Finally, in chapter 4 I turn to their antithesis, the vitalism of Toni Negri.

As this summary makes clear, the focus of part I is on contemporary French thought. Not all the thinkers reviewed are French: Habermas is German, Negri Italian, and Žižek Slovenian. But the latter two have been active participants in French philosophical culture, while, although no one would for a moment think of Habermas as anything but very German, one of his most important books – *The Philosophical Discourse of Modernity* – is a critical genealogy of French poststructuralism. My reason for concentrating on a cluster of theoretical interventions radiating from Paris is not that somehow the French have a monopoly of contemporary critical thought. On the contrary, in the crucial area of political economy, Anglophone Marxists are making a more important contribution.[8] But it seems as if the contemporary problem of transcendence has to be framed in terms defined by twentieth-century French thought. Rather than offering a general survey of contemporary styles of critical social theory, I have selected a group of thinkers who can be conceived as being in dialogue with one another in seeking to address this problem.

One way of thinking about this is as follows. The complaint I made about both neo-liberalism and postmodernism earlier was that neither takes into account the limits set to innovation by socio-economic structures. More broadly one could think about this as the burden of materiality: the extent to which imagination and action are confined by the material structures (physical as well as social but especially for these purposes social) that support them. Well, how then is this burden consistent with the possibility of transcendence? The dominant answer in contemporary French thought is that transcendence comes about through the negation of Being. Badiou offers the most systematic statement of this answer in his conception of truth-events as a subtraction from Being, emerging from the void, out of nothing. But arguably this is simply the most powerful and elegant version of an idea that has in different forms been held by various thinkers. Jean-Paul Sartre, for example, in the first volume of the *Critique of Dialectical Reason*, conceives the formation of a group-in-fusion as a sudden, literally apocalyptical event that breaks up the 'practico-inert' – the solid density of socio-economic structures that are themselves merely a kind of sedimentation of practice – only itself eventually to succumb to institutionalization and sink back into the practico-inert. Somewhat analogously Cornelius Castoriadis in *The Imaginary Institution of Society* posits a cyclical process in which creative irruptions surge up from the imagination only eventually to give rise to a new set of institutions that limits further innovation.

Even Derrida's concept of *différance* carries some of the same weight. Unlike vulgar postmodernists, Derrida does not simply celebrate difference. Difference involves a play of absence *and presence*: in other words, the process of differentiation inherent in, for example, signification includes the positing of a moment of presence – that is, of immediate access to the real – even though this moment is never attained but is instead constantly deferred as the transcendental signified. The neologism '*différance*' is intended to capture this necessary coexistence of absence and presence – presence is something that is necessarily posited but always deferred. In this sense, the difference, plurality, and heterogeneity celebrated by Lyotard cannot escape the burden of what Derrida calls the 'metaphysics of presence' – the idea, in other words, constitutive of the Western philosophical tradition that thought can attain direct unmediated access to the real. Finally, the well-known problems that Foucault faced in his 'middle period' (that of *Discipline and Punish* and the first volume of *The History of Sexuality*) in explaining how resistance can be inherent in power-relations when (according to him) these relations are inescapable and indeed, through, for example, the apparatus of the disciplines, constitute the very individual persons who are potentially the subjects of resistance imply a similar conception of Being as confinement.

There is, however, a minority view that refuses to conceive Being as closure. According to this position, held most notably by Deleuze and by Negri, innovation happens not despite but because of Being – thanks, as it were, to its generosity. This thought is expressed, for example, in the famous closing paragraph of *Empire*. Hardt and Negri write:

> There is an ancient legend that might serve to illuminate the future life of communist militancy: that of Saint Francis of Assisi. Consider his work. To denounce the poverty of the multitude he adopted that common condition and discovered the ontological power of a new society. The communist militant does the same, identifying in the common condition of the multitude its enormous wealth. Francis in opposition to nascent capitalism refused every instrumental discipline, and in opposition to the mortification of the flesh (in poverty and in the constituted order) he posed a joyous life, including all of being and nature, the animals, sister moon, brother sun, the birds of the field, the poor and exploited humans,

together against the will of power and corruption. Once again in postmodernity we find ourselves in Francis's situation, posing against the misery of power the joy of being. This is a revolution that no power will control – because biopower and communism, cooperation and revolution remain together, in love, simplicity, and also innocence. This is the irrepressible lightness and joy of being communist.[9]

Commentary on this passage has tended to focus on Hardt's and Negri's attempt to recruit the Christian concept of love to the cause of communism (or vice versa). But implicit here (and ruling out the possibility that they might be sliding towards any kind of theism) is a vitalist ontology invoked in phrases such as 'the joy of being' that is heavily indebted to Deleuze and his collaborator Félix Guattari in such works as *Mille plateaux*. One of my main concerns in this book, then, is to explore the polarity created if one counterposes Badiou and Negri – between conceiving Being as a barrier to transcendence and regarding transcendence as an effusion of Being's plenitude. Neither of these positions seems to me tenable: Badiou's ontology reduces transcendence to a miracle and licenses a version of the decisionism pervasive in contemporary left-liberal intellectual culture, while Negri's vitalism relies on philosophically indefensible assumptions and leads to a politics of passive waiting.

But if neither Badiou nor Negri delivers the goods, and if the other thinkers surveyed in part I also fail to do so, how is the possibility of transcendence to be explained? I sketch out an answer in part II. It has three main strands: critical realist ontology (chapter 5), a Marxist theory of social contradiction (chapter 6), and substantive principle(s) of justice (chapter 7). My strategy here introduces two more intellectual traditions into the argument. The first is Marxism. As I have already observed, Marxism has been relatively marginal to the contemporary revival of social critique and anti-capitalist contestation. The reasons are obvious enough – the political decline of both the far left and the Communist parties from the mid-1970s onwards, the victory of neo-liberalism during the 1980s, the collapse of the Soviet Union, the intellectual challenges posed by poststructuralism and its avatars, for example, postmodernism and postcolonial thought. But neither singly nor combined did this series of causes produce a definitive knockout, any more than had those behind the many preceding

crises of Marxism. There are plenty of signs of a renewal of intellectual energy and wider interest in Marxist theory, and many of
the thinkers surveyed – most obviously Badiou, Bidet, Habermas,
and Negri – conceive themselves as continuing what they consider
to be valid in Marxism; with the exception of Žižek, they can
indeed be described collectively as 'post-Marxist' in the sense that
Ernesto Laclau and Chantal Mouffe give the term – though intellectually indebted to some version or other of Marxism, they seek
to escape what they consider to be its limitations.[10] Not to treat
Marxism as an important reference point in the discussion of transcendence would therefore seem to be a serious mistake and its
profile will rise as my argument unfolds: in particular, how to
understand and to continue Marx's critique of political economy
is a recurring theme in this book. More generally, I try to show
the specific contribution that one strand in this tradition – what
has come to be known as classical Marxism – can make. The critical realist philosophy of science developed by Roy Bhaskar and
others since the 1970s, on which I draw in chapters 6 and 7, itself
bears a deep-seated relationship to Marxism.

The other tradition that I bring to bear in part II is egalitarian
liberalism – in other words, the style of thought inaugurated by
John Rawls's *A Theory of Justice* (1971) and embracing the work
of, among others, Brian Barry, G. A. Cohen, Ronald Dworkin, and
Amartya Sen that has sought to articulate egalitarian principles of
social justice. I have argued elsewhere that this body of work,
though primarily formulated in terms that take for granted the
existence of a market economy, offers valuable philosophical
resources for the contemporary anti-capitalist movement.[11] But I
also think that this body of writing can help to clarify the nature
of social critique. Why this should be so is something that I begin
to explain in chapter 1, in discussing Habermas and Bidet, but that
will only become clear near the end of the book in chapter 7.

One possible objection to this strategy might be that it lumps
together theorists and styles of thought that have nothing to do
with one another. What possibly do Rawls and Negri have in
common, or Davidson and Badiou, or Dworkin and Žižek?
One can indeed have a bit of fun imagining some odd encounters
or juxtapositions. And there is always the risk that a text comes
apart because those about whom one writes have nothing more
in common than the fact that one happens to have read them all.

I don't think that there is much risk of this here. This book is not a survey of schools, but the exploration of a problem – that of transcendence. The thinkers discussed here are chosen because of their relevance to this problem. Moreover, there is an important sense in which the strengths and weaknesses of the most sharply counterposed figures – the Continental critical theorists of part I and the Anglophone egalitarian liberals of chapter 7 – complement one another. There is, as I try to show, a large hole in all the theoretical perspectives discussed in part I (as there is in classical Marxism), where there should be a normative conception of egalitarian justice. The work of egalitarian liberal philosophers over the past generation has given us a much better idea of what such a conception might involve, but it has had very little to say about the kind of social world in which egalitarian justice might be realized, let alone about the ontological presuppositions of the normative ideals these authors seek to articulate – indeed, one of the main thrusts of Rawls's development after *A Theory of Justice* was to seek (in my view unsuccessfully) to detach his argument from any metaphysical entanglements. Badiou, Žižek, and Negri are particularly important because of the consequent way in which they have confronted the ontological questions that Anglophone egalitarian liberals typically seek to evade. The fact that they should all be able find common ground in the space offered by the Marxist critique of political economy (undergirded by a critical realist ontology) is hardly a surprise to anyone who continues to believe, with Fredric Jameson, that Marxism is 'the place of an imperative to totalize' that seeks to integrate the insights offered by other theoretical perspectives into a comprehensive understanding of a world still – indeed, more than ever – dominated by the capitalist mode of production.[12]

At the beginning of this introduction I described the question of transcendence as Kantian. I had in mind the fact that, in the *Critique of Pure Reason*, Kant asks what are the conditions of possibility of mathematics and physics. The answer he gives involves the construction of a transcendental argument that moves from the fact of conscious experience to the necessity of a categorial ordering of this experience as an objective, causally governed natural world. My question – what are the conditions of possibility of transcendence? – may be Kantian, but my answer isn't. It consists in a set of conjectural and, in part, empirical theories that have none of the apodictic character that Kant claims for his transcendental argument. Moreover, there is no deductive relationship between, in particular, the critical realist ontology outlined in chapter 5 and the two other strands of my argument – a Marxist theory of social contradiction and substantive principle(s) of justice. If I am right, all three are mutually consistent and mutually supporting, but the truth of each and the reasons for holding each true are independent of those of the others. This approach reflects a broadly naturalistic approach to philosophy, where the latter is conceived as continuous with the sciences and its sentences can claim no greater authority than those of the sciences. But some of the reasons for finding such a conception of philosophy attractive should become clearer when I discuss critical realism in part II.

As the foregoing should have made amply plain, this is a philosophical book. It proceeds by arguments that are intended to address some hard questions and that draw on interpretations of often difficult texts. But it does not follow that this book is conceived as purely a work of scholarship. Many of the theorists discussed here are also political actors – most obviously Negri throughout his career, but consider also Bourdieu's interventions from the 1995 public sector strikes onwards. I too have been actively involved in the contemporary movements against corporate globalization and imperial war. But activism is not enough. There are moments when reflection is necessary on the presuppositions of our beliefs and practices. Philosophy specializes in such reflection, both for its own sake and in the hope that conceptual clarification may help to make our lives better. Such, at any rate, is the hope informing *The Resources of Critique*.

Part I

Four Kinds of Impasse

1

Modernity and its Promises: Habermas and Bidet

1.1 Between sociological suspicion and the rule of law: Jürgen Habermas

What are the philosophical presuppositions of the new wave of social criticism? On the face of it, the very idea of critique implies some tacit or explicit appeal to a conception of the good or to a set of moral principles in terms of which liberal capitalism is found wanting. Yet one striking feature of the contemporary intellectual scene is the gap between, on the one hand, the kind of normative political philosophy that concerns itself with such conceptions and principles and their social implications and and, on the other, explanatory social theory, which seeks to uncover the mechanisms responsible for the injustice and suffering that continue to surround us. This theoretical dislocation is thematized in two of the most important contributions to social theory to have recently emerged from France – Jacques Bidet's *Théorie générale* and Luc Boltanski's and Eve Chiapello's *Le Nouvel Esprit du capitalisme*, both published in 1999. As Bidet puts it,

[c]ontemporary critical thought seems constantly to oscillate between resort to the sociologies of suspicion to which Marx opened the way, when it wants to think the world as it is, and a fascination with contractualism, with the doctrine of the rule of law, with the rights of man and of the citizen, when it seeks to formulate a project for society.[1]

The discrepancy between the explanatory and the normative in social thought is, of course, an old one. Both Marx and Weber in different ways register the existence of the problem, but fail to resolve it. One reason why it might seem especially acute today is because normative political philosophy has taken a quantum leap forward in the past generation. Egalitarian liberalism, whose founding text is John Rawls's *A Theory of Justice*, has greatly advanced our understanding of the prerequisites of a conception of social justice that would satisfy the demands of both equality and liberty – though, as so often in philosophy, progress has often consisted in arriving at a clearer insight into the difficulties of meeting these requirements.[2]

Egalitarian liberalism itself offers some conceptual resources by means of which it might be possible to connect explanatory and normative considerations. Thus, according to Rawls, the subject of a theory of justice (in the sense of that to which its principles are applied) is what he calls the basic structure of society – that is, the institutional arrangements that determine the distribution of social goods in the society in question. As Brian Barry has pointed out, this concept bears at least a family resemblance to key social-theoretical notions – in Marx, the relations of production, that is, the structures that determine access to productive resources, in Weber, the constellation of power-relations responsible for the distribution of life-chances.[3] Yet this point of contact remains largely unexplored.

In this chapter I consider the recent attempts by two contemporary philosophers, Jürgen Habermas and Jacques Bidet, to overcome the gap between critical social theory and normative political philosophy. Both stem from (very different) variants of Marxism – respectively the critical theory of the Frankfurt School and Althusserian Marxism. Both, however, seek to transcend Marx by moving from his critique of the capitalist mode of production to a more general theory of modernity. And both, albeit in quite distinct ways, seek in this theory to accommodate the requirements of both the explanatory and the normative. Though both these undertakings are, in my view, unsuccessful, by taking a closer look at them I hope to clarify the issues that will be addressed in the rest of this book.

Habermas has, of course, been a towering figure on the Western intellectual scene since the 1960s. *The Philosophical Discourse of*

Modernity (1985), perhaps his greatest book, established him as the premier philosopher of the Western left. This critical history of poststructuralism drew on and developed the broader account of modernity developed in *The Theory of Communicative Action* (1981).[4] Central to this account is a critique of Marxism (including the early Frankfurt School) for its reliance on the 'philosophy of consciousness', conceiving the subject as monological, constituted not by its relationship to other subjects, but by the struggle with nature that is expressed by the development of the productive forces given explanatory primacy in classical Marxism. Once the founders of the Frankfurt School, Max Horkheimer and Theodor Adorno, had radicalized Marx's critique of capitalism into a broader denunciation of the instrumental rationality that, following Weber, they regarded as intrinsic to any human appropriation of nature, then reason itself seemed compromised by its imbrication in relations of domination of both the natural world and human beings. Horkheimer and Adorno thereby pulled the rug from under their own feet, for how could reason then be used to criticize the very processes it had helped to produce? As Axel Honneth puts it, in Horkheimer's and Adorno's *Dialectic of Enlightenment* (1947), '[p]hilosophy is the reflective form of a critical theory that discovers in each step of conceptual reflection a piece of the continued history of domination. Therefore, strictly speaking, it prohibits itself.'[5]

Habermas seeks to resolve this dilemma by moving from a monologic to a dialogic, or communicative, conception of subjectivity and rationality; he enjoins us to

> give up the paradigm of the philosophy of consciousness – namely a subject that represents objects and toils with them – in favour of the paradigm of linguistic philosophy – namely that of intersubjective understanding or communication – and put the cognitive-instrumental aspect of reason in its proper place as part of a more encompassing *communicative rationality*.[6]

The philosophy of language developed in *The Theory of Communicative Action* is based on the claim that linguistic understanding presupposes an implicit orientation towards uncoerced agreement between speaker and hearer. Every speech act therefore implies the acceptance by the addressee of the 'redeemable validity claim' involved in the utterance. The speaker thus takes responsibility for, if necessary, providing the justification that would secure her hearer's agreement. This analysis privileges communicative action over other forms of human action, and reduces instrumental rationality – where reason is employed to determine the best means for achieving a given goal – to simply one mode of 'a subordinated moment' in a complex and primordially communicative rationality.[7] Habermas's theory of modernity proceeds along broadly similar lines. Following Weber, Durkheim, and Parsons he conceives modernization as essentially a process of differentiation. Its effect is to break up the lifeworld, the shared pre-understandings that form the taken-for-granted background presupposed by every speech act and, that, in the shape of tradition and religion, served in pre-modern societies as the cement of social life. On the one hand, science, law, morality, and art separate out into distinct 'cultural spheres'. On the other hand, there is the differentiation of system and lifeworld: the economy and polity separate out into specialized sub-systems that are no longer coordinated by linguistic communication but through their own media, respectively money and power. Habermas differs with Marx in that he regards these developments as an unvarnished good and, moreover, as an inescapable feature of modernity. Nevertheless, he warns that these can go too far: 'capitalist modernization follows a pattern such that cognitive-instrumental rationality surges beyond the bounds of the economy and the state into other, communicatively structured areas of life and achieves a dominance there at the expense of moral-political and aesthetic-practical rationality.'[8] This 'colonization of the lifeworld' represents the rational kernel in the critiques of modernity offered by Weber, the early Frankfurt School, and poststructuralists such as Foucault, but the remedy lies not in the refusal of reason or modernity but in the development of institutional means that can return the market and the state to their proper domains and protect the lifeworld from further invasions.

Granted this diagnosis, it is not surprising that Habermas should have subsequently devoted a major book to a philosophical sociology of law and democracy. It is on this text, *Between Fact and Norm* (1992), that I concentrate here. As we have already seen, Habermas regards the differentiation of law and morality as a consequence of the modernization process: 'at the post-metaphysical level of justification, legal and moral rules are *simul-*

taneously differentiated from traditional and ethical life and appear *side-by-side* as two different but complementary kinds of action norms.' But he further claims that law performs a privileged role in modern differentiated societies, where it 'functions as a hinge between system and lifeworld'. It is through transmission via the law that claims made in ordinary language become readable in the sub-systems of market and state: 'Normatively substantive messages can circulate *throughout society* only in the language of law. Without their translation into the complex legal code that is equally open to lifeworld and system, these messages would fall on deaf ears in media-steered spheres of action.'[9]

To understand why Habermas believes that law can play this critical integrative role, we need to triangulate his own account with what he regards as two mistaken approaches to law. The first is what Habermas tends to call the 'natural law' tradition, but which is perhaps better thought of as the contractualism common to Locke, Rousseau, Kant, Paine, and the Rawls of *A Theory of Justice*: here the demands of political justice and constitutional order are conceived as inferences from a moral theory that seeks to establish under what conditions free and equal human persons can exercise the rights they have by virtue of being such persons. One reason why this position is untenable, according to Habermas, is that, thanks to the success of the process of disenchantment constitutive of modernity in undermining the religious foundations of pre-modern world-views, liberal societies are confronted with what the later Rawls calls 'the fact of reasonable pluralism':

> A modern democratic society is characterized not simply by a pluralism of comprehensive religious, philosophical, and moral doctrines but by a pluralism of incompatible yet reasonable comprehensive doctrines. No one of these doctrines is affirmed by citizens generally. Nor should one expect that in the foreseeable future one of them, or some other reasonable doctrine, will ever be affirmed by all, or nearly all, citizens.[10]

In what Habermas calls the 'post-metaphysical' frame of thought that is one of our main debts to the Enlightenment, the exercise of reason gives rise to a plurality of different, equally defensible world-views. Moreover, with the development of modern social theory, the Enlightenment produced an alternative approach that also subverted 'the tradition of rational natural law'. Habermas describes the transformation of the concept of civil society begun by Smith and Ricardo, developed further by Hegel, and completed by Marx:

> Having begun as an ensemble of *authorizing* conditions that made freedom possible – conditions under which individuals could voluntarily and consciously join in association and bring the social process under their common control – it became an *anonymous* system independent of the intentions of unconsciously sociated individuals, a system that followed its own logic and subjected society as a whole to the economically decoded imperatives of its self-stabilization.[11]

Now, while Habermas thinks that this 'realistic model' of social relations is ultimately untenable, he also believes it contains a kernel of truth (as indeed he does the rival 'idealistic model'). As we have seen, he conceives modernity as functionally differentiated as a result of the emergence of independent cultural spheres and the separation out of the specialized sub-systems of the economy and polity. But what stops this society falling apart? Habermas follows Talcott Parsons in rejecting the idea that modern liberal societies can be held together simply by individual actors pursuing their own interests through some version of Adam Smith's hidden hand. In the conditions of modernity, social cohesion depends on normative integration – that is, on citizens sharing a common set of norms and values: 'If, as I assume along with Parsons and Durkheim, complexes of action cannot be stabilized simply on the basis of the reciprocal influence that success-oriented actors exert on one another, then *in the final analysis* society must be integrated through communicative action.'[12]

The phrase 'communicative action' here indicates the particular spin that Habermas puts on the concept of normative integration. Despite Habermas's debt to Parsons (to whom he owes, for example, the idea that power and money are the media of functionally differentiated sub-systems), he is highly critical of the way in which the systems approach developed in the latter's writings after the Second World War, and taken considerably further by Niklas Luhmann, tends to reduce law and communicative action more generally to objective social functions:

At the end of a long process of sociological disillusionment, systems theory has cleared away the last remains of the normativism found in modern natural law. Having withdrawn into an auto-poietic system, law stands before the defamiliarized sociological gaze and is stripped of all normative connotations, which in the final analysis refer to the self-organization of a legal community. Described as an auto-poietic system, a narcissistically marginalized law can react only to its own problems that are at most externally occasioned or induced. Hence law can neither perceive nor deal with problems that burden society as a whole.[13]

Habermas, by contrast, conceives communicative action as the medium of social integration: 'the functional specifications of the lifeworld proceed in such a way that, briefly stated, its components – culture, society, personality structure – differentiate themselves only *within their boundaries* of a multi-functional language, but remain *intertwined* with one another through this medium.' But how can communicative action perform this role, given the fact of reasonable pluralism?

how can disenchanted, internally differentiated, and pluralized lifeworlds be socially integrated if, at the same time, the risk of dissension is growing particularly in the spheres of communicative action that have been cut loose from the ties of sacred authority and released from the bonds of archaic institutions?[14]

Habermas's answer to this question is given at two levels. The first concerns the nature of communicative action itself, which does not directly generate prescriptive norms:

Communicative rationality is expressed in a decentred complex of pervasive transcendentally enabling structural conditions, but is not a subjective capacity that would tell actors what they *ought* to do.

Unlike the classical form of practical reason, communicative reason is not an immediate source of prescriptions. It has a normative content only insofar as the communicatively acting individuals must commit themselves to pragmatic presuppositions of a counterfactual sort.[15]

The critical contrast here, as the reference to 'practical reason' indicates, is with Kant. Communicative action does not give rise to categorical imperatives, universal laws of the kind that Kant

believes to be constitutive of moral thought. Its normative pertinence derives from the commitments that speakers and hearers
make to each other, inasmuch as every speech act presupposes the
offer by one and the acceptance by the other of a redeemable validity claim. But even what Habermas calls the 'weak transcendental necessity' of these presuppositions allows agents to take a
critical distance from their everyday beliefs and practices: 'A set
of unavoidable idealizations form the counterfactual basis of an
actual practice of reaching understanding, a practice that can
critically turn against its results and thus *transcend* itself. Thus
the tension between idea and reality breaks into the very facticity
of linguistically structured forms of life.'[16]

So communicative action somehow manages to carry a normative punch that does not rely on the moral generalizations on
which it is so hard to obtain agreement in the internally fractured
modern world. But law is a specific form of communicative action
that possesses distinctive properties. These properties, which
provide a second, more concrete reason for conceiving law as 'a
hinge between system and lifeworld', are best understood on the
basis of the requirements of social integration:

> if the orientations to personal success and to reaching understand-
> ing exhaust the alternatives for acting subjects, then norms suitable
> as socially integrating constraints on strategic interactions must
> meet two contradictory conditions that, from the viewpoint of the
> actors, cannot be simultaneously satisfied. On the one hand, such
> rules must present de facto restrictions that alter the relevant infor-
> mation in such a way that the strategic actor feels compelled to
> adapt her behaviour in the objectively desired manner. On the other
> hand, they must at the same time develop a socially integrative
> force by imposing obligations on the addressee – which, according
> to my theory, is possible only on the basis of intersubjectively
> recognized normative validity claims.[17]

There is, as it happens, one kind of norm that meets both the conditions, namely laws. Their observance is enforced by the state
(hence expressions such as 'having the force of law'); therefore
purely self-interested actors must adjust their calculations to take
into account the negative consequences that will flow from their
breaking the law. At the same time, however, the force of law is
more than simply the kind of threat that a gangster might make.[18]

Laws claim legitimacy: they purport to be norms that *ought* to be obeyed. The tension between 'the idea and reality' that Habermas claims to be inherent in communicative action thus takes the form, in the case of the law, of a duality, since it secures compliance '*simultaneously* by means of de facto constraint and legitimate validity'. This duality emerges fully in modern statute law:

> In contrast to convention and custom, enacted law does not rely on the organic facticity of inherited forms of life, but on the *artificially produced facticity* found in the threat of sanctions that are legally defined and can be imposed through action. On the other hand, the *legitimacy* of statutes is measured against the discursive redeemability of their normative validity claim – in the final analysis, according to whether they come about through a rational legislative process or at least could have been justified from pragmatic, ethical, and moral points of view.[19]

This analysis of law binds together two dimensions of Habermas's overall argument – on the one hand, his grounding theory of communicative action, and, on the other, the account of deliberative democracy that he develops towards the end of *Between Fact and Norm*. The first invites us to understand law as a species of communicative action; the second is mandated by the requirement that, to be legitimate, laws should be the outcome of 'a rational legislative process'. It is democracy, Habermas argues, that provides the institutional form in which this process unfolds. But properly to appreciate this treatment of democracy we must first critically consider Habermas's argument as outlined so far. It suffers from two strategic flaws that go to the very heart of his philosophical project.

The first concerns Habermas's reconceptualization of rationality. Once we make the linguistic turn, he argues, we come to realize that rationality consists not in any substantive principles but in the commitment, implicit in every utterance, to make a redeemable validity claim capable of eliciting the hearer's uncoerced agreement. This is, in other words, a *procedural* conception of rationality. For Habermas, proceduralism obtains in the moral realm just as much as it does in the physical and social sciences. Thus, like Hegel, he distinguishes morality, conceived as the kind of universal obligations on which Kant focuses, from the ethical, the commitments that actors undertake by virtue of participating in the practices specific to particular social forms. But, whereas Hegel conceives ethical life, 'the *actual spirit* of a family and a people', as rationally superior to morality, which he qualifies as abstract, subjective, and atomistic, Habermas argues that ethical practices, just like moral laws, are vulnerable to the dissolving effects of modernity.[20] Thus Habermas describes

> the dilemma in which every ethic claiming universal validity gets caught today under conditions of post-metaphysical thinking. Namely, so long as such an ethic makes substantive statements, its premises remain confined to the context in which particular historical or even personal interpretations of the self and the world arose. As soon as it is sufficiently formal, however, its substance at best consists in elucidating the procedure of ethical discourses aimed at reaching self-understanding.[21]

The validity of modern law similarly depends on a process of formalization that comes to focus on the procedures through which statutes are passed and judicial decisions are made: 'Positive law can no longer derive its legitimacy from a higher ranking moral law but only from a procedure of presumptively rational opinion and will-formation.'[22] But procedural rationality does not lack content. On the contrary: 'The Utopian perspective of reconciliation and freedom is ingrained in the conditions for the communicative sociation of individuals; it is built into the linguistic mechanism of the reproduction of the species.'[23]

But can a purely procedural conception of rationality carry such a heavy burden? Habermas argues that modern legal and constitutional orders derive their legitimacy from two normative conceptions, human rights and popular sovereignty. These are closely related to, respectively, the notion of 'moral self-determination' that is constitutive of the liberal tradition as Kant interpreted it and the idea of 'ethical self-realization' that informs the republican tradition most powerfully represented in the modern era by Rousseau, but are both rooted in the idea of political autonomy:

> human rights and the principle of popular sovereignty . . . represent the precipitate left behind, so to speak, once the normative substance of an ethos embedded in religious and metaphysical traditions has been forced through the filter of post-traditional justification. To the extent that moral and ethical questions have

been differentiated from one another, the discursively filtered substance of norms finds expression in the two dimensions of self-determination and self-realization.[24]

But why should the filtering process unleashed by the application of procedural rationality to previously unquestioned background beliefs leave such powerful substantive concepts as self-determination, self-realization, and autonomy unchallenged? The answer that Habermas can give consistent with his general approach is that the principles articulating these concepts are inferences from the ideal speech situation in which addresser and addressee implicitly orient themselves towards achieving an uncoerced agreement. The trouble with this response is that Habermas's theory of communicative action is highly disputable: I have argued elsewhere, following philosophers of language such as Wittgenstein, Quine, and Davidson, that, far from agreement being the telos of speech, large-scale agreement in substantive beliefs is a precondition of understanding.[25] In the concluding sentences of *Between Fact and Norm*, Habermas comes very close to endorsing such a position with respect to the philosophical foundations of law and democracy. Referring to 'the horizon of a pre-understanding within which everyone could take part in interpretation of the constitution', he writes:

> Certainly this understanding, like the rule of law itself, retains a dogmatic core: the idea of autonomy according to which human beings act as free subjects only insofar as they obey just these laws they give to themselves in accordance with insights they have acquired intersubjectively. This is 'dogmatic' only in a harmless sense. It expresses a tension between facticity and validity, a tension that is 'given' with the fact of the symbolic infrastructure of sociocultural forms of life, which is to say that *for us*, who have developed our identity in such a form of life, it cannot be circumvented.[26]

Given Habermas's premises, this is an absolutely disastrous move for him to make. Recall his analysis of law as having a dual nature: laws command obedience not simply because we can be sent to prison for breaking them but because they are legitimate, that is, because we *ought* to obey them. But if the idea of autonomy is the 'dogmatic core' of liberal-democratic norms, somehow bound up with the particular 'form of life' common to 'us' (presumably the inhabitants of Western liberal capitalist societies), how does it differ from the kind of context-bound ethics that Habermas claims is filtered out once the procedures of communicative rationality are unleashed on it? His position here seems dangerously close to that of Richard Rorty, who also aspires to a 'post-metaphysical culture', but who rejects the project of giving ' "philosophical foundations of democracy" '. Rorty argues that 'there is no standpoint outside the particular historically conditioned and temporary vocabulary we are presently using from which to judge this vocabulary' and that consequently we must abandon 'the idea that intellectual or political progress is rational, in any sense of "rational" that is neutral between vocabularies'. He therefore criticizes Habermas for thinking 'it essential to a democratic society that its self-image embody the universalism, and some form of the rationalism, of the Enlightenment'.[27] Now Habermas rejects what he calls Rorty's 'contextualism' in the name of 'a moral point of view that does not accrue to the privilege of a particular culture but goes deeper, in fact is ultimately anchored in the symmetries of the mutual recognition of communicatively acting subjects in general.'[28] But, in the passage cited above, he implies that the idea of autonomy may, after all, be 'the privilege of a particular culture'.

This ambivalence is closely connected to a second one that structures (and in my view subverts) *Between Fact and Norm* in its entirety. As we have seen, Habermas refers regularly to the tension between facticity (*Factizität*) and validity (*Gültigkeit, Geltung*). Indeed the original German title of the book is *Factizität und Geltung*, 'Facticity and Validity'. But why are there two German words that are both translated into English as 'validity'? The answer is to be found in one of the longest standing of Habermas's philosophical positions. He rejects the classical realist theory of truth, according to which sentences are true or false in virtue of the state of the world, in favour of a pragmatist conception of truth as warranted assertability. To say that a sentence is warrantedly assertable is to say that it is it justified. A weak version of justification would define a justified sentence as one that is entailed by our current beliefs. The difference between pragmatism and realism is that, according to the latter, any sentence, however well supported by our prevailing beliefs, may turn out to be false: the Ptolemaic theory of the planetary system was firmly entrenched in classical and mediaeval thought, but the world proved not to be how this theory asserted it to be. But a pragmatist conception of truth that relies on a weak notion of justification – for example, that sometimes defended by Rorty – would not allow us to say that a well-corroborated theory may be false. Following Peirce, Habermas defends a stronger notion of justification that maintains a tension between truth and assertability by equating the former with what *would* be finally accepted were discussion and research continued indefinitely. Peirce puts it like this:

> The real, then, is that which, sooner or later, information and reasoning would finally result in, and which is therefore independent of the vagaries of me and you. Thus, the very origin of the conception of reality shows that this conception essentially involves the notion of a COMMUNITY, without definite limits, and capable of an indefinite increase of knowledge. And so those two series of cognitions – the real and the unreal – consist of those which, at a time sufficiently future, the community will always continue to reaffirm, and of those which, under the same conditions, will ever after be denied.[29]

As Habermas puts it, 'Peirce explains truth as ideal assertability, that is, as the vindication of a criticizable validity claim under the communication conditions of an audience of competent interpreters that extends ideally across space and time.'[30] In this ideal interpretation community, Ptolemy would presumably turn out to have got the solar system wrong. Truth, like understanding, is thus folded by Habermas into the ideal speech situation. Corresponding to the tension between current beliefs and ideal assertability is that between two concepts of validity:

> The validity (*Gültigkeit*) claimed for statements and norms . . . conceptually transcends space and time, whereas the actual claim is, in each case, raised here and now, in a specific context in which acceptance or rejection has immediate consequences. The validity we claim for our utterances and for practices of justification differs from the *social validity or acceptance* (*soziale Geltung*) of actually established standards and expectations whose stability is based merely on settled custom or the threat of sanctions. The ideal moment of unconditionality is deeply ingrained in factual processes of communication, because validity claims are Janus-faced: as claims, they overshoot every context; at the same time, they must be raised and accepted here and now if they are to support an agree-

ment effective for coordination – for this there is no acontextual standpoint. The universalistic meaning of the claimed validity exceeds all contexts, but only the local binding act of acceptance enables validity claims to bear the burden of social integration for a context-bound everyday practice.[31]

So there are two kinds of validity – one that has the universalistic, context-transcending force of truth, understood as what would be accepted in an ideal speech situation should discussion be allowed to continue indefinitely (*Gültigkeit*), the other what is accepted in a specific social context and enforced by custom or coercion (*Geltung*). One way of restating the duality of law is to say that it brings together both kinds of validity: 'In the dimension of legal validity (*Rechtsgeltung*), the moment of normative validity (*Gültigkeit*) or rational acceptability is combined with the fact of social recognition or acceptance.'[32] Nevertheless, Habermas systematically privileges social acceptance – 'factual' validity, as it were – over normative validity. It is symptomatic in this regard that he calls his book *Faktizität und **Geltung***, not *Faktizität und Gültigkeit*. The effect is, as we shall see, to relax the tension between facticity and validity that Habermas constantly invokes and thereby to collapse social critique into the description of existing conditions.

This slide from *Gültigkeit* to *Geltung*, from universal acceptability to social acceptance, is evident in the following passage on truth and validity:

> The world as the sum total of possible facts is constituted only for an interpretation community whose members engage, before the background of an intersubjectively shared lifeworld, in processes of reaching understanding with one another about things in the world. 'Real' is what can be represented in true statements, whereas 'true' can be explained in turn by reference to the claim that one person raises before others by asserting a proposition. With the assertoric force of her statement a speaker raises a criticizable claim to the validity of the asserted proposition, and because no one has direct access to uninterpreted conditions of validity, 'validity' (*Gültigkeit*) must be understood in epistemic terms as 'validity (*Geltung*) proven for us'. A justified truth claim should allow its proponent to defend it with reasons against the objections of possible opponents; in the end she should be able to gain the rationally motivated agreement of the interpretation community as a whole.[33]

The last two sentences of this passage seem potentially in contra-diction with one another. The first moves from the premiss that the real is not directly accessible to humans independently of the interpretations that we put on it to the conclusion that universal, context-transcendent validity (*Gültigkeit*) must be equated with acceptance in a given social context (*Geltung*). Once again, this takes Habermas dangerously close to Rorty. In Rorty's postmod-ernist version of pragmatism '[t]ruth cannot be out there – cannot exist independently of the human mind' because 'truth is a prop-erty of linguistic entities, of sentences', and language is contingent human creation: consequently the truth or falsehood of a given sentence cannot be settled independently of the vocabulary that we happen to accept at a given time.[34] Both Habermas in the penultimate sentence and Rorty seem to be equating truth with justification in the weak sense of being implied by our prevailing beliefs. The final sentence of the passage quoted above, however, invokes a stronger conception of justification, one in which valid-ity derives from acceptance 'in the end' by an ideal interpretation community that transcends space and time.

It is fair to say that in *Between Fact and Norm* Habermas sys-tematically resolves this ambivalence in favour of *Geltung*. He does so because his overriding preoccupation in analysing law and democracy is to isolate the conditions of social integration. But, given this concern, morality is a relatively weak link in the chain: 'From the functional point of view it can be shown why the post-traditional form of principled morality depends on positive law as its complement. From the very start, then, questions of legal theory explode the framework of a purely normative way of looking at things.' Or again: 'Law, as it were, compensates for the functional weaknesses of a morality that, from the observer perspective, frequently delivers cognitively indeterminate and motivationally unstable results.'[35]

Now it is hardly controversial to say morality is *insufficient* to secure the reproduction of a differentiated modern society. The problem that, for example, Rawls in his later work seeks to address is precisely how to secure what he calls 'stability for the right reasons' (a stronger concept than social integration since, accord-ing to Rawls, in a well-ordered society 'everyone accepts, and knows that everyone accepts, the same principles of justice', which govern the basic institutional structure of that society) granted the fact of reasonable pluralism – i.e., granted that reasonable persons can be expected to develop different comprehensive doctrines about (*inter alia*) how society should be ordered.[36] Habermas says that '[w]ithout the view of law as an empirical action system, philosophical concepts remain empty.' In other words, normative political philosophy requires supplementation by functionalist sociology. One might have qualms about the particular version of social theory that Habermas endorses – for example, the idealist claim that 'social orders . . . *exist* through the recognition of normative validity claims'. All the same, who could in principle object to the basic point he makes here? But in one striking passage added in the 1994 Postscript to *Between Fact and Norm*, he goes much further, asserting that normative theory can be dispensed with altogether: 'Philosophy makes *unnecessary* work for itself when it seeks to demonstrate that it is not simply functionally recommended but also morally required that we organize our common life by positive law, and thus that we form legal communities.'[37]

Once again, then, *Geltung* triumphs over *Gültigkeit*, social acceptance (this time interpreted as normative integration) over universal validity. Normative political philosophy is no longer in need of supplementation; it can be dispensed with altogether. The trouble with saying this is that Habermas also argues that modern constitutional democracies derive their legitimacy from the paradigmatically normative concepts of human rights and popular sovereignty. Yet, when we consider how he puts these concepts to work in, for example, his theory of politics and democracy, we can detect yet another slide towards 'the functional point of view'. Recall that one of Habermas's criticisms of Luhmann's systems theory is that it conceives law as an autonomous, auto-poietic system whose development is driven by internally generated problems. Habermas starts from precisely the opposite position:

> the production of legitimate law through deliberative politics represents a problem-solving procedure that needs and assimilates knowledge in order to programme the regulation of conflicts and the pursuit of collective goals. Politics steps in to fill the functional gaps opened when other mechanisms of social integration are overburdened.[38]

Politics is thus 'the addressee for all unmanaged integration problems'. Habermas develops a version of the theory of deliberative democracy, according to which legitimacy derives from the quality of the procedures and, in particular, of the discussion – not simply in the formal institutions of the state, but in society at large – from which laws emerge. He endorses Bernhard Peters's 'sluice model' of democracy, in which 'binding decisions, to be legitimate, must be steered by communication flows that start at the periphery and pass through the sluices of democratic and constitutional procedures situated at the entrance to the parliamentary complex or the courts (and, if necessary, at the exit of the implementing administration as well).' On this model, the starting point of the democratic process lies outside the formal political system in the informal public sphere that acts as a bridge between civil society, 'those more or less spontaneously emergent associations, organizations, and movements that, attuned to how societal problems resonate in the private life spheres, distil and transmit such reactions in amplified form to the public sphere', and the representative and judicial structures of liberal democracy.[39]

Habermas thus conceives 'the political public sphere as a sounding board for problems that must be processed by the political system because they cannot be solved elsewhere. To this extent, the public sphere is a warning system with sensors that, though unspecialized, are sensitive throughout society.' He concedes, however, that this model of democracy involves a considerable degree of idealization, as is indicated by the following remark: 'the mass media ought to understand themselves as the mandatory of an enlightened public whose unwillingness to learn and capacity for criticism they at once presuppose, demand and reinforce.'[40] Up to a point, Lord Copper, one is inclined to rejoin. In the era of Fox News, Mediaset, and News International, there is more than a bit of a gap here between 'is' and 'ought'.

Part of the problem here lies in the concept of civil society, which Habermas conceives as connecting the genuinely 'private life spheres' of citizens and the informal public sphere. He writes: 'Civil society is expected to absorb and neutralize the unequal distribution of social positions and the power differentials resulting from them, so that social power comes into play only insofar as it *facilitates* the exercise of civil autonomy and does not restrict it.'[41] Once again a gap opens up, this time between the expectation that Habermas says we should have of civil society and the political economy of contemporary capitalism. Civil society, as the expression is used today, is a constitutively ambiguous concept, in that, on the one hand, it requires that its constituents are independent of the state (something that is, for example, not true of the major non-governmental organizations, which tend to be heavily dependent on government funding), and, on the other, it supposes that the unequal distribution of productive resources, wealth, and income will not affect the associational life of civil society and its influence on the political process. The latter supposition is, of course, also false, as is shown in all the evidence of the ways in which in the neo-liberal era corporate capital systematically shapes public policy.[42]

Habermas concedes that Peters's model of democracy rests on 'strong conditions' that aren't met by 'the normal business of politics'. But he argues that at moments of crisis the periphery can mobilize itself to play the initiatory role required by the model, on the assumption that the informal public sphere has 'the capacities to ferret out, identify, and effectively thematize latent problems of social integration (which require political solutions); moreover, an activated periphery must then introduce them via parliamentary (or judicial) sluices into the political system in a way that *disrupts* the latter's routines.' But this is, he says, a 'problematic assumption . . . It places a good part of the normative expectations connected with deliberative politics on the peripheral networks of opinion-formation.'[43] Given the extent to which, as Habermas himself has shown in his earlier work, the public sphere has been penetrated by the processes of commodification and the corporate media characteristic of late capitalism, this indeed seems a doubtful assumption.[44]

One might, however, equally contend that even Habermas's ideal model of deliberative democracy rests on remarkably *weak* conditions. He claims to be offering a synthesis of the liberal and republican traditions: 'Discourse theory takes elements from both sides and integrates these in the concept of an ideal procedure for deliberation and decision-making.'[45] Classical liberalism approaches the political process chiefly with the concern to limit the capacity of the state to interfere in individual freedom. But, in the republican tradition, freedom is conceived as the property of a collective subject, as something that can only be exercised by citizens together when they actively participate in the political process.[46] In a brilliant critical history of republicanism from

Machiavelli to Lenin, Toni Negri develops an account of constituent power – *pouvoir constituant*, the creative power from
which new constitutional orders arise:

> To speak of constituent power is to speak of democracy. In the
> modern era the two concepts have been most often coexistensive
> . . . In other words, constituent power has not been considered only
> as the all-powerful and expansive source from constitutional norms
> emanate in all juridical orders, but also as the subject itself of this
> production, as an activity that is itself all-powerful and expansive.
> From this point of view constituent power tends to identify itself
> with the concept of politics itself, under the form in which it is to
> be understood in a democratic society.[47]

Now Habermas has no time for *this* kind of republicanism. His
conception of deliberative democracy sublimates the traditional
conception of popular sovereignty, which 'ascribe[s] the citizens'
practice of self-determination to a macro-social subject' into 'the
higher-level intersubjectivity of processes of reaching understanding.' 'The "self" of the self-organizing legal community disappears
in the subjectless forms of communication that regulate the flow
of discursive opinion and will-formation.' This shift is partly
required, Habermas believes, by his rejection of 'the philosophy
of consciousness' in favour of a communicative conception of
rationality. But it is also mandated by more specifically political
and economic considerations:

> If deliberative politics is supposed to be inflated into a structure
> shaping the totality of society, then the discursive mode of socia-
> tion expected in the legal system would have to expand into a self-
> organization *of society* and penetrate the latter's complexity as a
> whole. This is impossible, for the simple reason that democratic
> procedure must be embedded in contexts it cannot itself regulate.[48]

This requirement that the scope of democracy must be restricted
may be implied by Habermas's conception of modernity, but it
doesn't follow that its necessity is self-evident. He argues that
'political steering . . . must . . . leave intact the modes of operation
internal to functional systems and other highly organized spheres
of action. As a result, democratic movements emerging from civil
society must give up holistic aspirations to a self-organizing

society, aspirations that also undergirded Marxist ideas of social revolution.'[49] As the reference to Marxism indicates, limiting the range of democratic decision-making follows from Habermas's evolutionary philosophy of history, according to which the differentiation of autonomous sub-systems from the lifeworld is a welcome and irreversible feature of modernity. But politics occupies an ambiguous position in Habermas's overall conception of society since it is both one such sub-system with its own specialized medium (power) and the point at which problems of social integration can be thematized with the help of the informal communicative networks that are at once embedded in everyday language and hooked up to the formal political system via the public sphere.

But Habermas's concern to limit the scope of democracy is bound up with yet another ambivalence. On the one hand he argues that law can 'tame the capitalist economic system, that is, to "restructure" it socially and ecologically in such a way that the deployment of administrative power can simultaneously be brought under control.' But, on the other hand, the problem with welfare-state legislation is that 'satisfying the material conditions for an equal opportunity to exercise individual liberties alters living situations and power positions in such a way that compensation for disadvantages is associated with forms of tutelage that convert the intended *authorization* for the use of freedom into a *custodial supervision*.'[50] This sounds awfully like the standard neo-liberal criticism of the welfare state for allegedly encouraging a culture of dependency. To the extent that Habermas endorses this critique, one can see why he should reject any idea of 'a self-organizing society' and insist that democratic processes should respect the autonomy of one particular sub-system, namely the market economy. For Bidet such a move is inherent in Habermas's counterposition of system and lifeworld, which presupposes the adoption of a neo-classical conception of economic rationality: 'The result of this approach is, it seems to me, to produce a perfect naturalization of the market. If the capitalist economy is thus defined as a systemic sphere of exchanges . . . , there is no longer at this level any conceptual resource available to talk about the phenomenon of exploitation.'[51]

The upshot is a strange conception of democracy, in which an etiolated popular sovereignty is exiled to the decentred communicative networks at the periphery of the political system where it is commanded to restrain its ambitions, while at the same time Habermas concedes that the conditions under which the public sphere might initiate policy are unlikely to be met save in exceptional crisis situations. Habermas's deliberative politics is at once too weak to bear the democratic aspirations of the republican tradition and too strong to be realized in actually existing liberal capitalist societies. This self-denying account of democracy is symptomatic of what Bidet calls 'a *critical functionalism*' that, as we have seen, systematically privileges the effective acceptance required for social integration over the normative validity on which legitimacy depends.[52] Fusing the normative and the explanatory threatens to deprive critical theory of its charge. Thus Habermas endorsed both the 1991 Gulf War against Iraq and the 1999 NATO intervention in Yugoslavia as evidence of 'the trends towards the dissolution of the sovereignty of the state. Against the horizon of an emerging global public sphere, such trends could signal the beginning of a new universalistic world order.'[53] Against the much darker horizon that has loomed over global politics since 11 September 2001, one might instead suggest that the appeals to human rights made to justify both these wars are best approached from the standpoint of sociological suspicion, as ideological legitimations of contemporary imperialism. Perry Anderson indeed accuses Habermas (along with Rawls and Norberto Bobbio) of, in their eagerness to discern glimpses of the cosmopolitan democracy-to-come in 'the disgraced reality of interstate relations' today, providing 'a licence for the American empire as placeholder for human progress'.[54] Too hasty an attempt to clamp together normative political philosophy and explanatory social theory may end up by collapsing into what Marx once called 'uncritical positivism'.[55]

1.2 With and against Marx and Rawls: Jacques Bidet

The ambivalences and limitations that I have identified in Habermas's philosophy of law and democracy help to set an agenda for the rest of this book. Two issues in particular stand out. First, there is the problem of realism and truth. Habermas has developed an epistemology that seeks to be at once anti-realist and anticontextualist. In other words, he denies that sentences are true or false in virtue of the state of the world but he wants to reject Rorty's version of pragmatism, which asserts that there are no context-independent standards to allow us to judge the relative merits of different vocabularies. Rorty says: 'It seems to me that I am just as provincial and contextualist as the Nazi teachers who made their students read *Der Stürmer*; the only difference is that I serve a better cause, I come from a better province.'[56] It is Rorty's implication that 'better' here invokes no universal criteria that would allow us to determine whether or not he is right to prefer liberal democratic America to National Socialist Germany that Habermas most fiercely resists. He insists: 'What we hold true has to be defendable on the basis of good reasons, not merely in a different context but in all possible contexts, that is, at any time and against anybody.'[57] But the constant slide from validity (*Gültigkeit*) to acceptance (*Geltung*) that I have traced in *Between Fact and Norm* suggests that Habermas's identification of truth with ideal assertability may not be a stable position and may be liable to collapse into contextualism. Such indeed in Rorty's view: 'I am not sure how people like Habermas and [Albrecht] Wellmer, who have given up on correspondence theories of truth and consequently cannot distinguish between a claim to report a habit of action and a claim to represent reality, can draw this distinction between context-dependence and context-independence.'[58] There may, in other words, be a closer connection between realism and universalism than Habermas is prepared to admit.

As the example that Rorty gives of German professors under Hitler indicates, at stake here are not simply philosophical issues in epistemology and ontology, but also the fundamentally political problem of the tenability of critical theory. Is it possible for philosophy and social theory to establish sufficient distance from prevailing beliefs and practices to provide a vantage point for social criticism? Here we touch on a second issue. Habermas's theory of communicative action is intended not merely to ground context-transcendent inquiry into the world but also to establish the rationality of a 'moral point of view' that can claim universal validity. Once again, however, a conceptual instability emerges. Having insisted that both the ethical outlooks embedded in specific social forms and Kantian universalist morality must be subjected to a filtration process that removes any substantive principles, Habermas nevertheless claims that human rights and popular sovereignty constitute the 'dogmatic core' on which the legitimacy of liberal democracy rests. This apparent slide into contextualism is accompanied by a systematic tendency to replace the normative criterion of legitimacy with the functionalist problem of how beliefs and practices contribute to social integration, producing a disturbingly weak model of deliberative democracy that nevertheless succeeds in idealizing the actual conditions prevailing in Western political systems. This suggests that, first, any attempt to ground social critique should seek to establish a greater distance between normative principles and prevailing beliefs and practices than Habermas succeeds in doing and that, secondly, pursuing such a strategy may well entail renouncing his failed attempt to banish substantive doctrines from moral discourse.

Both these questions will be addressed at length in part II. In the remainder of this chapter, however, I consider another attempt to develop a general theory of modernity that, in parallel with but in important respects at odds with Habermas, seeks both to build on and to transcend Marx; this project, worth discussion for its own sake, also throws more light both on Habermas's enterprise and on the issues I have highlighted. Jacques Bidet describes himself as writing 'with-and-against' Marx.[59] But, as editor of the journal *Actuel Marx* and chief organizer of the triennial International Marx Congresses that have met in Paris since 1995, he operates in an intellectual context much more deeply rooted in Marxist debates than does Habermas. Moreover, since his first brilliant study of Marx's economic writings, *Que faire du 'Capital'?* (1985), Bidet has sought to develop his own theory of modernity through a close critical reading of *Capital* – an enterprise that was, in its early stages, welcomed by Louis Althusser as a continuation of the project that he and his collaborators in *Reading Capital* (1965) had inaugurated.[60] But, as the title of one of Bidet's articles – 'For a Revolutionary Contractualism' – indicates, his dialogue with Marx has taken him beyond the bounds of orthodoxy to an engagement with egalitarian liberalism and in particular with Rawls.[61] Like Habermas, then, he operates in an intellectual terrain where explanatory social theory and normative political philosophy meet.

Also like Habermas, Bidet has sought to develop a general theory of modernity capable of overcoming the limitations of

Marxism. Thus he writes: 'Marxism, with its succession of modes of production, its linear and teleological vision of history, has deprived us of the concept of modernity, understood as an ensemble of possibilities which exist as such only in their quasi-contemporaneity.' Unlike Habermas, however, Bidet seeks to develop a broader account of modernity that thematizes the full range of possibilities, not through a theory of communicative action, but starting from a deconstructive reading of *Capital*. This critical stance towards Marx does not amount to a root-and-branch demolition of Marxist economic theory. On the contrary, Bidet strongly condemns Habermas for simultaneously misunderstanding and abandoning the labour theory of value; as a result, he contends, the structural antagonism of class exploitation 'loses its strategic place' in *Between Fact and Norm*, and is subordinated to the functional requirements of system integration.[62]

The real problem with Marx's critique of political economy lies elsewhere, Bidet contends. Fundamentally Marx fails sufficiently to reflect on the presuppositions of his own argument in parts 1 and 2 of *Capital*, volume I. Here he first develops (in part 1) an analysis of commodities and money in which the labour theory of value (according to which commodities exchange in proportion to the socially necessary labour-time required to produce them) is presented. Marx's rationale for starting with the commodity is, as the famous opening sentence of *Capital* has it, that '[t]he wealth of societies in which the capitalist mode of production prevails appears as an "immense collection of commodities"; the individual commodity appears as its elementary form.' But it is only in part 2, 'The Transformation of Money into Capital', that Marx identifies the *differentia specifica* of capital – namely its capacity for self-expansion, which means that money is invested in the expectation that it will grow by securing a profit – and argues that what makes this self-expansion possible is that 'peculiar commodity' labour-power. Labour-power, like any other commodity, has a value, but its use-value consists in the creation of new value through the performance of labour. The transformation of labour-power into a commodity involves its separation from the means of production, which are concentrated in the hands of the capitalists; consequently the worker is 'free in the double sense that as a free individual he can dispose of his labour-power as his own commodity, and that, on the other hand, he has no other commodity for sale, i.e., he is rid of them, he is free of all the objects needed for the realization of his labour-power.' The resulting inequality between worker and capitalist on the labour market compels the former to strike a bargain that leads to her exploitation. The secret of capital's self-expansion is to be found in the surplus-value – the value created by the worker in excess of what is required to replace her wages – that is appropriated by capital.[63]

Bidet argues that Marx's treatment of this crucial transition from the commodity to capital undergoes a transformation across successive economic drafts. In the *Grundrisse* (written in 1857–8), Marx essays (through an analysis of the concept of money, which forms an intermediary stage in his exposition between the commodity and capital) what Bidet calls a 'dialectical' treatment of the transition. The thought seems to be that in the *Grundrisse* Marx seeks to show that the concept of capital is contained in that of the commodity, or that there is a deductive relationship between the levels of analysis pertaining respectively to the commodity and to capital. But, by the time we get to *Capital*, volume I, first published in 1867, Marx's 'discourse does not proceed from part 1 to part 2 in analytical continuity, but by means of a constructive intervention'. The introduction of the concept of labour-power in part 2 involves 'a constructivist initiative, which consists in adding a new determination to the preceding categorial system, the commodity system. Marx "determines" a commodity of the system as "labour-power".'[64]

Bidet draws very radical conclusions from this interpretation. Once the relationship between commodity and capital is no longer conceived by Marx as a deductive one, '[i]t becomes impossible to conceive capitalism as (at the logical level) the unique and necessary development of the market. The operator of the connection is "labour-power" and the strategic question is that of its status as a "commodity". It is to the extent that this status is realized that one can truly speak of capitalism.'[65] But Marx fails to recognize the indeterminacy introduced by the changes he makes in his method of presentation between the *Grundrisse* and *Capital*, volume I. For Bidet, however, this indeterminacy signifies the presence, buried in Marx's discourse, of the concept of a 'metastructure' of modernity that transcends the more specific structures of the capitalist mode of production: 'A concept of metastructure is in effect implicated in the idea that properly capitalist social rela-

tions are inscribed in a more general "envelope", that of commodity relations; and that one cannot expound the capitalist
system without having first expounded, in all its abstraction, the
commodity system.'[66]

The metastructure is Bidet's central concept. It signifies that
'field of possibilities', broader than capitalism, that is modernity.[67]
But it is not a transhistorical concept. On the contrary, the metastructure is a 'historical transcendental', 'the general "presupposition", common to diverse forms of modern society – from the
most free-market capitalism to the most collectivist statism – of
whose virtualities each diversely develops.' Bidet calls the metastructure a *'trinome'* because it consists of three elements. The first
(and most obscure) is what Bidet calls 'the *immediate* discursive
relationship of liberty–equality–rationality': the great founding
declarations of modern democratic politics (1776, 1789, etc.)
articulate what Habermas argues is inherent in communicative
action as such, namely that speech takes place between subjects
who recognize each other as free, equal, and rational. But this then
requires two '"contractual" mediations' or 'relays' that form the
second and third elements of the metastructural 'trinome'. 'Contractuality', Bidet argues, is inherent to the market that, as we have
seen, belongs to the metastructure constitutive of modernity.
But it has two forms. One is 'inter-individual contractuality',
which is present notably in the transactions between market
actors. The other is 'central contractuality', or 'centricity', namely
the constitution of the state on the basis of a social contract.
Bidet stresses the interdependence of these two forms of contractuality: 'The free inter-individual contractuality of a commodity
type cannot exist without a central will that assures it, nor can
central contractuality without the autonomy of inter-individual
contractuality.'[68]

As the foregoing should make clear, Bidet does not exactly give
a perspicuous account of his key concepts. It may be easier to
extract their cash-value if we take a look at how they are used.
Bidet argues that the more concrete homologues of inter-individual and central contractuality are, respectively, the market and
organization. He insists on 'the radical co-originarity of inter-
individuality and centricity'. Market and organization necessarily
coexist and imply the necessity of the state, which Bidet conceives
as *'supreme* centricity, as a fact of global organization dominat-

ing the whole of civil society'. Marx's mistake was therefore not simply to have believed that the market was inseparable from capitalism but also to have underestimated the significance of organization, treating it as a secondary consideration rather than as a constitutive feature of modernity. Therefore: 'An – abstract – theory of the state is found, as we can see, necessarily implicated in the first, metastructural, moment of the exposition of a theory of modern society.'[69]

His conceptualization of the metastructure thus allows Bidet to give equal weight to the dimensions of bureaucracy and the state that critics from Bakunin and Weber onwards have argued that Marx neglected. A number of moves follow from this initial theoretical reorientation. First, Bidet seeks to show that his theory 'doesn't propose a simple typological reorganization of Marx's problematic, but a theoretical refoundation, which defines the properly modern *dynamic* of class relations starting with the articulation of two *class factors* (market and organization) and the interference of their two *faces*, reasonable (contractuality) and rational (coordination).' Class structuration in modernity is a result of the '*structural* interference' of both these factors: 'the class relation is not constructed unilaterally on the commodity relation of exploitation, but correlatively on the hierarchical element of organization that impregnates society as whole.'[70]

The distinction Bidet makes here between the reasonable and rational is a symptom of the extent to which he operates in a wider intellectual universe than that of Marxism. He owes the contrast to Rawls, for whom '[r]easonable persons . . . desire for its own sake a social world in which they, as free and equal, can cooperate with others on terms all can accept', while [t]he rational . . . applies to a single, unified agent . . . with the powers of judgement and deliberation in seeking ends and interests peculiarly its own.'[71] The reasonable is thus intended to capture the core of contractualism, namely the idea that just societies are the product of uncoerced agreements between free and equal subjects, while the rational pertains to the instrumental rationality of self-interested actors. Bidet seems to be saying that *both* the market and organization belong to the dimension of the reasonable, inasmuch as they involve contractuality, but also to the rational, since they are modes of coordination by means of which economic systems can reproduce themselves on a simple or extended scale.

The fact that market and organization are simultaneously mutually interdependent and the bearers of these two dimensions leads, secondly, to a philosophy of history. Bidet presents us with 'a radical antinomy: what is given to the determination of the centre is withdrawn from inter-individual commodity determination.' The ' "antinomy of modernity" ' is that economic coordination must take the form of either a centralized plan or a decentralized market. Consequently, modernity has a cyclical structure: Bidet outlines a cycle in which decentralized market relations give rise to a state whose domination by capital is contested by the developing labour movement; under working-class pressure state regulation of the market increases until a limit is reached with communism, where the market is abolished altogether, that gives rise not to the eradication also of exploitation, but to what Bidet more recently has called 'a patrimonial form of appropriation in the hands of a managerial class'; the eventual reaction then reinstates the market, and so we go round again.[72] Capitalism and communism (or what he now calls 'collectivism') are now conceptualized not as stages in an evolutionary sequence, but as alternative possibilities inherent in the metastructure of modernity. It does not, however, follow that we are bound to repeat the cycle that has brought us back to *laissez-faire* 150 years after the 1848 Revolutions: the metastructure 'furnishes the principle of circularity proper to modernity, which however is realized in an irreversible history.'[73] There is, as we shall see, a progressive directionality in modernity that may allow us to escape this infernal cycle, or at least to control it.

Thirdly, Bidet's theory of the metastructure forms the basis of a larger conceptual architectonic. There are, in fact, three principal levels of his analysis. First, there is the metastructure, the matrix of possibilities constitutive of modernity. Second, there is the structure, the point at which the promise of liberty–equality–rationality inherent in the metastructure is reversed thanks to the relations of class exploitation and domination that arise from the conjoint action of market and organization. But, third, there is the system. The structural tendencies inherent in modernity give rise to the formation of an articulated totality, an integrated economic and political space encompassing the entire globe. Bidet's argument here is heavily indebted to the world systems theory variously developed by Fernand Braudel, Immanuel Wallerstein,

Giovanni Arrighi, and others. Accordingly he conceives the system, even more than the structure, as a domain of domination and violence. But he criticizes Marx and classical theorists of imperialism such as Luxemburg, Kautsky, Lenin, Hilferding, and Bukharin for conceptualizing the global purely through the category of world economy: *'it is because Marx doesn't provide an adequate idea of the structure as articulation of market and organization (notably the state) that he cannot describe the "world" as it is: a market with a non-state form of organization, namely a "system", the world-system.'*[74]

The world system is thus more than a market: it involves a political order, though that still takes the predominant form of inter-state relations. There is thus no 'central contractual instance', no global state. 'There is thus, in the *global* framework . . . , an anteriority of the era of "inter-individual contractuality" over an era of potential central contractuality.' The implication is that there is, however, a progressive movement towards a global state. The growth of transnational economic and cultural relations increasingly poses the necessity of such a state. Various concrete institutions, from the United Nations to the *lex mercatoria* regulating the global transactions between corporations, bear witness to this striving towards a transnational centricity. The very idea of a social contract also implies the demand for a global state, 'since it is only at the level of the concrete totality of humanity, and with respect to the shared use of the planet that bears it, that the genuinely universal character of the principles governing the social order can be established. *The contractual order is geo-contractual or it does not exist.* The state is global or it is not contractual.' To some extent like Habermas, Bidet reads the 1991 Gulf War (which, unlike more recent American military expeditions, was authorized by the UN Security Council) as 'signifying a decisive evolution in the direction of the world state, as that in which the two figures of centrality – that, still largely potential, of the *super-state [sur-Etat]*, and that, all too real, of *imperialism* – happened to become identified': even if the second figure predominated over the first, the effort by the United States to secure the legitimacy provided by a Security Council resolution indicated that the idea of a world state was more than an 'ideological cover: when the appearance is necessary, it is something other than a simple appearance.'[75]

If, as Bidet puts it, he begins, unlike Dante, in Paradise, with the promise of liberty and equality inherent in modernity, his general theory doesn't quite return us there. But neither does it consign us to the 'terrestrial Hell' of exploitation and domination; rather it leaves us in 'a problematic Purgatory' where the embryonic forms of a world state at least offer us the prospect of regulating global capitalism.[76] Bidet's refusal simply to renounce Marx's critique of political economy undoubtedly gives his theory of modernity a harder, more critical edge than Habermas is able to sustain on the basis of his functionalist conception of social systems. But naturally a theorization of such ambition and intelligence gives rise to many questions. Perhaps the most important from a substantive point of view is Bidet's claim that a market economy (in Marx's sense of 'generalized commodity production', where most goods and services are produced for sale on the market) is inherent in the nature of modernity and dissociable from capitalism. I have criticized this claim elsewhere: here I simply wish to reaffirm that Bidet is, in my view, mistaken and that, moreover, there is no 'antinomy of modernity', since democratic planning offers an alternative to (dare one say, a third way between) both Western-style liberal capitalism and a Stalinist command economy.[77]

My concern here is rather with what Bidet regards as his major philosophical innovation, the concept of the metastructure. Though he is correct in detecting a shift in how Marx treats the relationship between the commodity and capital between the *Grundrisse* and *Capital*, this does not of itself justify separating the two by including the market in a metastructure broader than capitalism. In *Capital*, volume I, chapter 1, Marx does indeed analyse the commodity in abstraction from the existence of the capitalist mode of production. But this is an instance of his more general procedure in *Capital*, which involves conceiving capitalism as an articulated, multi-levelled structure that can be conceptualized by progressively introducing step by step more complex determinations.[78] It would be a mistake, however, to imagine that each level of this theoretical construction has some distinct reality corresponding to it: to borrow a term of Althusser's, the real object of *Capital* is the capitalist mode of production as a whole, reconstructed conceptually as 'a rich totality of many determinations and relations'.[79] Therefore, simply because Marx does not posit the existence of capitalist relations of production at the start of *Capital* doesn't mean that the analysis of the commodity in chapter 1 corresponds to a social reality – the market – distinct from capitalism. This analysis allows Marx to construct a model of generalized market production, that is, of an economy of inter-dependent but autonomous commodity producers, that he seeks to establish, as the discourse of *Capital* unfolds, can only exist if labour-power itself is a commodity – that is, if capitalist relations of production exist.

Marx makes this point explicitly when criticizing the classical political economist Robert Torrens for formulating an early version of what has come to be known as the historical interpre-tation of the labour theory of value, which claims that commodi-ties exchange in proportion to their values (i.e., the socially necessary labour-time required to produce them) only in a pre-capitalist economy of simple commodity producers who control the means of production themselves (and thus have not been reduced to the status of wage-labourers):

> This means ... that the law which applies to commodities qua commodities, no longer applies to them once they are regarded as capital or as products of capital, or as soon as there is, in general, an advance from the commodity to capital. On the other hand, the product wholly assumes the form of a commodity only as a result of the fact that the entire product has to be transformed into exchange-value and that also all the ingredients necessary for pro-duction enter it as commodities – in other words it wholly becomes a commodity only with the development and on the basis of capi-talist production. Thus the law of value is supposed to be valid for a type of production which produces no commodities (or which produces commodities only to a limited extent) and not to be valid for a type of production which is based on the product as a commodity.[80]

Marx clearly sees this as a *reductio* of the historical interpreta-tion. Far from portraying a social form historically antecedent or (on Bidet's version) ontologically prior to the capitalist mode of production, the labour theory of value allows Marx to construct a model of the system of generalized commodity production that requires capitalist relations of production to become operative. Thus it is only when the direct producers have been transformed into wage-labourers that they become dependent exclusively on the market to meet their subsistence needs; except under very special conditions, simple commodity producers are likely to rely on production for use (typically within the framework of the household) in order to meet the bulk of their needs. Consequently, it is where capitalist relations of production prevail thanks to the transformation of labour-power into a commodity that most output is produced for sale on the market: as Marx puts it, 'it is only from this moment that the commodity-form of the products of labour becomes universal.'[81] Bidet, then, is right in suggesting that, by the time of *Capital*, Marx no longer conceives the relationship between the different levels of his analysis as a deductive one, but he fails to see that one aspect of the relationship this analysis seeks to conceptualize is the functional interdependence between a market economy and the institution of wage-labour constitutive of the capital-relation.[82]

Of course, the philosophical tenability of Bidet's concept of the metastructure cannot be settled by the kind of challenge I have posed to his interpretation of *Capital*. But it is very hard to understand what the ontological status of the metastructure is supposed to be. Recall that Bidet conceives it as a matrix of possibilities that define the limit conditions within which concrete modern societies take shape. He also calls it a 'historical transcendental', an expression that resonates with Foucault's concept of the 'historical a priori'.[83] Such formulations evoke Kant's notion of transcendental argument, whose aim is to establish the conditions of possible experience. But Kant is very concerned his arguments establish universal conclusions. Foucault's formulation is, among other things, an attempt to subvert such a conception of transcendental argument. The historical, by virtue of being tied to a specific time and place, is by definition not universal: the implication is that the presuppositions of our beliefs and practices are a priori just in the sense of being presupposed, but that they do not have universal validity. This isn't a problem for Foucault since, like Rorty, he wants to move our thinking in a contextualist and anti-universalist direction. But Bidet *is* trying to ground universal principles: thus, as we have seen, he claims that the 'universal character' of contractualist principles requires that they have a planetary extension based on the establishment of a world state.

Bidet insists that 'the metastructural presupposition' is 'far from being only a preliminary of the exposition, a simple logical antecedent'. The best way of understanding it is in terms of the promise inherent in modernity as a historical formation. Modernity is 'this moment (process) when the structural forms of domination can only *conceive* themselves by starting from the position where the universal declares itself.' Thus Bidet repeatedly insists that (a) the metastructure starts from the distinctively modern structures of exploitation and domination inaugurated by capitalism, and that (b) it is, or begins as, a declaration: 'The metastructure is thus to be taken as the modern "declaration", which has two faces, that, rational, of truth-efficacy, and that, reasonable, of justice.'[84]

Bidet tries, in order to meet the requirements of his conception of modernity, to pack too much in here when he says that the declaration through which the metastructure announces itself embraces, on the one hand, truth and instrumental rationality, and, on the other, the reasonable that Rawls claims is constitutive of contractualism and that is based on the desire of the citizens of a democratic polity to treat each other as free and equal. Bidet offers nothing resembling an argument for truth and rationality being presuppositions of modernity. But if we stick to the second aspect the status of the metastructure makes a bit more sense. The idea of the metastructure as a declaration then evokes the actual, historical declarations through which, for example, the English, American, and French Revolutions affirmed the rights of citizens. The idea that this *political* modernity has a permanent subversive potential has been powerfully articulated by Etienne Balibar, who has coined the portmanteau word '*égaliberté*' as part of an argument that the ideals of equality and liberty have the same historical conditions of realization and that the affirmation of these ideals by the great bourgeois revolutions offers a permanent incitement to challenge existing institutions and overcome whatever structures of oppression and exclusion prevent the treatment of all as free and equal.[85]

It is tempting then to develop this argument into the historical thesis that capitalism, in subverting feudal hierarchies and drawing the entire world into its universalizing influence, creates the conditions in which these ideals can be affirmed, but in doing so creates a double that accompanies its progress but also constantly draws attention to the constitutive gap between the promise of liberty and equality and the exploitive realities of capitalist social relations. Marx says something along these lines when he argues that 'the concept of human equality' could acquire 'the permanence of a fixed public opinion . . . only in a society where the commodity-form is the universal form of the product of labour', and different kinds of labour are therefore treated as equivalent: the capitalist mode of production thus produces the historical context in which the ideal of equality can gain widespread acceptance, but at the same time capitalism constantly subverts this ideal because the exploitation of wage-labour depends on worker and capitalist being in real economic terms unequal.[86] Some of Bidet's formulations seem to offer a gloss on this argument: 'The contractualist pretention is inscribed . . . in a realist social ontology: the metastructure always advances only in the conditions of the structure, in conflict.'[87]

But Bidet resists any attempt historically to situate the ideals of liberty and equality. Thus, in his fullest attempt to explicate the nature of the metastructure, he writes:

> The metastructure is not to be understood as a superstructure . . . It defines a 'moment' of the social institution, which is neither a pure order of discourse nor a distinct institution. The 'declaration' has an ontological status, an index of reality, in the sense that it marks, determines, impregnates, in whatever degrees of strength, concrete historical institutions. On the one hand, in their effective legal or customary status, in their material inscription in a common symbolic space. On the other hand, in the fact that that the declaration, across these determinations and inscriptions, which recall its indefinite openness (at the same time as they tend to fix it), constitutes a constant provocation that can be read by all those whom it excludes as an intervention to force their way into the common space of citizenship.[88]

The bulk of this passage seems very close to Balibar's conception of *égaliberté* as a permanent incitement to revolutionize relations and institutions that stand in the way of its realization. But one can accept that the ideals of liberty and equality, affirmed in revolutionary declarations, have a historical reality through *both* their institutionalization *and* the subversive potential they retain despite this institutionalization without concluding that they must therefore be posited as constituents of a metastructure that is pre-supposed by the structures of modern capitalist societies. One reason why Bidet insists on this conclusion is given in the first sentence of the passage last cited, where he denies that the meta-structure is a superstructure.[89] Maybe he fears that historically contextualizing the ideals of liberty and equality reduces them to the reflex of the relations of production. But this fear is unjusti-fied: normative sentences of the kind that affirm, for example, that all humans are free and equal have a truth-value just like any other kind of sentences. The reasons that one might have for asserting such sentences are independent of the historical context in which they first gained currency and of the social conditions that continue to sustain (or subvert) them.

Like Habermas, Bidet is trying to construct a theoretical space in which the kind of explanatory social theory traditionally pursued by Marxists can cross-fertilize with normative political philosophy as it has been practised, for example, by egalitarian liberals. And he is right to reject the kind of relativist meta-ethics frequently championed by orthodox Marxists, which reduces moral and political beliefs to the functional requirements of the prevailing relations of production. But this rejection does not justify conjuring up, as a kind of shadow accompaniment to these relations, a metastructure into which are packed the moral imper-atives characteristic of contractualist political philosophy. In one respect, also like Habermas, Bidet's strategy has the effect of marginalizing moral and ethical discourse. For the propositions making up the metastructure are treated not as moral affirmations, but as a statement of the presuppositions of the structure of modern societies, and therefore as having the same epistemic status as, say, the labour theory of value, which Bidet follows Marx in treating as the starting point for uncovering capitalist relations of production and as an explanatory theory that dis-avows normative commitments. But if the metastructure is simply an objective matrix of possibilities, what reason does one have to seek to realize one possibility rather than another? And if the requirement that we treat our fellow humans as free and equal is merely a presupposition of modern societies, what reasons can we give someone who wishes to follow Nietzsche and condemn modernity *tout court*? In other words, though Bidet wants to reject standard reductionist treatments of moral and political discourse, his own argument is in its own way just as reductive, since it ignores the strictly evaluative nature of such discourse, focusing instead on the role that some of its propositions allegedly play in the constitution of modern societies. He seeks to continue 'the philosophical project of thinking in the unity of the concept what is and what it is appropriate to do, a project illustrated to the highest degree by Spinoza and Hegel', but in fact ends up collapsing 'ought' into 'is'.[90]

Two conclusions are suggested by these criticisms of Bidet's general theory of modernity. The first is simply to reinforce one of the thoughts presented at the beginning of this section, namely that constructing a philosophically robust basis for social critique is likely to involve taking normative theory seriously and seeking, with its help, to establish free-standing substantive principles of justice. I return to this topic in chapter 7 below. Secondly, how helpful is the idea of modernity in this context? Let us grant for the sake of argument that the great bourgeois revolutions opened up an imaginary space that extends beyond capitalism and that is constituted by the ideals of universal liberty and equality. Nevertheless, the actually existing form taken by modernity is capitalism. Bidet himself treats the only candidates with any plausible historical claim to represent a non-capitalist modernity – the Stalinist societies – as aberrant cases.[91] The attempts to delineate modernity as a distinct social form that we have considered in this chapter either essentialize tendencies characteristic of capitalism (in Habermas the differentiation of society into autonomous subsystems, and the colonization of the lifeworld) or posit a shadow metastructural accompaniment of capitalist structures (Bidet). Fredric Jameson recently proposed, as a 'therapeutic . . . recommendation', 'the experimental procedure of substituting capitalism for modernity in all the contexts in which the latter appears'.[92] Certainly, as we shall have further reason to see in the next chapter, the main target of social critique remains capitalism.

2

Between Relativism and Universalism: French Critical Sociology

2.1 Capitalism and its critiques: Boltanski and Chiapello

The debate on modernity that Habermas has dominated no longer seems to be in the vanguard of critical theory. Habermas's position gave him a pivotal role in an intellectual and political conjuncture in which, on one hand, the great renaissance of Marxist theory in the 1960s and 1970s had ended in crisis and collapse, and, on the other, poststructuralism mounted a root-and-branch challenge to the Enlightenment project.[1] But the 1990s were marked by a significant shift in the intellectual and political environment. The very scale of the triumph of liberal capitalism after the end of the Cold War and the attempts via international financial institutions such as the IMF and the World Bank to universalize the neo-liberal economic package known as the Washington Consensus made how – and whether – to live with capitalism an increasingly urgent issue. This change in the agenda became politically visible at the very end of the decade, when the Seattle protests signalled the emergence of the international movement for another globalization, but there were also in the intellectual world important signals that the great *querelle* of moderns and postmoderns was no longer at the cutting edge of theoretical debate.

Surprisingly enough, one of those to sound this signal was Rorty, who started to denounce the narcissism of what he called the 'cultural left' in the American academy and to call for a return to 'class politics' that would address the growing inequalities produced by neo-liberal globalization.[2] The fact that Rorty, by popularizing poststructuralist themes in the idiom of American pragmatism, had helped to legitimize the introversion of post-modernist academics didn't make his criticisms any less pertinent. But much more significant was what happened in France – not only the homeland of poststructuralism but also the country where the crisis of Marxism had first become visible with the emergence of the *nouveaux philosophes* in 1976–7.[3] In 1993 two books were published in France. The first was *The Weight of the World*, a collective work headed up by Pierre Bourdieu that sought, by recording, collecting, and analysing a mass of individual narratives, to convey the material and spiritual suffering induced by twenty years of neo-liberal economics. The second was Jacques Derrida's *Spectres of Marx*: in a political and ideological context where Marx had apparently been consigned permanently to oblivion by the victors of the Cold War, Derrida denounced the evils constitutive of the 'new world order' – unemployment, exclusion, competition, debt, the arms trade, nuclear proliferation, war, globalized crime, the domination of international institutions by the Great Powers and the big corporations – and affirmed: 'There will be no future without this. Not without Marx, no future without Marx, without the memory and the inheritance of Marx: in any case of a certain Marx, of his genius, of at least one of his spirits.'[4]

Daniel Bensaïd has written that the two books 'inflicted a check on the triumphant liberal rhetoric, announcing a renaissance of social resistances and helping to modify the geography of the decade.'[5] This renaissance first surfaced in France with the mass public sector strikes of November–December 1995, which pushed the centre of gravity significantly to the left and accelerated the development of new political networks organizing against neo-liberalism; the most internationally significant of these was ATTAC, founded in 1998, which campaigns for the regulation of global financial markets.[6] It was also during the 1995 strikes that Bourdieu emerged as the leading intellectual champion of these new movements of resistance. Deploying (to use his own vocabulary) the considerable symbolic capital of an internationally renowned professor at the Collège de France, he launched a determined literary campaign against the neo-liberal *pensée unique* and convened a group of scholar-activists, Raisons d'agir, to pursue a research agenda that could address the needs of the movements.[7]

Bourdieu's intervention in the years between the 1995 strikes and his death in January 2002 gave a strongly political inflection to the critical sociology that he had developed in the previous thirty years. But the status of social critique at the end of the twentieth century was most systematically explored not by Bourdieu himself, but by Luc Boltanski, a fellow sociologist and former collaborator with Bourdieu who subsequently distanced himself from the latter. *Le Nouvel Esprit du capitalisme*, a massive study co-authored by Boltanski and the management theorist Eve Chiapello and published in 1999, seeks 'to contribute to the relaunching of critique' by exploring both the general relationship between capitalism and its critique and the particular vicissitudes of this relationship in France since 1968.[8] Both the richness of the research on which this book is based and Boltanski's and Chiapello's explicit problematization of *capitalism* – underlining the broader intellectual shift away from the debate on modernity and postmodernity – make it sensible to start with *Le Nouvel Esprit du capitalisme* before, prompted by its aporias, going on to consider Bourdieu's account of the status of social theory in §2.2 below.

We have already seen in both Habermas and Bidet a preoccupation with transcending the polarity of critical social theory and normative discourse. It is interesting therefore to discover just such a concern expressed also by Boltanski and Chiapello:

> The notion of the spirit of capitalism, as we define it, allows us henceforth to overcome the opposition, which has dominated a large part of the sociology and philosophy of the last 30 years ..., between theories, often of Nietzscheo-Marxist inspiration, that see in society only violence, relations of force, exploitation, domination and conflicts of interest, and, on the other hand, theories that, inspired rather by contractualist political philosophies, have emphasized democratic forms of debate and the conditions of social justice.[9]

If the latter pole of the opposition alludes to Rawls and Habermas, the former surely evokes not only Foucault but also Bourdieu, whose most influential sociological writings thematized symbolic domination and structural violence. The concept of the spirit of capitalism that is meant to allow us to escape this polarity refers us to yet another major social theorist, Max Weber. For Weber, however, 'the spirit of capitalism' refers to the stylization of life required for the accumulation of capital socially to prevail – the systematic subordination of all life-activities to instrumental rationality that, through the vehicle of the 'inner-worldly asceticism' encouraged by Calvinism, was historically necessary for modern capitalism first to get a hold, but became dispensable once humankind was subordinated to 'the technical and economic conditions of machine production which today determine the lives of all the individuals who are born into this mechanism, not only those directly concerned with economic acquisition, with irresistible force.'[10]

For Boltanski and Chiapello, by contrast, the 'spirit of capitalism . . . plays a central role in the capitalist process that it serves by constraining it.' The necessity of such a constraint is inherent in the nature of capitalism itself, which they define as *'a need for the unlimited accumulation of capital by formally peaceful means'*. This is

> an absurd system: the wage-earners have lost their ownership of the product of their labour and the possibility of conducting an active life beyond subordination. As for the capitalists, they find themselves chained to an endless and insatiable process that is totally abstract and dissociated from the satisfaction of consumption needs, be those for luxuries. For these two kinds of protagonists, insertion in the capitalist process is singularly lacking in justification.[11]

This assessment recalls, of course, Marx's critique of capitalist exploitation and alienation. But Boltanski's and Chiapello's preoccupation is with another Weberian theme – the legitimation of social order. 'Systemic constraints' are insufficient to motivate actors to participate in capitalism: enter the spirit of capitalism – 'this ensemble of beliefs associated with the capitalist order that contributes to justifying this order and, by legitimizing them, to sustaining the modes of action and the dispositions that are coherent with it.' This might make the spirit of capitalism seem like an ideology in the Marxist sense, which legitimizes capitalism by masking its contradictions. But Boltanski and Chiapello deny that the capitalist spirit is a superstructure.[12] Moreover, in *De la justi-*

fication (1991), which he wrote with Laurent Thévenot, Boltanski specifically criticizes even Weber's conception of legitimation because it

> tends to confuse justification with deception by dismissing the constraints of coordination in favour of taking refuge in a value-relativism. Justifiable acts are what interest us, as we draw all the consequences of the fact that persons are confronted with the need to have justified their actions, that is to say, not to invent, after the event, false reasons to disguise secret motives, in the way that one finds an alibi, but to perform them in a way that allows them to stand up to a test of justification.[13]

This problem-shift – from ideology and legitimation to justification – occurs at two levels. The first and more abstract is that of Boltanski's and Thévenot's theory of justification, which is reprised in *Le Nouvel Esprit de capitalisme*. As in this later text, Boltanski and Thévenot are minded 'to abandon the systems that, in a realist or critical perspective, make all social relations rest on domination or on force in favour of constructions seeking to build equilibrium in a city, which aims in common to give shape to a world where humans are sharply distinguished from other beings and also brought together in a fundamental equality.' This reference to equilibrium underlines once again that Boltanski, while hostile to the kind of sociological suspicion that reduces social relations to hierarchies of domination, wishes to avoid lapsing into normative political philosophy. Thus he and Thévenot seek to bring together the explanatory and the evaluative in a play on the French root-word *juste*:

> Thus we are led to pass over the distinction between the two definitions of *adjusted* [*ajusté*] oriented in one case towards *justice* [*justice*], in the other towards *soundness* [*justesse*], and to treat with the same conceptual instruments situations in which a maladjustment will be entered into the register of injustice or rather, for example, of that of dysfunction.[14]

So Boltanski and Thévenot's aim is to bring together in the same theoretical space the problem of normative integration – the concern of functionalist sociology common, for example, to Durkheim, Parsons, and Habermas to establish how shared norms and values secure the reproduction of a social order – and that of justification, which, as we have seen, they insist cannot be treated as a matter of ideology or on the basis of value-relativism. One critical difference between Boltanski and Thévenot, on the one hand, and functionalist sociology, on the other, is that the former, unlike the latter, do not privilege consensus. On the contrary, Boltanski and Thévenot are particularly interested in *dis*agreement. Hence the significance of those cases – what they call tests (*épreuves*) – where disagreements are regulated. These disagreements are, in particular, evidence that there is a plurality of principles of justification to which parties in dispute can appeal. Thus there are 'two major difficulties in the construction of legitimacy' – first, the conflict between inequalities of various kinds and 'what can appear as a principle governing the totality of legitimate forms of justification . . . what we call the *principle of common humanity*', and, secondly, 'the apparent plurality of these forms of agreement. How is this plurality possible when universality appears to be a requirement of legitimacy, and one that is often placed first?'[15]

This is a good question, though it goes without a satisfactory answer. In both books Boltanski and his collaborators concentrate on what they conceive to be the irreducible plurality of forms of justification. They argue that '[s]ix logics of justification, six "cities", have been identified in contemporary societies.' These cities, or political communities, whose essential character can be culled from widely diffused classics of political philosophy, are the inspired city (Augustine), the domestic city (Bossuet), the city of opinion or renown (Hobbes), the civic city (Rousseau), the market city (Smith), and the industrial city (Saint-Simon). Boltanski and Chiapello add a seventh city that is emerging and that makes possible the kinds of justification appropriate to the 'network world' being produced by contemporary capitalism.[16]

Each city is constituted by a 'superior common principle'; it is these principles 'to which individuals, today in France, most often appeal to establish an agreement or pursue a dispute.' But the forms of justification have a complex structure. Boltanski and Thévenot list a series of 'axioms' defining a city. These start out from 'the principle of the *common humanity* of the members of *the city*', but also posit a plurality of different conditions in which members of the city may find themselves, even though they are assumed to be equally capable of gaining access to these conditions. In order to 'coordinate actions and justify distributions', each city must have 'a *scale of values* for the goods or happiness attached to these conditions'. But the resulting hierarchy of valuations seems to be in tension with 'the axiom of *common humanity*'. This contradiction is resolved by two further 'axioms'. The first, 'a *formula of investment*', 'links the benefits of a *superior condition* to a *cost* or a *sacrifice* demanded to attain this' condition. The second 'posits that *happiness*, to the extent that it grows as one moves towards *superior conditions*, profits the entire city, that this is *a common good*.' The ordering of conditions in a scale of values is thus 'an *order of greatness* [*grandeur*]. The *common good* is opposed to the egoistic enjoyment that must be sacrificed to achieve a position of superior *greatness*.'[17]

The thought seems to be that – contrary to the famous slogan of the French Revolution – the great do not seem great because we are on our knees. The great are great to the extent that they have sacrificed to achieve their superior position and that they benefit us all: 'The condition of the great is not differentiated from that of the small [*petits*] only because it dispenses more wellbeing to those who accede to it, but also because it rebounds on the wellbeing of the small.'[18] The nature of greatness, however, varies between cities – in the inspired city it is sanctity, in the domestic city position in a hierarchical chain of personal dependence, in the city of opinion honour or public esteem, in the civic city commitment to the common good, in the market city commercial wealth, and in the industrial city inventiveness and expertise. But since these are all social qualities to which it is assumed all are equally capable of gaining access, it is always open to argument whether the current distribution of conditions among the members of the community corresponds to their respective greatness.

It is this that makes possible 'a *dispute* [*litige*], that is to say, a disagreement about greatness of persons, and thus about the more or less appropriate [*juste*] character of their distribution in the situation'. Such a dispute leads to a test whose function is to settle the disagreement 'by achieving a new disposition of persons and of valued objects'. Tests are able to resolve conflicts to the extent that they can appeal 'to a superior common principle to establish the relative greatness of people'. Agreement is, however, much harder to achieve when disputes involve appeals to *different* worlds – different cities and the larger social contexts sustaining

them. Such conflicts are unavoidable in modernity: 'in a differentiated society, each person every day must confront situations
referring to distinct worlds, know how to recognize them and
show herself capable of adjusting to them.'[19] But there is no standpoint superior to the individual cities from which appeals to different common superior principles can be adjudicated. Hence the
necessity of compromises where agreement is reached to suspend
a dispute without the issues being tested by appeal to a common
principle, even though the absence of a successful test makes such
a solution inherently fragile.

But the plurality of logics of justification is also what makes critique possible. Critique, in fact, depends on two conditions – first,
'the presence of beings of another world', and, second, the capacity of human beings 'to subtract themselves from the hold of the
situation, and contest the validity of the test'. Such a challenge
involves an *'unveiling'* that 'denatures the situation' by 'bringing
out the value of beings of another nature whose interference introduces foreign forms of greatness into the test'. The effect is to
expose those who were initially conceived to be the great by
demonstrating that their role does not produce the benefits attributed to it. The possibility of critique may complicate the resolution of disputes because of the absence of any independent
standard capable of assessing the claims of rival cities, but critique
plays an essential role in the practice of justification:

> Taking into account several worlds allows us to make the con-
> straint of justification more precise. Persons are not subject to it if
> they have not been faced with critique. The possibility of with-
> drawing from the present situation and denouncing it by taking
> support from an external principle and, in consequence, from the
> plurality of worlds, therefore constitutes a condition of justified
> action.[20]

Critique is also functional at a second, more concrete level, that
of the spirit of capitalism. For Boltanski and Chiapello, this
concept 'permits the articulation . . . of the two central concepts
on which our analyses rest – that of *capitalism* and that of *critique* – in a dynamic relationship.' Capitalism is the active party
to this relationship, constantly outdistancing its critiques, but it
also depends on them in order to meet its need for legitimation:
'Capitalism, unable to find its moral basis in the logic of the insa-

tiable process of accumulation (left to itself, amoral) must borrow from the orders of justification (named here *cities*) that are external to it the principles of legitimation that it itself lacks.'[21] The emergence of new critiques forces transformations in the spirit of capitalism that allow capitalism to draw on new normative resources, themselves derived at least in part from these critiques, and thereby to renew itself.

The emergence of the new spirit of capitalism that is the subject of Boltanski's and Chiapello's book is a case in point. They argue that there have been three capitalist spirits, 'in phase with' different kinds of capitalism – respectively, family, managerial, and globalized capitalism. The first spirit, focused on the individual bourgeois proprietor, drew its forms of justification from the domestic city. The second, whose central figure is the manager, was 'a compromise between the industrial city and the civic city'. It is the genealogy of the third spirit, whose normative resources contemporary capitalism draws from a new city, 'the *city of projects*' (la *cité par projets*), which evokes a 'flexible world of multiple projects pursued by autonomous persons', that Boltanski and Chiapello trace. Their analysis is based on a study of management literature, which, they argue, provides 'the most direct access to the representations associated with the spirit of capitalism of an epoch'.[22]

This study reveals a remarkable discontinuity between the 1960s and the 1990s. This is reflected in very different practices that the managerial discourses of these two periods identify as problematic: 'the management texts of the 1960s criticize, explicitly or implicitly, family capitalism while the texts of the 1990s are repelled principally by big hierarchical and planned organizations.' In other words, the later literature stigmatizes precisely the organizational forms that the managerial discourse of the 1960s seeks to vindicate against its petty capitalist precursors and also to render effective by ensuring that managerial personnel (*cadres*) are properly motivated and by addressing the organizational problems produced by the '*gigantism of enterprises*'. The discourse of the 1990s offers indeed a programme of liberation from the stultifying practices of the big corporation whose main themes are '*lean* enterprises, working in *networks* with a multitude of participants, team-working, or work organization *on the basis of projects*, oriented towards the satisfaction of a client, and a general mobilization of workers thanks to the *visions* of their leaders.' The manager is no longer a bureaucrat, but 'network man' (*l'homme des réseaux*), a figure whose essentially creative qualities allow him to take on 'the qualities of the artist and the intellectual'.[23]

This new discourse has become familiar enough to anyone who consults the business press (indeed the *Financial Times* has been running for some years quite a funny weekly column devoted to sending it up). The originality of Boltanski's and Chiapello's *démarche* lies in the argument that this managerial ideology is heavily indebted to the anti-capitalist discourse of the 1960s. They argue that critiques of capitalism draw on four 'sources of indignation' produced by capitalism – (a) disenchantment and inauthenticity, (b) oppression, (c) misery and inequality, and (d) opportunism and egoism. These in turn make possible two kinds of critique – the 'artistic', which relies on sources (a) and (b), and the 'social', which focuses instead on (c) and (d). The first condemns capitalism for the ways in which it violates the autonomy of persons, their capacity to live a life that they have genuinely chosen and that is meaningful to them. It has therefore been attractive to aesthetic rebels from Baudelaire onwards. The second targets the *social* evils induced by capitalism – poverty, suffering, injustice, and the corruption of solidarity, and is therefore more morally motivated. Marx's 'two concepts of alienation and exploitation refer to these two different sensibilities.'[24]

Boltanski and Chiapello argue that what they call 'neo-management seeks to respond to the two demands for authenticity and for freedom historically conjoined in . . . the "artistic critique", and sets aside the questions of egoism and of inequality traditionally associated in the "social critique".' This discursive shift is, moreover, an important part of the legacy of 1968. Boltanski and Chiapello describe the worker and student revolt of May–June 1968 in France as 'a profound crisis that imperilled the functioning of capitalism . . . But it is also, on the other hand, in recuperating some of the themes of the contestation that were expressed in the course of the May events that capitalism disarmed its critique, regained the initiative and found a new dynamism.' The social critique was traditionally dominant in the French workers' movement, but in 1968 a rehabilitated artistic critique found itself 'at the heart of the contestation'.[25] The themes of autonomy, creativity, alienation, and the like had been explored during the post-war years by small groups of radical intellectuals such as Socialisme ou barbarie and the Situationists; the emergence in 1968 of a radical student movement outside the control of the traditional left gave these ideas a new, vast audience. More threatening still for the employers, these ideas spilled over into the workplaces both during the events themselves and in an aftermath that extended well into the 1970s. While the social critique – taking the form, for example, of demands for higher wages – was pursued by the Communist Party, its allies in the Confédération Général du Travail, and the far left groups, the artistic critique found expression in the so-called refusal of work – the rebellion against Taylorist methods of mass production especially by young workers.

Employers initially 'interpreted the crisis *in terms of the social critique*' and offered material concessions designed to re-establish the post-war compromise between capital and labour. But, faced with a crisis of authority in the workplaces and with the rising cost of concessions against the background, from the mid-1970s onwards, of global recession, the *'advanced fractions of the bosses*' reframed the problem in terms of the artistic critique. In the course of the 1980s managerial control over the workplaces was restored under the slogan of flexibility 'by substituting *self-control for control* and by externalizing the very high costs of control by placing the burden of the organization on wage-earners'. This involved a variety of measures that, on the one hand, flattened managerial hierarchies, reduced the size of enterprises, and shifted responsibilities onto teams of workers, and, on the other, through practices such as sub-contracting, replaced centralized corporations with networks of apparently autonomous enterprises and subjected individual workers to direct market pressures. The latter 'appeared as an external factor that could not be controlled', and was therefore a 'more powerful and more legitimate' disciplinary mechanism than that offered by a hierarchical structure in which managers issued orders to their subordinates.[26]

Resistance to this 'deconstruction of the world of work' was weakened by political factors – for example, the crisis that overtook the French left in the late 1970s, whose outcome was a radical weakening of the Communist Party, the force that had hitherto organized the most militant sections of the manual working class. But it was also undermined by the way in which 'those who were in the vanguard of critique in the 1970s often appeared as promoters of the transformation.' This was true in the world of philosophy. Boltanski and Chiapello note that 'the metaphor of the network is tending progressively to assume the role of a new general representation of societies' and argue that the way was prepared for this by avant-garde philosophers such as Deleuze, who championed against the concepts of structure and system the idea of multiplicities whose ramifying, decentred, lateral relations are best captured by the metaphor of the rhizome. Deleuze and other theorists who became prominent after 1968 – for example, Bourdieu, Derrida, and Baudrillard – also deprived critique of an essential tool when they, from different perspectives, sought to dismantle the very idea of authenticity out of 'the desire to finish with the responsible subject to whom the choice between authenticity and inauthenticity presented itself as an existential choice, [which was] denounced as pure illusion or as an expression of the bourgeois *ethos*.' At a more mundane level, the entry of the Socialist Party into government after François Mitterrand's election as President of the Republic in May 1981 permitted the integration of many left-wing activists in the state and in the public sector more broadly. In the context of the Mitterrand government's embrace of neo-liberalism from 1983 onwards, their intellectual baggage, heavily indebted to the artistic critique of the 1960s and to the problematization of power in Foucault's enormously influential writings of the 1970s, took on a different meaning. 'Enunciated in a libertarian rhetoric, the critique of the state of the 1970s could not recognize its proximity to liberalism: it was in some way liberal without knowing it.'[27] In the course of the 1980s this naïveté was replaced by an all too knowing – sometimes cynical – self-consciousness.

Though greatly reinforced during the same decade by legislation and an ideological climate hostile to trade unionism, and by the increasing marginalization of the concept of class itself, the new capitalism began to face new challengers. Boltanski and Chiapello explore the multiple sources of 'the renewal of social critique' during the 1990s with which this chapter began – the increasing politicization of the previously neutral concept of exclusion, a reorientation of the modes of humanitarian action that had developed in the 1970s and the 1980s around issues pertaining to the global South (Médecins sans frontières, for example) towards combating the domestic effects of neo-liberalism, and, in 1994–5, the convergence of the new activist networks that had developed out of these processes with trade-union militants, particularly those from the radical SUD unions. Boltanski and Chiapello high-light the adoption of the network metaphor as a self-description of the new activism, reflected, for example, in the following remark by Christophe Aguiton, a militant in SUD-PTT and before long one of the key figures in the emerging international move-ment for another globalization: 'One form of organization is sym-bolic of this situation: the network, a flexible system, where people work together while maintaining their own identity.' Boltanski and Chiapello take this as evidence of 'the morphological homol-ogy between the new protest movements and the forms of capi-talism that have been put in place over the past twenty years'. The network form claimed by both capitalism and its opponents pro-vides the starting point for Boltanski's and Chapiellio's attempt to provide the new social critique with the concepts that it needs.[28]

Even this very selective summary should make plain the scale and the sophistication of *Le Nouvel Esprit du capitalisme*. Even though the book is too long and at points disorganized and repet-itive, we are dealing here with a major work. It is likely to remain an important reference point if only for the interpretation of the trajectory of French society in the final third of the twentieth century that it offers. But *Le Nouvel Esprit du capitalisme* invites a series of critical questions. In the first place, Boltanski and Chia-pello offer precisely a thick *French* narrative of a process that is surely of more universal import. The 'deconstruction of the world of work' that they describe was pioneered elsewhere, notably in the United States and Britain. The incorporation of *soixante-huitards* into a capitalism that adopted a mellow libertarian rhetoric isn't by any means purely a French phenomenon. Thomas Frank writes of contemporary American business culture: 'We live in a time, after all, when hard-nosed bosses compose awestruck disquisitions on the nature of "change", punk rockers dispense leadership secrets, shallow profundities about authenticity sell luxury cars, tech billionaires build rock 'n' roll museums, man-agement theorists ponder the nature of coolness, and a former lyricist for the Grateful Dead hails the dawn of New Economy capitalism from the heights of Davos.'[29] (Though Thatcherism and Reaganism on the whole employed a rather different cadre with a much more hard-nosed ideology, in many respects the ancestor of contemporary neo-conservatism.) It is a pity that, as Sebastian Budgen notes, '*Le Nouvel Esprit* lacks any comparative dimension' that might have facilitated a winnowing out of the local and the genuinely universal.[30] But the real difficulties with the book lie at a deeper theoretical and political level.

The central issue concerns the idea of critique itself. Once again, this is best explored first at a philosophical level before we consider the more concrete difficulties of Boltanski's and Chiapello's argument. As we have seen, they wish to develop an account of justification that avoids the value-relativism they condemn in Weber but that also recognizes the irreducible plurality of political communities (or, as they call them, cities). But it is not clear whether such a position is actually available. Boltanski and Chiapello on a number of occasions cite Michael Walzer, who has developed an influential pluralist theory of justice. Thus Walzer argues that '[j]ustice is relative to social meanings', that '[e]very substantive account of distributive justice is a local account', and that '[j]ustice is rooted in the distinct understanding of places, honours, jobs, things of all sorts, that constitute a shared way of life. To override these understandings is (always) to act unjustly.'[31] The implication of this conception of justice – though in a confused way Walzer has tried over the years to resist it – is that there are no context-transcendent principles of justice common to different ways of life.

Boltanski and Thévenot struggle with precisely this difficulty in *De la justification*. Towards the end of the book they write: 'The reference to a fundamental equality among human beings rules out *definitively* creating hierarchies on the basis of a hierarchy, whatever it might be, that defers humanity by directing it into a continuum of the more or less human.' And indeed, as we have seen, the first 'axiom' defining a city is 'the principle of the common humanity of the members of *the city*'. Accordingly Boltanski and Thévenot saw that a city could not include slavery or serfdom, and say that eugenics is an '*illegitimate order*'.[32] But it is not clear on what basis this stipulation can be justified. Why are cities required to respect the common humanity of their members? Boltanski and Thévenot say that the six logics of justification they discuss are implicit in disputes among individuals in contemporary France. But the substantial votes that the Front

National consistently receives in French elections suggest that there is a seventh logic, very different from that of the new 'connexionist' world, that precisely denies the principle of common humanity, namely racism.

In fact, what contemporary racist discourse tends to do is less explicitly to say that people of non-European origin belong to biologically inferior races but rather to argue that their 'culture' makes it impossible, whatever the legal formalities of citizenship, to be genuine members of European political communities. The principle of common humanity extends only to 'members of *the city*', which might seem to offer a let-out clause. Thus Walzer treats the right to limit the membership of a community as fundamental: 'Admission and exclusion are at the core of communal independence . . . Without them there could not be *communities of character*, historically stable, ongoing associations of men and women with some special commitment to one another and one special sense of their common life.'[33] But if 'common humanity' applies only within the city, then Boltanski and Thévenot seem arbitrary in banning slavery and serfdom. Why should these institutions be proscribed if they were restricted to non-citizens? After all, it was often in precisely this way that historically such practices were legitimized. Boltanski and Thévenot would of course resist such a conclusion, but it is hard to see on what basis they can do so as long as they deny that there are any principles common to the different cities.[34]

A similar tension between universality and inequality runs through their detailed account of justification. Justice, on this account, is a matter of securing an ordering of valued conditions that corresponds to the distribution of greatness in the city in question. As Jacques Bidet observes, greatness 'functions here in the mode of a "weak" philosophico-political presupposition, which allows the integration of "cities" that are hardly modern.'[35] Another way of making the same point would be to say that Boltanski and his collaborators are concerned with the legitimation of unequal distributions. The significance of these inequalities is meant to be limited by the assumption that members of the city are equally capable of attaining the unequally rewarded conditions that the city contains. The same thought is presumably expressed when Boltanski and Thévenot, in a passage cited a little earlier, say that human equality 'rules out *definitively* creating

hierarchies'. But it is very doubtful that these restrictions can do
the job intended for them. For example, the domestic city involves
a hierarchy of personal dependence: to the extent that places in
this hierarchy follow from family positions that are at least
partly a consequence of biological differences and properties – say,
being a father or mother or child or woman – is it *really* the case
that everyone has the same chance of gaining access to these
conditions?

More fundamentally, it is a misunderstanding of egalitarianism
to associate it with a requirement of equal capacities that plainly
does not correspond to the facts. The real challenge is rather how
to realize the ideal of equality granted that human persons differ
in their needs, goals, and abilities (see §7.2 below). In this context,
it seems to be that Bidet is right to argue that 'to approach the
question of justice in terms of *degrees of greatness* [*grandeurs*]
. . . seems to me contrary to the modern idea of justice. This consists in the establishment of differences against the background of
equal greatness.'[36] Indeed, the conception of justice developed by
Boltanski and Thévenot seems to tie justice to desert. The requirement that the great can be shown to have sacrificed in order to
achieve the benefits of their superior position and that this situation serves the common good implies that justice involves a distribution that corresponds to the moral merits of members of the
city. By contrast, Rawls refounded egalitarian thought by seeking
to disjoin justice and desert, arguing that the different productive
contributions made by members of society reflect 'the accidents of
natural endowment and the contingencies of social circumstances'.
His difference principle indeed requires that social and economic
inequalities should only be tolerated when they work to the benefit
of the least advantaged, but this proviso presumes a default position of fundamental equality, as is indicated by the 'more general
conception of justice' of which Rawls's two principles are specifications: 'All social values – liberty and opportunity, income and
wealth, and the social bases of respect – are to be distributed
equally unless an unequal distribution of any, or all, these values
is to everyone's advantage.'[37]

Of course, Rawls's having said it doesn't make anything true.
But it is still worth considering what motivated Boltanski and his
collaborators in implicitly giving the idea of desert such an important role in their account of justification and thereby distancing it

from the most powerful contemporary strand of thinking about justice. Once again, it seems to me that Bidet is right to say that 'the notion of "great" appears surreptitiously here as simultaneously a category of realism and of justification.'[38] As we have seen, Boltanski and Thévenot's concept of justification relies on a notion of equilibrium that appeals to both the normative concept of justice and the sociological concept of functionality. The same fusion of the normative and the explanatory informs *Le Nouvel Esprit du capitalisme*, where Boltanski and Chiapello call cities 'simultaneously operators of justification and critical operators'. But in fact there seems to be a more or less explicit tendency on their part to subordinate critique to functionality, as the following gloss indicates: 'The city thus appears as a *self-referential critical arrangement*, internal, immanent to a world in the process of making itself and that must limit itself to last.'[39]

This conception of critique, where it serves to make a particular version of capitalism viable by causing it to restrain its destructive tendencies, represents a restriction also of the ambitions of critique itself. Early on in the book Boltanski and Chiapello distinguish between two kinds of critiques of the tests through which a city is articulated with respect to particular cases, '*corrective*' and '*radical*': 'corrective critique is a critique that takes seriously the city with respect to which the test is constructed . . . a critique internal to the city. Inversely, radical critique is a critique that operates in the name of other principles, relevant to another city.' In *De la justification* Boltanski and Thévenot seem to make radical critique the paradigm of all critique, since they argue that critique involves the coexistence of more than one world. But *Le Nouvel Esprit du capitalisme* moves in the opposite direction, making all critique corrective. Thus Boltanski and Chiapello regard exclusion as too limited a concept to support a form of critique appropriate to the city of projects, but dismiss the Marxist concept of exploitation as too tied to nineteenth-century capitalism. What is needed is an account of '*a form of exploitation that develops in a connexionist world*'. They present at length a contrast between two modes of action in a network. On the one hand, 'the great in the city of projects' is characterized not simply by such qualities as adaptability and flexibility, but by his using these abilities to benefit more than himself: 'The team trusts him to the extent that he shows himself to be a *connecter*, an *extender* [*passeur*], who doesn't keep to himself the information gleaned in the network but redistributes it among the members of the team.' On the other hand, the 'networker [*faiseur de réseaux*]' is 'an opportunistic personage, who, while possessing all the qualities required in this world, uses them for purely egoistic purposes' – in particular, by taking advantage of information asymmetries for personal benefit.[40] Boltanski and Chiapello go on to broaden out their account of network exploitation: 'In a connexionist world, where greatness implies displacement, the great derive a part of their strength from the immobility of the small, which is the source of the latter's misery. But the least mobile actors are an important factor in the formation of the profits that the mobile derive from their displacements.' They offer some examples of 'relations of exploitation based on differentials of mobility . . . : financial markets vs. countries; financial markets vs. enterprises; multinationals vs. countries; big customer vs. small sub-contractor; global expert vs. enterprise; enterprise vs. precarious person; consumer vs. enterprise'.[41]

This attempt to develop the conceptual tools needed for the self-criticism of network capitalism prompts two objections. In the first place, the reconceptualization of exploitation in terms of mobility/immobility cuts across the distinction between extender and networker. Both the latter have the necessary qualities to succeed in the connexionist world, which crucially involves or is expressed in their mobility. The difference between them lies in their motivations: the networker is egoistic, out just to benefit herself, while the extender shares information with the whole team. Moreover, even the benefits the latter brings seem to flow only to fellow teamworkers, who are themselves among the mobile, but greatness is supposed to work to the common good – that is, to the advantage of the small as well as the great. Here we seem to see exactly the kind of surreptitious shift from an appeal to normative principles to realistic sociology for which Bidet criticizes the treatment of greatness by Boltanski and his collaborators.

Secondly, it is far from clear that the mobility/immobility opposition can support a defensible account of exploitation. It is undoubtedly true that immobility is a prime source of disadvantage and suffering in contemporary capitalism. Think, for example, of the ex-mining communities in Britain that, with the

virtual disappearance of the industry that brought them into existence, have been abandoned to unemployment, drug addiction,
and crime. In this kind of case, to be immobile is to be condemned
to suffering. But to be exploited is more than to suffer. Exploitation involves a relationship of interdependence between exploiter
and exploited: thus in the classical Marxist theory of exploitation,
the profits of capital derive from the surplus-labour performed by
wage-workers. Boltanski and Chiapello are perfectly aware of this
requirement: 'The denunciation of exploitation in effect inverts the
maxim "The happiness of the great produces the happiness of the
small", which constitutes the keystone of the axiomatic of cities,
by affirming that it is on the contrary *the unhappiness of the small
that produces the happiness of the great.*'[42]

But they do not show that immobility is necessarily the source
of the profits secured by the mobile. It has become a cliché to say
that neo-liberal globalization has freed capital to roam globally
while labour remains tied down. But the situation is much more
complicated than this simple contrast suggests. Boltanski and Chiapello offer a detailed account of 'precarization' – the emergence, as
a result of the construction of more flexible labour markets, of a
layer of low-paid, temporary, often part-time workers employed
particularly in small sub-contractors supplying large corporations.[43] Plainly these workers are particularly vulnerable to inten-
sified exploitation. But this kind of vulnerability doesn't seem
necessarily related to immobility. On the contrary, these workers
may be particularly mobile because they are migrants. In 2003 it
is estimated that there were 98 million itinerant workers, who had
left rural areas to work in the cities, in China.[44]

Many migrant workers are particularly vulnerable because they
are illegal. Consider another contemporary British case of *la
misère du monde*, the twenty-three illegal Chinese workers who
drowned in Morecambe Bay while picking cockles in February
2004. Here it was their mobility – itself a function of poverty –
that produced their suffering. Hardt and Negri in their theory of
the multitude make much of the mobility of labour today; this has
its own weaknesses, but it captures an aspect of the contemporary
social world ignored by Boltanski and Chiapello.[45] The problem
is at least in part a conceptual one. Exploitation is a relational
concept. Now mobility and immobility are best defined relative to
one another, but this doesn't generate the right kind of relation-

ship, since being mobile doesn't make one *dependent* on the immobile in the way in which, in Marx's theory of exploitation, the
capitalist is dependent on the worker's labour. Boltanski and
Chapiello dismiss the latter theory as a legacy of nineteenth-
century industrialism, but there is no reason why the exploitive
relationship Marx posits should require the exploited to perform
manual labour or even to help make a physical product.[46]
  These reflections suggest that the conceptual resources of the
connexionist world as it is revealed by the management literature
of the 1990s are insufficient to support a critique of capitalism.[47]
While this conclusion is, on the face of it, hardly surprising, it
invites the thought that Marxist *Ideologiekritik*, which among
other things draws a contrast between how society presents itself
in the discourses that seek to legitimize it and its real structures
constituted by exploitation and class antagonism, is still an essential critical tool. This would represent a particular problem for
Boltanski and Chiapello, since their focus is on corrective critique
– that is, critique internal to a particular city, in this case the city
of projects. There is moreover generally an anti-realist drift to
their argument. In a striking passage Boltanski and Thévenot
declare: 'Objectivity implies the definition of attestable relationships and of acceptable forms of evidence that are thus relative to
a world and to the resources of the great who are attached it.'
They go on to say that, 'outside an orientation towards justification, the question of the existence of things in the universe does
not concern us.'[48] This seems to be a contextualist conception of
objectivity where existence is defined relative to the standards of
a given city. *Le Nouvel Esprit du capitalisme* in fact ranges wider
than this would indicate, following procedures standard in the
social sciences and in historiography to draw on a variety of
sources and construct a narrative of the transformations of capitalism in the last third of the twentieth century.
  But Boltanski and Chiapello still seem largely to conceptualize
this history from the perspective of the plurality of cities that are
the sources of critique. At one point they seem to restrict the scope
of this perspective. 'The dynamic of capitalism itself is only partially related to critique', they note, pointing to the role of competition among capitalists in prompting technological innovation
and the processes of creative destruction on which Schumpeter
focused. But this restriction is then withdrawn by the rider that

competition is itself a form of critique, but one that operates (here Boltanski and Chiapello draw on the work of Albert Hirschmann) on the basis of exit – the threat or actuality of withdrawal from the market concerned – rather than voice – the collective attempts at reform that may seek to legitimize themselves by appealing to one of the logics of justification.[49] Competition is thus internalized within the process of critique. This is perhaps related to the fact that Boltanski and Chiapello make little effort to develop an account of capitalism as an economic system that goes beyond its minimalist definition as 'the unlimited accumulation of capital by formally peaceful needs'. Indeed, they seem to argue that capitalism's main problems are not economic. They dismiss any idea that capitalism was in crisis during the 1980s and 1990s: 'we consider that the last 20 years have been marked rather by a flourishing capitalism.' The rate of growth may have slowed down, but the return on capital has risen. 'So world capitalism . . . is doing fine. Societies . . . are doing rather badly.'[50]

There is therefore a marked contrast between Boltanski's and Chiapello's account of the strains of capitalism and the assessment independently arrived at by a variety of Marxist political economists that the advanced economies have been struggling since the late 1960s with what Robert Brenner calls 'the long downturn' caused by a chronic crisis of profitability.[51] These offer accounts of the structural contradictions of the capitalist mode of production that treat the latter as a system that has an existence and a dynamic irreducible to its discursive justifications. Boltanski's and Chiapello's ambivalent treatment of competition, which plays an important role in these Marxist theories of profitability crisis, indicate that they acknowledge that capitalism exists independently of these justifications. But they certainly under-theorize its economic logic and externalize the tensions between this logic and the prevailing mode of legitimation – '[t]he dialectic between capitalism and its critiques . . . [,] necessarily without end, insofar as we remain within the regime of capital, which seems to be the most probable medium-term prospect.'[52]

Bidet therefore seems entirely justified in concluding that Boltanski's and Chiapello's sociology 'presents itself, strangely, all at the same time as the critique of capitalism, and as its therapy'.[53] The reforms that they suggest – for example, the institution of 'a *right to employability*' that would allow workers to maintain themselves across successive projects – are inferred from the nature of the connexionist world. Moreover, Boltanski and Chiapello concede that the city of projects, as the conception of justice appropriate to this world, 'does not justify actions whose effect would be to limit the extension of commodification. It is however there perhaps that the only critical perspectives that capitalism cannot recuperate are situated because it is in some way of its essence to be connected with the commodity.' A little earlier they say that a new spirit of capitalism is required, 'not only from a humanist perspective – to limit the suffering caused by an unrestrained capitalism, but also from a perspective to some degree internal to the process of accumulation whose pursuit has to be assured.'[54] But if the new spirit cannot restrain commodification, these two perspectives are likely to come into conflict with one another rather than remain in harmony. For the strongest motivation to anti-capitalist resistance today is probably the relentless spread of commodification, both because of its deadening spiritual consequences (artistic critique) and because of its destructive effects on the physical and social worlds alike (social critique). Given the trajectory of contemporary capitalism, justice and functionality will find it hard to live together.[55]

2.2 The dialectic of universal and particular: Pierre Bourdieu

One can to some degree see Boltanski's and Chiapello's ambivalence about the status of critique as emblematic of broader political uncertainties in the *altermondialiste* movement. The aim of one substantial wing of the movement, represented particularly by ATTAC in France, is to impose new regulations on an increasingly unrestrained free-market capitalism. This is, if you like, a form of corrective critique that seeks to rein in capitalism's destructive – and self-destructive – tendencies; the idea of a radical critique that doesn't simply draw on normative resources foreign to the prevailing form of capitalism but might try to get rid of capitalism *tout court* is off the agenda for those who take this broadly reformist approach. For them, as Bidet observes of Boltanski and Chiapello, 'capitalism is the unsurpassable horizon of our time.'[56]

The allusion here to Sartre's famous description of Marxism as 'the unsurpassable philosophy of our time' is indicative of the enormous ideological upheaval that separates the present radicalization from its forebear a generation ago.[57] But it should be clear from the foregoing discussion that there are deeper philosophical and methodological difficulties with *Le Nouvel Esprit du capitalisme*.

In the first place, the theory of justice developed by Boltanski and his collaborators has a strong tendency to slide into normative functionalism. Though, unlike Parsons or Habermas, they privilege disagreements (*épreuves* and *litiges*) rather than consensus, the role of the critique that engages with these conflicts is to remedy evils and *thereby* to render capitalism more viable. This conception is no doubt sustained by the political considerations to which I have just alluded, but theoretically it develops from a broadly contextualist account of justice – or better, given the plurality of cities, of justices – that cannot without further argument sustain the minimal universal requirements that Boltanski and Thévenot insist are common to modern political communities. As in the case of the discussion of Habermas and Bidet in chapter 1, the moral is that normative principles need to be developed at a greater distance from explanatory social theory. But, secondly, the conception of sociology implicitly endorsed by Boltanski and his collaborators is an anti-realist one that focuses primarily on eliciting the concepts implicit in actors' practices rather than on developing an independent account of these practices and of the structures that sustain them. The result is a weak conception of social contradictions in which the main conflict is that between an under-theorized capitalism and the normative tissue in which it is embedded. The implication – which will be pursued much further in part II – is that one dimension of the realist ontology that, it is beginning to appear, is needed to sustain social critique is a considerably more emphatic theory of social structure than we have so far encountered.

It may, however, be helpful here briefly to consider a contrasting approach to critical sociology to that pursued by Boltanski and his collaborators, namely that developed by Bourdieu. His was, of course, a vast and complex enterprise pursued over four decades with a variety of co-researchers. My interest here is, however, with a very specific aspect of Bourdieu's work, namely the account of the status of the sciences that he gives, especially in *Pascalian Meditations* (1997).[58] This work serves not simply as a lucid and combative *summa* of his social theory, but also represents his most systematic exploration of what seems to have been one of Bourdieu's major preoccupations during his final years of political engagement, namely, how to situate socially, philosophically, one might even say ethically, intellectual work itself.

'I do not like the intellectual in myself', he wrote. This reflected his sense of '[t]he *fundamental ambiguity* of the scholastic universe and of all their productions – universal acquisitions made accessible by an exclusive privilege – [that] lies in the fact their apartness from the world of production is both a liberatory break and a disconnection, a potentially crippling separation.' For Bourdieu the secret of scholarship is revealed by the etymology of the world itself – '*skholè*, the free time, freed from the urgencies of the world, that allows a liberated relationship to those urgencies and to the world'.[59] This ambivalence about the social place of intellectual work did not lead Bourdieu to argue for abandoning the academy. On the contrary, in his last years he seems to have been seeking a new way of being an intellectual. In the immediate aftermath of the great demonstrations at Seattle in November 1999, he called for 'scholarship with commitment, that is to say . . . a politics of intervention in the political world that obeys, as far as possible, the rules in force in the scientific field'.[60]

As an intellectual increasingly actively engaged in politics, Bourdieu sought to develop a theory of such engagement. One means of entry into that theory would be via the Hegelian concept of the universal class, a class for whom 'the private interest is satisfied through working for the universal'.[61] Hegel thought that the modern state bureaucracy performed this role, but Marx in the 1843 Introduction to *A Contribution to the Critique of Hegel's Philosophy of Right* provides probably the most celebrated discussion of that concept of the universal class, one that, as we shall see in the next chapter, continues to resonate with contemporary radical thought: 'Only in the name of the general rights of society can a particular class claim to general domination.' He laments the German bourgeoisie's lack of 'that revolutionary audacity' – displayed by the French Third Estate in 1789 – 'which flings at the adversary the defiant words: *I am nothing and I should be everything.*' Marx famously concludes that only the proletariat can play this role – 'a class with *radical chains*, a class of civil society which is not a class of civil society, an estate which is the dissolution of all estates, a sphere which has a universal character by its universal suffering and claims no *particular right* because no *particular wrong* but *wrong generally* is perpetrated against it . . .'[62]

So a universal class is one that is able to represent its interest as the universal interest. The proletariat, according to the young Marx, represents a kind of limit-case: it is its position of exclusion from society and its 'universal suffering' that make it the universal class.[63] Crucial, then, to the conception of the universal class is the idea that a particular social position can embody the universal interest. The same dialectic of universality and particularity is be found in Bourdieu. Thus he talks of 'agents who . . . have a *particular interest in the universal*'.[64] How are they able to perform this role? Consider Foucault's critique of the 'universal intellectual' who 'spoke and was acknowledged the right of speaking in the capacity of master of truth and justice. He was heard, or purported to make himself heard, as the spokesman of the universal.' Sartre was the classic instance to this kind of intellectual. Foucault claimed he was being replaced by the 'specific intellectual', whose political involvement sprang from her particular competence with the modern apparatus of 'power-knowledge'. Thus: 'Magistrates and psychiatrists, doctors and social workers, laboratory technicians and sociologists have become able to participate, both within their own fields and through mutual exchange and support, in a global process of politicization of intellectuals.'[65]

Bourdieu's position is more complex. In *Pascalian Meditations* he undertakes what he calls 'the most radical historicization' of reason, hoping thereby to avoid the two false poles of abstract rationalism and postmodernist relativism. On the one hand, he develops a critique of 'scholastic reason' – of the way in which intellectuals fail to acknowledge the very particular and privileged social conditions that allow them to pursue 'work that is freed, in its rhythm, movement and duration from every external constraint and especially from the constraint over direct monetary sanctions'. Bourdieu traces the characteristic fallacies produced by the failure to recognize these social conditions of intellectual work, which he characterizes as 'scholastic epistemocentrism', 'moralism as egoistic universalism', and 'aesthetic universalism'.[66]

On the other hand, he argues that intellectuals, by virtue of this very social position, can become champions of the interests of the universal. This idea seems first to have emerged in *The Rules of Art* (1992), where Bourdieu offers a contrasting analysis of the 'universal intellectual' to Foucault's. He argues that this figure was made possible by the development of literature into an autonomous 'field of production' particularly as a result of the activities of Flaubert and Baudelaire as both critics and exemplars under the Second Empire. But it was Zola who played the decisive part in 'the invention of the intellectual'. Through his intervention in the Dreyfus Affair,

> he constituted, as a deliberate and legitimate choice, the stance of independence and dignity appropriate to a man of letters, by putting his own kind of authority at the service of political causes. To achieve that, Zola needed to produce a new figure, by inventing for the artist, a mission of prophetic subversion, inseparably intellectual and political.[67]

What is specific to this form of intervention in public life is that it implies, not the subordination of the cultural to the political, but rather the former's attainment of full independence: 'Thus, paradoxically, it is the autonomy of the intellectual field that makes possible the inaugural act of a writer who, in the name of norms belonging to the literary field, intervenes in the political field, thus constituting himself as an intellectual.'[68] It is Zola's achievement as a novelist – as it would later be Sartre's as a writer and a philosopher and Foucault's as a philosophical historian – that provides him with the authority to intervene, beyond the literary field, in politics. The conclusion to *The Rules of Art* makes it clear that Bourdieu is offering more here than a historical or sociological account of a particular form of connection between the intellectual and public life. Here he generalizes this account:

> Intellectuals are two-dimensional figures who do not exist and subsist unless (and only unless) they are invested with a specific authority, conferred by the autonomous intellectual world (meaning independent from religious, political or economic power) whose specific laws they respect, and unless (and only unless) they engage this specific authority in political struggles. Far from there existing, as is customarily believed, an antinomy between the search

for autonomy (which characterizes the art, science or literature we call 'pure') and the search for political efficacy, it is by increasing their autonomy (and thereby, among other things, their freedom to criticize the prevailing powers) that intellectuals can increase the effectiveness of a political action whose ends and means have their origin in the specific logic of the fields of cultural production.[69]

But the autonomy of these cultural fields, Bourdieu argues, is now threatened by neo-liberalism, which he regards as a form of economic reductionism. In response he advocates rehabilitating the figure of the universal intellectual, this time to preserve the autonomy of the cultural production from which (usually) his authority derives. 'One therefore has to appeal to a *Realpolitik* of the universal, a specific form of political struggle aimed at defending the social conditions of the exercise of reason and the institutional bases of intellectual activity, and at the same time endowing reason with the instruments which are the conditions of its fulfilment in history.'[70] Gérard Mauger has sought to underline the continuities between this account of the universal intellectual and Foucault's analysis: 'The appeal for "a corporatism of the universal" is addressed to "specific intellectuals": artists, writers or scholars recognized in their own domain who intervene in the political field in the name of the skills and values associated with their work.'[71] Now, there is something to this claim: for Bourdieu, the public authority of intellectuals derives from their positions within autonomous cultural fields. In that sense, they are universal intellectuals by virtue of being specific intellectuals. Nevertheless, their claim to be heard publicly transcends the particular cultural field in which they function. As he puts it, they intervene politically 'in the name of a particular form of ethical and scientific universalism which can serve as foundation not only for a sort of moral magisterium but also for a collective mobilization to fight to promote these values.'[72] This magisterium is epistemological as well as moral. Thus Bourdieu justifies his interpretation of the oppression of women as an instance of symbolic domination by appealing to 'the universalism that, notably through the right of access to the totality of objects, is one of the foundations of the Republic of sciences'.[73] It is thus hard not to conclude that Bourdieu still sees intellectuals as, in Foucault's words, 'spokesmen of the universal'.

But intellectuals can only legitimately claim this status if they can vindicate their 'right of access to the totality of objects'. The key to Bourdieu's attempt to offer such a vindication is provided by an intriguing passage hidden away in the methodological appendix to *Distinction* (1979):

> Objectification is only complete when it objectifies the site of objec-
> tification, the unseen standpoint, the blind spot of all theories – the
> intellectual field and the conflicts of interest in which sometimes,
> by a necessary accident, an interest in truth is generated – and also
> the subtle contributions it makes to the maintenance of the sym-
> bolic order, even through the purely symbolic intention of subver-
> sion which is usually assigned to it in the division of the labour of
> domination.[74]

So to complete the process of objectification inherent in the scientific study of the world we must objectify 'the intellectual field' whose perspective is the presupposition of objectification itself. The tools of objectification in this case are the concepts of social theory – and, in particular, the mutually implicated concepts of habitus and field. It is through the metaphor of the field that Bourdieu believes social structure must be conceptualized: each field involves a struggle for recognition whose specific character is a consequence of the nature of the scarce and unequally distributed resource (or capital) that is the object of competition in the field in question; meanwhile, the habitus is the set of dispositions through which individual subjects perceive and act on the world, dispositions formed through a process of adjustment to the fields into which the individual is inserted and therefore pre-adapted, thanks to the expectations the subject forms during this process, to reproduce the prevailing social structures. This is a conception of the social in which these structures weigh very heavily on persons who indeed (according to a metaphor to which Bourdieu has constant resort), through their habitus, incorporate these structures. Nevertheless, out of the competitive struggles in the scientific field, 'sometimes, by a necessary accident, an interest in truth is generated'. How is this possible?

The answer that Bourdieu gives in *Pascalian Meditations* is that the particular form taken by competition in the scientific field constrains researchers to rely on methods selected solely by their propensity to provide 'realistic representations' of the world:

> The fact remains that, despite everything, the struggle [within the
> scientific field] always takes place under the control of the consti-

tutive norms of the field and solely with the weapons approved within the field, and that, claiming to rely on the properties of the things themselves, their structures, their effects, etc., and therefore to have the status of truths, the propositions engaged in this struggle recognize each other tacitly or explicitly as amenable to the test of coherence and the verdict of experiment.[75]

The social mechanisms of the scientific field therefore give its agents an interest in pursuing scientific objectivity:

> If the universal does advance, this is because there are social microcosms which, in spite of their intrinsic ambiguity, linked to their enclosure in the privilege and satisfied egoism of a separation by status, are the site of struggles in which the prize is the universal and in which agents who, to differing degrees depending on their position and trajectory, have a *particular interest in the universal*, in reason, truth, virtue, engage themselves with weapons that are nothing other than the most universal conquests of the previous struggles.[76]

Theoretical progress is thus the result of a social mechanism that, rather like Smith's hidden hand, gives self-interested participants in the scientific field an incentive to pursue the truth. Bourdieu has here provided an intriguing analysis that seeks to transcend the conventional dichotomy between scientistic objectivism and sociological relativism by incorporating into his theory of fields the conception developed by Gaston Bachelard, founder of the French 'epistemological' tradition, of the *cité savante*, the community of scholars, as the site of scientific objectivity.[77] In contrast to Boltanski's idea that our conceptions of political community are necessarily plural, Bourdieu is saying that there is a particular, socially determined site from which we can gain access to the universal: the scientific field is 'a historical place where transhistorical truths are produced'.[78] Nevertheless, his argument invites a number of questions. In the first place, what is the precise status of objectivity here? The closest that Bourdieu comes to answering this question is in the following passage:

> The scientific field is an armed struggle among adversaries who possess weapons whose power and effectiveness rises with the scientific capital collectively accumulated in and by the fields (and therefore, in the incorporated state, in each of the agents) and who

agree at least to appeal to the verdict of experience, the 'real', as a kind of ultimate reference. This 'objective reality' to which everyone else explicitly or tacitly refers is ultimately no more than what the researchers engaged in the field at a given moment agree to consider as such, and it only ever manifests itself in the field through the *representations* given of it by those who invoke its arbitration.[79]

Bourdieu seems here to be endorsing a version of the pragmatist conception of truth discussed in §1.1 above where 'reality' and 'truth' are defined in terms of the standards to which researchers agree to subject themselves. In his final *cours* at the Collège de France, he goes further in this direction, declaring that 'the truth is the totality of representations considered as true because produced according the rules defining the production of the truth', and that '[i]t is . . . in a Kantian perspective, but totally excluded by Kant, in the name of the break between the transcendental and the empirical, that I have placed myself, in giving myself for an object the search for the *social-transcendental conditions of knowledge*.'[80] Bourdieu seems close here to the kind of socialized Kantianism developed by Habermas (see §1.1 above). The question is, as we have seen, whether such an epistemology can sustain a notion of objectivity strong enough for Bourdieu's purposes. His aim in taking objectification to the limit by objectifying the scientific field is not to dissolve the latter into a relativist morass. But to make truth and reality a matter of intersubjective agreement is to deprive oneself of the ability to say that whatever passes the currently prevailing 'rules defining the production of the truth' may turn out to be false. The whole idea of participants in the scientific field having 'a *particular interest in the universal*' would lose its paradoxical force if the universal were whatever researchers happened to take as universal at a given time. The anti-realist conception of truth and reality that Bourdieu espouses relaxes the tension in the idea that one can simultaneously be socially situated and have access to the universal and thereby makes it uninteresting. Developing his suggestive analysis of the scientific field requires a more robust form of realism of the kind outlined in chapter 5 below.[81]

Secondly, universality in this sense – scientific objectivity – is not the same as ethico-political universality. Bourdieu includes 'reason, truth, virtue' in 'the universal', but, without further argument, this looks like an illicit conflation of distinct concepts. One of the main themes of the early Frankfurt School was to stress that scientific rationality can be employed for barbarous ends, as the Holocaust bears witness. One might try to characterize ethico-political universality by appealing to Etienne Balibar's principle of '*égaliberté*' discussed in §1.2 above – the conditions of the fullest possible realization of liberty are co-extensive with those of the fullest possible realization of equality, which implies an ethical imperative to eliminate all forms of domination and exploitation. But *this* kind of universality is not equivalent to or implied by the scientific objectivity that Bourdieu claims is at stake in intellectual fields, or at least not without further argument which he does not provide.

Thirdly, Bourdieu's explanation of scientific objectivity on the basis of the specific properties of the scientific field is one symptom of the very emphatic conception of social structure that he – by contrast with Boltanski and his collaborators – employs. Consider, for example, the following account of why competition is endemic to social fields:

> To explain why all fields are the site of competition and conflicts, there is no need to invoke a selfish or aggressive 'human nature' or a 'will to power'. As well as the investment in the stakes that defines participation in the game and which, being common to all the players, sets them against and in competition with each other, it is the very structure of the field, that is, the structure of the (unequal) distribution of the various kinds of capital, which by generating the rarity of certain positions and the corresponding profits, favours strategies aimed at destroying or reducing that rarity, through the appropriation of rare positions, or conserving it, through the defence of those positions.[82]

It is thus on the structural properties of social fields that the entire burden falls of explaining conflict and its consequences (which, as we have seen, include scientific objectivity). One question that this provokes returns us to the very beginning of this book: how, according to Bourdieu, is transcendence – social and intellectual innovation – possible? In general, he insists on the obstacles to change – for example, 'the extraordinary *acceptance* that the established order manages to obtain':

> Because dispositions are the product of the incorporation of objective structures and because expectations always tend to adjust

themselves to chances, the instituted order always tends to appear, even to the most disadvantaged, if not as self-evident, natural, at least as more necessary, more self-evident than might be thought by those who, not having been brought up in such pitiless conditions, can only find them spontaneously unbearable and revolting.[83]

Thus their habitus – the embodied dispositions that adjust individuals' thought and action to the requirements of social structures – tends to bind the masses to the status quo. Bourdieu says 'it would be wrong to conclude that the circle of expectations and chances cannot be broken', first because of what he calls 'the Don Quixote effect', which arises when, say, changes in the occupational structure introduce a discrepancy between actors' expectations and the actual positions available to them, causing frustration and resentment, and, secondly, thanks to 'the relative autonomy of the symbolic order, which in all circumstances and especially in periods in which expectations and chances fall out of line, can leave a margin of freedom for political action aimed at reopening the space of the possible.'[84] Like Boltanski and his collaborators, Bourdieu sees conflict as inherent in social structures, in his case because of the relative scarcity and unequal distribution of different kinds of resources. Like them also, however, he has a relatively weak conception of systemic contradiction, which arises mainly when the evolution of society cheats the expectations incorporated in the habitus of a class of actors. Bourdieu wants to open up 'the space of the possible', but believes the cards are stacked against this. Let us now move on to consider theorists for whom, by contrast, transcendence is paradigmatic.

3

Touching the Void:
Badiou and Žižek

3.1 The exception is the norm

So far we have been dealing with thinkers who focus on *regularities* – systems, structures, long-term patterns and trends. The formation of modern social theory in the era of the Enlightenment and the French Revolution depended on the identification of a domain of being midway between the universal human characteristics and cyclical movements that preoccupied classical Greek thought and the occurrences that are the stuff of chronicles and larger scale historical narratives. Now there hove into sight social regularities whose scope was less than universal but that possessed a solidity, a capacity for self-reproduction, an internal logic demanding a particular kind of theoretical attention. Thus Adam Smith, in isolating systemic regularities at work in civil society, made it possible for Marx to formulate the concept of the capitalist mode of production, a historically specific social system. Whatever their differences with their predecessors and among themselves, Habermas, Bidet, Boltanski, and Bourdieu are all recognizably committed to this same intellectual enterprise, the theoretical study of social regularities that imperatively govern the limited zone of time and space over which they extend.

One striking intellectual reconfiguration that has taken place over the past generation is an increasing preoccupation with, instead of regularities, singularity, instead of structures, the *event*.

Of course, the enemies of social theory as an intellectual genre have long privileged the historically unique as the signifier of a life that resists confinement in structures: this was, for example, one of the main moves made by German *Lebensphilosophie* at the end of the nineteenth century in seeking to found a contrast between the physical and the human sciences that would make social theory illegitimate. But the interesting development has taken place outside the terms of this rather tedious debate. The beginnings of this shift are already registered in Foucault's inaugural lecture at the Collège de France in 1970. Braudel, one of the founders of self-consciously structural history, at the beginning of his great book on the Mediterranean, famously dismisses '*l'histoire événementielle*, that is, the history of events', as dealing with 'surface disturbances, crests of foam that the tides of history carry on their backs'.[1] Foucault, by contrast, seeks to displace this opposition between structure and event:

> Contemporary history is rightly often praised for having abolished the privileges accorded in the past to the singular event and to have made the structures of *la longue durée* appear. But I am not sure that historians have worked precisely in this direction ... what is important is that history does not consider an event without defining the series to which it belongs, without specifying the mode of analysis that it requires, without seeking to know the regularities of phenomena and the limits of the probability of their emergence, without interrogating the variations, the inflections and the appearance of the curve, without wishing to determine the conditions on which they depend.[2]

Foucault goes on to note that the concept of the event has 'rarely been taken into consideration by philosophers'. The event has none of the properties normally assigned to bodies, but

> it is not at all immaterial; it is always at the level of materiality that it takes effect, that it is effect; it has its place and it consists in the relation, coexistence, dispersion, intersection, accumulation, selection of material elements; it is not at the action or the property of a body; it produces itself as effect of and in a material dispersion. Let us say that the philosophy of the event must at first glance advance in the paradoxical direction of a materialism of the incorporeal.[3]

Foucault's main aim here is to desubstantialize the concept of structure by reducing it to probabilistic distributions of events, a move that would make it easier for him subsequently to develop a Nietzschean conception of history as 'the hazardous play of dominations'.[4] But in doing so he treats the event itself as an essentially statistical phenomenon: events are necessarily plural and are to be studied in the various relations they take up towards each other. But 'the philosophy of the event' that has come subsequently to dominate discussion treats the event *in the singular* and *out of relation* to other events and to any subtending structures and tendencies. This shift is reflected in Derrida's insistence in his later writings, for example, *Spectres of Marx*, on an experience of history as (in Hamlet's words) 'out of joint' – heterogeneous, disjunctive, out-of-synch, contretemps – as a precondition of the openness requisite for justice and democracy to be more than legitimations of existing manifestly unjust and undemocratic polities, an openness to the event whose actual occurrence can only be a complete surprise, ungrounded, inherently other, lacking any guarantee, an advent unsupported by any divine purpose or historical teleology. Derrida argues that deconstruction therefore represents not, as Marxist critics have often claimed, a depoliticization of avant-garde thinking but rather 'the condition of re-politicization, perhaps of another concept of the political', through

> thinking another historicity – not a new historicity or still less a 'new historicism' but another opening of event-ness as historicity that permitted one not to renounce, but on the contrary to open up access to an affirmative thinking of the messianic and emancipatory promise as *promise* and not as onto-theological or teleo-eschatological programme or design.[5]

Associated with this increasing focus on the event, conceived as singular and a-relational, has been the attention paid to two major German thinkers of the Weimar period – Carl Schmitt and Walter Benjamin. Benjamin's presence here is hardly surprising. His 'Theses on the Philosophy of History', written after the Hitler–Stalin Pact of August 1939, resonated with a new time of historical disillusion, as the crisis of the Western left that began in the second half of the 1970s climaxed in the collapse of the Soviet Union and the eclipse of 'historical Communism'. Benjamin offers in this text a critique of the orthodox Marxist conception of history as an inevitable progress, portraying this movement instead as 'one single catastrophe', and arguing that the task of the 'historical materialist' is 'to brush history against the grain', a reading of Marxism that, however heterodox, has had much to recommend it in an era marked by the apparently definitive triumph of liberal capitalism. The peculiar fusion of revolutionary Marxism and Jewish Messianism in the 'Theses', where socialist revolution is conceived not as the fated culmination of the development of the productive forces, the appointed conjunction of objective and subjective conditions, but as 'a Messianic cessation of happening', the violent interruption of the 'homogeneous empty time' of bourgeois normality by proletarian insurrection, is one source of Derrida's concept of 'messianicity without Messianism', of a Messianism without guarantees.[6]

Schmitt, however, is another matter. Leading legal philosopher of the Weimar right, close associate of the authoritarian militarist Schleicher circle in the months before Hitler took power, prominent apologist for the National Socialist regime in its early years, disgraced conservative *éminence grise* in the first decades of the *Bundesrepublik*, Schmitt has nevertheless become a major intellectual reference point for the liberal and radical left over the past two decades. Thus, at the same time as opening up to Marx, Derrida also interrogates Schmitt's political writings:

> lucidity and fear not only drive this terrified and insomniac watcher to anticipate the storms and seismic movements that would wreak havoc with the historical field, the political space, the orders of concepts and countries, the axiomatics of European law, the bonds between the tellurian and the political, the technical and the political, the media and parliamentary democracy, etc. Such a 'watcher' would thereby have been more attuned than so many others, to the fragility and 'deconstructible' precariousness of structures, borders and axioms that he wished to protect, restore and 'conserve' at all costs.[7]

Gopal Balakrishnan in an outstanding Marxist study of Schmitt offers a similar take on his thought, which 'took shape in the intertwining timelines of civil and world wars'. Balakrishnan argues that, '[u]nable to integrate his disconnected insights and judgements into a unified theoretical framework, Schmitt opted for a jagged and exemplary clarity over a smooth and featureless system.' The insight most influential on contemporary critical thought is Schmitt's attempt in *Political Theology* (1922) to use the state of exception (*Ausnahmezustand*), or state of emergency when the executive assumes special powers, to rethink the concept of political sovereignty. As Balakrishnan puts it,

> [e]mergency situations are like X-ray flashes which suddenly reveal the antinomies of legal reason. At such moments it becomes clearer that the state is more than a set of legal rules which define jurisdictions. In the rule-warping context of an emergency, an extra-legal surplus of discretionary power accrues to a 'sovereign' agent; in legal language, terms like 'threat', 'danger' and 'enemy' are the vectors of an anticipated transgression of legality.[8]

'Sovereign is he who decides the exception', declares Schmitt. Sovereignty resides in that instance of the state that decides that an emergency situation exists and accordingly suspends the constitution in order to save the state. Moreover, this decision cannot consist in the application of a norm (say, of a constitutional clause that defines the conditions under which a state of emergency can be declared) precisely because it addresses a situation that is abnormal, that falls outside the operation of general rules: 'The decision on the exception is a decision in the true sense of the word. Because a general norm, as represented by an ordinary legal prescription, can never encompass a total exception, the decision that a real exception exists cannot therefore be exactly derived from this norm.' Consequently 'the essence of the state's sovereignty . . . must be juristically defined correctly, not as the monopoly to coerce or to rule, but as the monopoly to decide.' The state of emergency thus reveals the arbitrary core of state power: beneath norms, the decision, beneath generality, the exception. The rediscovery of this reality is of not simply political but metaphysical significance for Schmitt, since '[t]he rationalism of the Enlightenment rejected the exception in every form.'[9] The sovereign decision is the hard kernel of singularity that cannot be accommodated in the generalities of the social contract and the categorical imperative.

Schmitt formulated this theory of sovereignty in the embattled conditions of the Weimar Republic, the famous article 48 of whose constitution made provision for the president to assume special powers, in all probability to crush a resurgence of the left-wing insurrectionism that in 1918–19 nearly made Germany the second chapter in the global revolutionary process that October 1917 in Russia was intended to initiate. In *Die Diktatur* (1921) Schmitt envisioned a temporary 'commissarial dictatorship' to defend the existing order against the threat of proletarian dictatorship. In *Political Theology* he radicalized this argument, making what he had earlier called 'sovereign dictatorship', which does not simply suspend the constitution to save it, but affirms the right to institute a new constitutional order, the paradigm of sovereignty. The spirit in which both books were written is summed up in these words of Donoso Cortés, one of the counter-revolutionary thinkers whom Schmitt embraced as ancestors in the struggle against the Enlightenment: 'It is a question of choosing between the dictatorship from below and the dictatorship from above. I choose the one from above because it comes from regions which are pure and more serene.'[10]

Extracted from these historical conditions, Schmitt leaves us with what Giorgio Agamben calls the 'paradox of sovereignty': 'the sovereign is, at the same time, inside and outside the juridical order.' The exception is not simply outside the norm, but founds it. 'The exception does not subtract itself from the rule; rather, the rule, suspending itself, gives rise to the exception and maintaining itself in relation to the exception, first constitutes itself as a rule. The particular "force of law" consists in the capacity of law to maintain itself in relation to an exteriority.'[11] But, as Agamben acknowledges in his recent book *Etat d'exception*, the exception is more than a philosophical problem. Benjamin, Schmitt's great interlocutor on the Weimar left, writes in his 'Theses': 'The tradition of the oppressed teaches us that the "state of emergency" in which we live is not the exception but the rule.'[12] Over fifty years later Derrida echoed him: 'The exception is the rule'.[13] For Derrida this reflects the fact that the application of any rule requires a decision that of necessity goes beyond that rule: 'the decision always marks the interruption of the juridico- or ethico- or politico-cognitive that precedes it and that *must* precede it.'[14] But, of course, Benjamin's remark had for him primarily a concrete political meaning: the catastrophic breakdown of the norms of liberal Europe that ushered in a global disaster of which he himself was one among tens of millions of victims. For Agamben, *mutatis mutandis*, Benjamin's statement has a contemporary actuality with its own urgency. He takes the emergency measures imposed under the state of permanent global war declared by George W. Bush after 11 September 2001 as confirmation of the state of exception as the 'constitutive paradigm of juridical order' since 1914:

> what I have tried to show is precisely that it has continued to function nearly without interruption starting with the First World War, across Fascism and National Socialism, right up to our own day. The state of exception has even attained today its most extensive planetary deployment. The normative aspect of law can thus be obliterated with impunity and contradicted by a governmental violence that, while ignoring international law abroad and producing a permanent state of exception at home, nevertheless claims still to be enforcing the law.[15]

3.2 Miracles do happen: the ontology of Alain Badiou

If we are indeed condemned to live under the sign of the exception, then it might be helpful to be able to place it philosophically as well as politically. Schmitt himself appeals to the familiar categories of *Lebensphilosophie*: 'In the exception the power of real life breaks through the crust of a mechanism that has become torpid by repetition.'[16] Balakrishnan calls him 'a *bricoleur* weaving a political programme of his own, without any fixed image of its final shape or of its immediate application to contemporary German realities'; an analogous judgement of eclecticism could also be passed against Schmitt's theoretical efforts, despite the arresting quality of the specific insights they offer.[17] But the most powerful philosophical appropriation of the exceptional was developed, at a considerable distance intellectually and politically, as well as chronologically, from the Faustian world of the interwar German intellectual right.

It is precisely in the context of a discussion of Schmitt's theory of sovereignty that Agamben introduces Alain Badiou's major philosophical work, *L'Etre et l'événement* (1988): 'Badiou's thought is, from this perspective, a rigorous thought of the exception. His central category of the event corresponds to the structure of the exception. Badiou defines the event as an element of

the situation such that its membership of the situation is undecidable from the perspective of the situation.'[18] Slavoj Žižek,
whose own recent work has engaged very closely with some of the
major themes of Badiou's writing, relates him more directly to the
contemporary political and intellectual scene:

> The fundamental lesson of postmodernist politics is that *there is no
> Event*, that 'nothing really happens', that the Truth-Event is a
> passing, illusory short circuit, a false identification to be dispelled
> sooner or later by the reassertion of difference or, at best, the fleet-
> ing promise of the Redemption-to-come, towards which we have
> to maintain a proper distance to avoid 'catastrophic' totalitarian
> consequences; against this structural scepticism, Badiou is fully jus-
> tified in insisting that – to use the term with its full theological
> weight – *miracles do happen*.[19]

Badiou's ontology is now the subject of an excellent detailed critical exposition by Peter Hallward to which I, like anyone who
chooses to struggle with an austerely compelling but also, at
points, intimidatingly arcane body of thought, am much
indebted.[20] But here I approach *L'Etre et l'événement* via a discussion of the philosophical and political trajectory that led to its
writing: it is, to my mind, a weakness, not merely of Hallward's
book, but of other Anglophone commentary on Badiou, that it
fails to give sufficient weight to the formation of his mature
thought against the background of what must have seemed to
most participants to have been the death agony of French
Marxism in the late 1970s and early 1980s. So I devote some
attention to an earlier book, *Théorie du sujet* (1982), that is best
seen as Badiou's philosophical working through of that crisis.

Like other French Marxists of his generation, Badiou moved in
the course of the 1960s from Sartre's attempt to reconcile exis-
tentialism and Marxism in the *Critique of Dialectical Reason* to
Althusser's project of a 'return' to a Marx stripped of humanist
and Hegelian residues. Badiou was indeed the author of an important essay seeking to situate Althusser's project, as well as of a
book in the 'Théorie' series that Althusser edited for Maspéro.[21]
Also like many of his generation around 1968, particularly those
influenced by Althusser, he broke with the mainstream left and
rallied to Maoism, becoming an activist in the Union des com-
munistes de France (marxistes-leninistes). During the 1970s

Badiou was known as the author of a series of stridently partisan texts that sought to formulate a theoretical approach appropriate to his Maoist politics (one legendary pamphlet denounced Deleuze's and Guattari's little book *Rhizome* as 'fascist'; the memory of such interventions – and of his support for Pol Pot's murderous regime in Cambodia – undoubtedly complicates the response of Badiou's French contemporaries to his more recent work).[22]

But the years 1975–8 brought a dramatic change in the political and intellectual conjuncture. The defeat of the Portuguese Revolution in November 1975 signified that the high watermark of the post-1968 radicalization had been passed; the leftist tide was receding. Mao's death, the overthrow of the Gang of Four, and the coming to power of Deng Xiaoping marked the end of the radical hopes raised (outside China at least) by the Cultural Revolution of 1966–9. In France, the Union of the Left between the Communist and Socialist parties collapsed, allowing the right to win the legislative elections of 1978; by the time François Mitterrand finally achieved the presidency three years later, the Communists had been reduced to a junior partner to a Socialist Party that would soon embrace neo-liberalism. This outcome was facilitated by the emergence of the *nouveaux philosophes*, ex-Maoist intellectuals who now, often appealing to vulgarized versions of the theory of power-knowledge being developed by a complaisant Foucault, denounced Marxism as the philosophical legitimation of the Stalinist camps immortalized in Aleksandr Solzhenitsyn's *The Gulag Archipelago*. By 1983 Perry Anderson could describe Paris as 'the capital of European intellectual reaction'.[23]

Théorie du sujet is a series of lecture notes (*séminaires*) composed between January 1975 and June 1979 that record Badiou's philosophical evolution in the face of what must have been a very painful political experience. Though, by the end, he still affirms 'an unconquerable nostalgia' for the late 1960s and early 1970s and 'the "cult of Mao"' that then reigned, he is already not far removed from the definitely post-Marxist stance of *L'Etre et l'événement*.[24] One way of capturing the logic of Badiou's itinerary is to consider one of the many ambiguities constitutive of Althusser's reconstruction of Marxism. On the one hand, Althusser offers an anti-humanist reading of Marx, in which history is 'a process without a subject' and individual subjects are formed within ideology to act as the supports of the prevailing relations of production. On the other hand, Althusser, particularly in his most strongly Maoist phase after 1968, insists on the primacy of the class struggle as the motor of historical change and denounces any attempt to give an explanatory role to the development of the productive forces. These two emphases pull in opposite directions: the former tends to objectivize the historical process, portraying it as the impersonal movement of structural forms; the latter, by contrast, subjectivizes history by giving the main causal role to the clash of rival class wills. It is probably fair to say that most of those influenced by Althusser tended to resolve this tension by radicalizing the subjectivizing tendency: Badiou certainly did, though in a characteristically idiosyncratic way.[25]

Thus, towards the end of *Théorie du sujet* he declares: 'The time of Marx, the time of Freud, consists in the fact that the subject is not given, but must be found.' Badiou acknowledges that this stance implies a reconfiguration of Marxist orthodoxy. He dismisses the critique of political economy ('the elephant-capital'), insisting that 'the texts of Marxism are first of all those where politics is being practised.' But this movement of subjectivization becomes more radical in the course of the book. The early sections contain discussions of the dialectic that offer a gloss on the Maoist slogan of the mid-1960s 'The One divides into Two'. 'The dialectic affirms that there are Two'; contradiction is conceived as a correlation – better a conflict – between two inherently heterogeneous forces. But even here there is a strong undertow tugging Badiou away from any version of Marxism. He reads the paradigm case of contradiction as that between not proletariat and bourgeoisie but proletariat and capitalist society as a whole, conceived as antagonistic subjects. This reflects the fact that the dialectic begins with the contradiction 'between the being [*l'étant*] and its place', in this case between the proletariat and its confinement within an exploitive imperialist society.[26]

To underline this point Badiou invents two virtually untranslatable portmanteau words – *le horlieu* and *l'esplace*: the first combines *hors* (apart from, outside) and *lieu* (place), meaning out-of-place, the second *espace* (space) and *place* (place) – 'splacement', perhaps. 'The dialectic', Badiou says, '. . . is the *horlieu* against the *esplace*'. This is a crucial move that more than anything else lays the basis of Badiou's mature ontology: contradiction no longer occurs between structures (say, the forces and relations of production) or as the clash of antagonistic class subjectivities. It is the struggle of a being against its confinement in spatialized structures. But what is this being? By 1977 Badiou has largely stripped away the carapace of orthodox Maoism. Contradiction must not be seen as a correlation of forces: we must reject 'a vision of politics as subjective duel . . . There is one place, one subject.' Moreover, 'just as there is only one subject, so there is only one force, whose existence always produces the event.'[27]

This poses the question of what Badiou means by the subject. Althusser's anti-humanism was part of a much larger philosophical movement in post-war France that challenged what Habermas calls 'the philosophy of consciousness' – the conception of the individual subject as a self-transparent, coherent unity that is the starting point for the construction of knowledge and the world. Badiou clearly does not regard the subject as foundational, but he takes his distance from anti-humanism because, in giving discourse a 'constituent function', it tends towards linguistic idealism (*idéalinguisterie*), one of his abiding dislikes. He seeks instead 'a conceptual black sheep – a materialism centred on a theory of the subject'. It is important to see that Badiou's preoccupation with the subject is in its original impulse political. He insists repeatedly on the difference between the working class and the proletariat – between, in other words, the empirically existing sociological class of wage-labourers and the revolutionary subject. The working class belongs to *l'esplace*, to the situating of being in social structures, while '[t]he proletariat exists wherever a political *horlieu* is created. It is thus in purging itself that it exists. It has no existence anterior to its organization of political survival.'[28]

Thus (rather ironically, given that one of the main themes of Badiou's recent writings is the obsolescence of the party as a political form) the proletariat exists in *Théorie du sujet* as the Marxist-Leninist party. At one level, this is a familiar enough case of what the young Trotsky called substitutionism, in which the actual working class disappears into its self-appointed representative, the party: this ideological operation played an important role in legitimizing Mao's regime, particularly during the Cultural Revolution.[29] But Badiou gives this ideologeme a characteristic twist of political extremity and metaphysical sophistication. The party 'is of the subjective': its function is to free force from the impurities it necessarily acquires through being placed in social structures. Indeed, 'the party *is* purification', seeking to combat the effects of the working class's situation in *l'esplace* of bourgeois society. (Badiou approvingly quotes Stalin on the need for the party to strengthen itself by purging opportunist elements, but adds the qualification that 'cutting off heads' led Stalin to 'nothing but disaster'.) Consequently, in a formulation that implicitly repudiates Althusser's claim that Marx's significance lay in his opening up 'the continent of History' to scientific knowledge, Badiou writes: 'Science of history? *Marxism is the discourse through which the proletariat sustains itself as subject.*'[30]

It might seem tempting to dismiss such formulations as belonging merely to Badiou's Mao-Stalinist juvenilia, and therefore best forgotten. But this would be a mistake, for two reasons. First, the reception of French thought in the English-speaking world has already suffered badly enough from a tendency to detach texts from their highly specific intellectual and political contexts to perpetuate this practice in the case of a thinker whose highly politicized work is only beginning to receive serious Anglophone attention. Second, the continuities in Badiou's thought between his Marxist and post-Marxist periods are very striking. Thus, to take the case in point, Hallward notes: 'In Badiou's work, both early and late, a politics of disciplined purification prevails of a politics of alliance and negotiation.' Moreover, as Hallward also observes, for Badiou '[t]ruth and subject are occasional, exceptional.'[31] This idea is also present in *Théorie du sujet*. As early as February 1976, Badiou writes: 'Every subject is an exception, who comes in second place.'[32] One can see why he should have come to develop this conception of the subject. Given his preoccupation to tear French workers from the deadening normality of the bourgeois *esplace*, to construct a party through which a revolutionary subjectivity could assert itself, it was entirely natural that Badiou should see the subject as inherently abnormal (in the words of a much later text), 'rare and heroic'.[33]

Even though politics is thus often in command in Badiou's thought, he draws on a variety of sources in developing this key notion that the subject is an exception. He first formulates this idea in the course of a detailed discussion of Mallarmé's poems (Hallward indeed calls his a 'philosophy conditioned by Mallarmé').[34] But there are two more strictly theoretical sources

of Badiou's conception of the subject. One is Jacques Lacan's reinterpretation of psychoanalysis. At different points in *Théorie du
sujet*, Badiou compares Lacan to Lenin, Hegel, and the Maoists:
his significance is thus the subjective reinvigoration of Freud's
thought, rescuing it from 'Yankee psychoanalysts'. There are,
notoriously, two Lacans: the one that interests Badiou is the
second, who thematizes the Real as the inherent breakdown of the
Symbolic order to which the subject is tied down through language
and the Oedipus complex (see §3.3 below). But the other critical
source of Badiou's theory of the subject is provided by the sub-
field of mathematical logic known as set theory. These two sources
aren't necessarily clearly distinguished. Badiou approvingly quotes
Lacan's remark: 'In the first place the Real is for us woven by
numbers.'[35]

It is, however, over *L'Etre et l'événement* that set theory reigns.
By the time this book appeared in 1988 Badiou had concluded
that 'the "age of revolutions is over"', though he continues to
invoke also the 'post-Cartesian doctrine of the subject' that he
associates with 'the names of Marx (and of Lenin), of Freud (and
of Lacan)'.[36] Having distilled from Maoism its subjectivism,
Badiou now transforms the latter into an ontology. To justify his
reliance on set theory he explains that, 'if it is true that it was the
philosophers who have formulated the question of Being [*l'être*],
it was not they, but the mathematicians, who have produced the
reply to this question.' The attraction of set theory seems to a significant degree to be that it allows Badiou to pursue the project
of purification that emerges in his earlier Marxist writings. Thus
he taxes even Heidegger, who sought to pose the question of Being
distinct from that of the nature of specific beings, for suffering
from 'nostalgia for presence and for repose', poeticizing Being by
conceiving it as directly given in nature, but somehow now lost
or concealed. He contrasts this with 'ontology proper, as the native
figure of Western philosophy', 'the Greek event, that thinks Being
subtractively, in the mode of an ideal axiomatic thought. The distinctive invention of the Greeks was that all being is sayable once
a decision of thought subtracts it from all instances of presence.'[37]

Badiou therefore follows the Greeks – above all, Plato, who
'*interrupted* the poem with the matheme'.[38] This philosophical
strategy leads him to organize his account of Being and the event
around the interpretation of a series of proofs in set theory. In

expounding Badiou, Hallward follows the same path, giving detailed and very helpful accounts of such figures in the development of modern mathematical logic as Georg Cantor and Paul Cohen. I don't intend myself to repeat any of this, partly because I lack the competence, but partly also because I must admit to being sceptical about the status given set theory by Badiou. It seems to me that his main philosophical claims can be stated and assessed without a deep immersion in mathematical logic. This, in any case, is how I shall proceed.

Badiou posits a fundamental opposition between Being and the event; therefore, 'of the event, ontology has nothing to say.' This opposition is recognizably the descendant of that between *esplace* and *horlieu* in *Théorie du sujet* – that is, between confinement in structures and the purifying moment of a subject. The suitably refined version of *l'esplace* in *L'Etre et l'événement* is the situation, 'the place of having-a-place' (*le lieu d'avoir-lieu*). Badiou declares: 'There are only situations. Ontology, if it exists, is *a situation*.'[39] But what is a situation? What had been evoked by metaphor in Badiou's earlier writings now becomes the object of sustained analysis. As Hallward puts it, 'mathematics provides Badiou with a language for describing the general situation of all conceivable situations, regardless of their particular contexts or contents.'[40]

The starting point for understanding the situation is not the presence beloved of poeticizing ontologies, but presentation: 'what is *presented* is essentially multiple, *what* is presented is essentially one.' In the ancient philosophical dispute between the Many and the One, Badiou has now opted for the many, though in a distinctive fashion: 'there is no one, there is only counting-as-one.' The multiple is given in presentation, but it is presented *as* a multiplicity. In other words, the multiple, when presented, is unified, counted-as-one. But, since what is presented is multiple, this unification is the result of an '*operation*'. This result is a situation, a 'presented multiplicity . . . Every situation receives an operator of counting-for-one that belongs to it. This is the most general definition of a *structure* as being what prescribes, for a presented multiplicity, the regime whereby it counts-as-one.'[41]

Because the multiple is presented as multiplicities through the operation of counting-for-one, there is no direct access to the multiple. The operation of counting-as-one, since it is subject to the laws of arithmetic, produces consistent multiplicities; the multiple as inconsistent multiplicity can only be inferred indirectly, and not experienced or known:

> the multiple is the inertia that can be retroactively deciphered start-ing from the fact that the operation of counting-as-one must effec-tively operate for there to be a one. The multiple is the inevitable predicate of what is structured, for structuration, i.e. counting-as-one, is an effect. That the one, which is not, cannot be presented, but only operates, establishes 'behind' its operation that presenta-tion takes place under the regime of the multiple.[42]

Inconsistent multiplicity, though only 'a horizon of uncapturable [*insaisissable*] Being', introduces an instability into the situation. Because it cannot be presented, it lacks any positive quality. Indeed, 'the pure multiple, absolutely unpresentable according to the count, is *nothing*', but that doesn't mean that it has no onto-logical pertinence. Insofar as the unity of the situation is a result of an operation of counting-as-one, ' "something" of the multiple must not be in absolute coincidence with the result.'[43] This 'some-thing' is, precisely, nothing. As Hallward puts it, 'the void, or nothing, is that absent "no-thing" upon which any conceivable count or presentation is effectuated.'[44] In fact, the void is a lot more than nothing taken literally: it is 'the name of Being – of inconsistency – according to a situation, insofar as presentation gives us there an unpresentable access, thus a lack of access to this access, in the mode of what is not-one, nor composable of ones, and thus cannot be qualified in the situation except as the wan-dering of nothing.' The void is thus best thought of less as literal nothingness, certainly not in the sense of not-being, than as indif-ference, since Being is 'neither one . . . nor multiple', or as the inef-fable, since, being beyond presentation, it has no qualities.[45]

It is at this point in Badiou's argument where it is most plausi-ble to say that set theory plays an ineliminable role. He appeals to the distinction between membership or belonging, 'which indi-cates that a multiple is counted as an element in the presentation of another multiple', and inclusion, 'where one multiple is a subset [or part] of another'. A situation is defined by the relationship of belonging: it is composed of elements. But there is at least one subset of every set that does not belong to it: '*no multiple can make-one of everything that it includes* . . . Inclusion is in irremediable excess over membership.' Moreover, the void is a subset of all sets and itself includes a subset, namely the void itself. So, '[i]t follows from everything that is not presentable that it is everywhere present in its lack.'[46]

Badiou takes this as a kind of formal proof of the constitutive instability of the situation, and therefore of the necessity of a further dimension of being to nail the situation in place:

> All multiple-presentation is in danger of the void, which is its Being-as-such [*son être en tant que tel*] . . . For the apparent solidity of the world of presentation is only a result of the action of the structure, even if *nothing* is outside such a result. It is necessary to forbid the catastrophe of presentation that would be the encounter with its own void – i.e. the presentative advent of inconsistency as such, or the ruin of the One.[47]

To encounter Being, the void = pure inconsistent multiplicity in presentation would be like those moments in Greek myth when a visiting god gives way to the importunities of his human lover, and, dropping his mortal guise, reveals himself as he really is, which withers and blasts her into inexistence. The structure of the situation is the weak link in the chain that could allow such a devastating apocalypse, the irruption of the void, to occur. Itself the transparent result of the structuring operation that counts the multiple as one, and thus

> a-structured, the structure itself is the point where the void should be given. To ban the void from presentation, *it is necessary that the structure should be structured*, that the 'there is a one' applies for the count-as-one. The consistency of presentation thus requires that all structure should be *redoubled* with a metastructure, which closes it to any fixation of the void.[48]

This metastructure is what Badiou calls the '*state of the situation*', 'through which the structure of a situation – of whatever structured situation – is counted-as-one.' This reduplication is secured through what (by contrast with the original presentation constitutive of the situation) is characterized as representation: everything that is included in a situation is a member of its state, thus avoiding the excess that threatened the invasion of presentation by the void. The state is able to perform this function because it is 'intrinsically a structure *separated* from the originary structure of the situation' that gives the situation 'a fictional being, which dismisses, it seems, the peril of the void'.[49] The political resonances of this account of the state of the situation are quite intentional. As Hallward puts it, '[t]he state is thus a kind of primordial response to anarchy. The violent imposition of order, we might say, is itself an intrinsic feature of being as such.'[50]

But if the reduplication of structure in the state stops up one hole through which the void might gain access to presentation, the event offers it another, albeit highly unpredictable route to experience. Badiou draws a distinction between normality and singularity. A normal term is one that is both presented and represented, that is both an element of a situation and (thanks to the reduplication of the structure in the state) included in it as well. A singular term is one that is presented, but not represented: it belongs to the situation but somehow escapes the reunifying function of the state. Badiou maps this distinction onto that between nature and history. 'The natural is the intrinsic normality of a situation', he says. History, by contrast, is 'the a-normal': 'the place where that-which-is-not-being is the non-nature that is presented as *other* than natural, or stable, or normal . . . I call *historical* what is thus determined as the opposite of nature.'[51] It is interesting to see here an austerely classical philosopher, concerned to subtract his concepts from any naturalistic taint, reproduce the opposition familiar in *Lebensphilosophie* between nature and history, generality and singularity.

'That-which-is-not-being' is the event. Events are outside situations, whose composition, structures, and states exhaust the subject matter of ontology. As Hallward puts it, 'what is encountered through the event is precisely the void of the situation, that version of the situation that has absolutely no interest in preserving the status quo as such.'[52] But, although the event transcends the situation, its condition of existence is to be found in the situation. This is what Badiou calls the 'evental site': this is a multiple that is presented in the situation; none, however, of its elements are and it is not a subset of the situation. It is thus 'totally a-normal', since it belongs to, but is not included in, the situation. It is thus 'on the edge of the void'.[53]

This peculiar relationship to the situation gives the event an ambiguous quality. Badiou defines the '*event of site X* [as] *a mul-*

tiple such that it is composed in part of elements of the site, in part of itself.' He gives the example of the Great French Revolution, of which 'one must say at the same time that it presents the infinite multiple of the sequence of facts situated between 1789 and 1794, and *beyond this* that it presents itself as immanent resumé and trait of its own multiple'. An event has a surplus quality that cannot be reduced to the succession of facts from which it emerges. This isn't just because of the familiar problem that historical knowledge has an inherently retroactive dimension – that, for example, one couldn't know that one was fighting in the Thirty Years' War at the time. Because the event isn't a subset or part of the situation, there is no objective way of determining its relationship to the situation: 'If an event exists, *its membership of the situation is undecidable from the point of view of the situation itself.*'[54]

This undecidability means than an 'interpreting intervention' is required for an event to become discernible. It is through the event that the inherent excess that is the void present in every situation can become visible; the interpreting intervention is a response to this: 'By affirming that the event belongs to the situation, it bars the irruption of the void. But this is only to force the situation itself to own up to its void, and thus to bring forth, from inconsistent being and interrupted counting, the glare, that does not partake of Being, of an existence [*l'éclat non-étant d'un existence*].' The event is where Being as the situation, consistent multiplicity, breaks down. Its discursive recognition through an interpreting intervention therefore involves going beyond knowledge (*savoir*), which takes the form of what Badiou calls the encyclopaedia, 'a classification of parts of the situation that groups together terms having such or such explicit property'. But the event pertains to precisely what is not explicit, what is indiscernible in the situation. Acknowledging it, naming it through an interpreting intervention, requires a 'generic procedure' through which a *truth* is recognized:

> 'Generic' positively affirms that what does not allow itself to be discerned is in reality the general truth of a situation, truth of its distinctive being, considered as foundation of all knowledge to come. 'Generic' reveals the truth-function of the indiscernible. The negation implicit in the 'indiscernible' however preserves the fol-

lowing essential point, that a truth is always something that makes a hole in a knowledge.[55]

Perhaps one can detect here, in the idea that a truth tears into the knowledge that merely identifies and classifies what pertains to the normal in a situation, a faint echo of Althusser's concept of the epistemological break through which a science constitutes itself in opposition to the theoretical ideology from which it emerged. But for Althusser both science and ideology are generalities, bodies of concepts; for Badiou, however, it is always a matter of *a* truth, specific, exceptional, and localized, since an event depends for its existence on its eventical site in a situation but also necessarily exceeds that situation. More than that, whereas for Althusser scientific practice is a process without a subject, for Badiou a truth is always subjective, since recognizing an event requires a decision: 'Because an event is essentially a multiple whose membership of the situation is undecidable, to decide that it belongs to it is a wager that one cannot hope will ever be legitimate, since all legitimacy depends on the structure of the situation.' This unfounded decision isn't just subjective: through it a subject is constituted: 'I call *subject* every local configuration of a generic procedure through which a truth procedure is sustained.'[56]

As we have seen, Badiou conceives the subject as exceptional: 'A subject is not a result – any more than it is an origin. It is the *local* status of the procedure, an excessive configuration of the situation.'[57] It follows that not all human individuals are subjects. As Hallward puts it, '[a] subject is an individual transfigured by the truth she proclaims.' But since, as he also notes, '[a]n event is the unpredictable result of chance and chance alone', and since the decision to acknowledge an event is a wager that can never be shown to have been justified, it is probable that most individuals will never experience this transfiguration.[58] In this respect, there is an analogy between Badiou's conception of the subject and Nietzsche's insistence that self-realization can only be achieved by a few exceptional individuals. Badiou indeed approvingly quotes Nietzsche's injunction 'Become who you are': 'If it is necessary to become a subject, this is because one isn't one. The "who you are" as a subject is nothing but the decision to become it.' And he opposes '*a formalized in-humanism*' to what he contemptuously dismisses as the 'animal humanism' of the contemporary liberal orthodoxy.[59] Badiou's thought is of course quite free of the Lam-arckian biologism that Nietzsche uses to shore up his aristocratic contempt for the mass of humanity. Becoming a subject does not depend on any imaginary racial qualities; it requires rather what Badiou calls fidelity to the event. Fidelity is the stance or orienta-tion that a subject takes up in order to sustain a particular truth through time. It is 'a *discipline* of time', 'the arrangement that sep-arates out, in the set of presented multiples, those that depend on an event. To be faithful is to assemble and identify a chance that is becoming legitimate [*le devenir legal d'un hazard*].'[60]

There is a tension then in fidelity. The notion of a chance becoming legitimate implies a tendency towards institutionaliza-tion, rather like Weber's idea of the routinization of charisma, in which the original creative impulse that founds a movement is pro-gressively drained away as bureaucracy and tradition come to predominate. But the fact that the decision to name an event can never be legitimized because legitimacy pertains to the situation that an event of its nature exceeds suggests that any such process of institutionalization is always contestable. Badiou calls this deci-sion an 'interpreting intervention'; since interpretation is an infi-nite process, what fidelity to a particular event implies is always open to argument. Badiou's career as a Maoist activist would have taught him this. Nevertheless, the most interesting case study he gives of fidelity – his remarkable little book *Saint Paul* (1997), which offers the most accessible way into Badiou's thought – sug-gests that when choosing this term to characterize the orientation of a subject he did not simply reject its literal meaning.

Badiou's interest in St Paul is another sign of the continuities in his thinking: already in *Théorie du sujet*, he sketches out the main themes of *Saint Paul*, and names Paul 'the Lenin' of 'the Universal Church'.[61] In the later book Badiou puts his interest in Paul in the context of his 'search for a new militant figure' to replace the figure of the party activist constructed by Lenin and the Bolsheviks. He rejects the commonplace view of Paul as the agent of the routinization of charisma, 'the indefatigable creator of the Church', through whom the original fire of early Christianity is damped down and contained by an ecclesiastical hierarchy whose terminus was the Vatican bureaucracy. Badiou's Paul is 'a thinker-poet of the event', who sought to universalize Christianity by dissociating it from both Jewish law and Greek metaphysics and stripping it down to the Resurrection, 'pure event, opening of an epoch, change in the relations between the possible and the impossible'. For Badiou, Paul's role in the debate over whether gentile converts to Christianity should have to conform to the Jewish law by becoming circumcised exemplifies the relationship between an event and its eventual site. Paul recognized that, if Judaism was the site of the 'Christ-Event', the event nevertheless transcended its site. By becoming the apostle to the gentiles and preaching a 'New Law' in which the gift of divine grace is available to all, Paul became 'one of the very first theoreticians of the universal'.[62]

Whatever one finally makes of all this, no one can doubt that Badiou is one of the most formidable of contemporary thinkers. His great merit is to have explored with great rigour and imagination the implications of a widely held idea of the event. His commitment to precise conceptualization means that, for all its difficulty, his thinking compares favourably with, for example, the treatment of the event offered by Derrida, where the event becomes one of the many names of what is beyond the categories of Western metaphysics but that, because these categories are at once inadequate and inescapable, can only be evoked, alluded to, indirectly approached. Although Badiou's conception of Being as the void that is beyond but implicit in all presentation is his own particular version of negative ontology, he does offer a clear account of the event. Moreover, this account captures two important features of the phenomenology of events that are highlighted notably in Benjamin's 'Theses on the Philosophy of History'.

First, there are occurrences that constitute breaks in normality, interruptions in 'homogeneous empty time'. This is surely an important part of modern historical experience. If one thinks not simply of the great revolutions (France 1789, Russia 1917) that Badiou treats as paradigm cases of political events (as opposed, for example, to events in art such as Cézanne's transformation of Impressionism or in science such as Cantor's development of set theory) but of more recent upheavals such as the collapse of the Stalinist regimes in 1989–91 or 11 September 2001, what they all share is the quality of exceeding the causal sequence that preceded them and to which, when trying to explain why they took place, the historian tracks back. A historical interpretation that simply dissolves the event into this sequence causes to disappear the surplus quality that makes the event an event, the property that

Badiou conceptualizes as being partly composed of itself and not just of the elements of the situation from which it emerged.[63] Second, just because of this quality of exceeding the situation, an event demands interpretation: identifying the elements that do belong to it is a matter of judgement that can always be contested and revised, not the predictable outcome of the application of an algorithm. For example, what are the decisive constituents of the French Revolution – the constitutional reforms of the propertied elites that somehow 'skidded off course' thanks to the interference of Jacobin ideologues and the mob, as François Furet argued, or the self-organized invasion of high politics by the *menu peuple* of town and country, as Albert Soboul devoting his life to trying to show? Moreover, just because these contestable interpretations seek to outline the lineaments of something that has *happened*, they are necessarily retroactive. And it is through this 'interpreting intervention' that events become visible. As Benjamin argues, the historian who seeks 'to blast open the continuum of history' turns her back on the future to face the past.[64]

But if Badiou's intervention helps us to conceptualize the event, must we take on the attendant metaphysical baggage? There are good reasons to doubt that we must. In the first place, there is Badiou's starting point, the claim that mathematical logic provides the key to ontology. Hallward says that this is one of the 'fundamental decisions' through which 'Badiou's mature ontology is established'. This reflects the fact that '[w]hat comes first is the decision and its decider, the subject who asserts the axiom.'[65] If this is right, that Badiou's is a much more radical decisionism than, say, Schmitt's: it's decisions all the way down. But if one rejects the idea that thought is somehow grounded in the order of Being or in the self-transparent Cartesian subject, one does not therefore have to treat ontology as simply the product of a series of decisions. The rational kernel of Badiou's equation of Being with number is the fact that modern physics took shape and still develops from Galileo's essentially Platonist declaration that 'this grand book, the universe, . . . is written in the language of mathematics.'[66] But this is sustained not by any decision but by the success of the scientific research programmes that have started from, *inter alia*, the assumption that this declaration is true. That the physical world has a mathematical structure is not an axiom of ontology, but a testable empirical hypothesis, albeit one that, through its numerous confirmations, is now deeply entrenched in the web of scientific beliefs. It follows that the empirical reference of any particular mathematical truth is a matter of conjectural research, not philosophical assumption.

This objection need not be thought too damaging from Badiou, since the basic outlines of his ontology predate its casting in set theory. The organizing contrast between Being qua situation and event in *L'Etre et l'événement* is a refined, etiolated version of the opposition between *l'esplace* and *l'horlieu* that runs through *Théorie du sujet*. In his latest book, *Le Siècle*, Badiou argues that the twentieth century was characterized by a 'passion for the real' that all too often took the form of destruction (the Stalinist Terror, for example), but that also found expression in efforts at sub-traction – that is, in attempts to measure 'the minimal, but absolute difference between the place and that which has taken place in the place, the difference between place and having place.'[67] Badiou's thought is structured by this struggle to escape the confinement of what exists. Hallward rightly notes: 'There is more than a passing resemblance between Badiou's subtractive tenacity and Sartre's essentially tragic confrontation, in the *Critique de la raison dialectique*, of true subjective praxis with the deadening accumulation of the practico-inert.'[68] But this is the second reason for rejecting Badiou's ontology. Daniel Bensaïd makes the point well: 'Detached from its historical conditions, pure diamond of truth, the event . . . resembles a miracle.'[69]

As we have seen, Žižek indeed sums up Badiou's thought as the idea that *'miracles do happen'*. He also suggests that 'Badiou . . . can be read as the last great author in the French tradition of Catholic dogmaticists.'[70] Taken literally, this is false. In *Saint Paul* Badiou makes it clear that as far as he is concerned the Resurrection is a 'fable'. Nevertheless, one of the most interesting aspects of this book is the extensive and sympathetic discussion of grace. It is a central Christian dogma that salvation is a gift of God that exceeds whatever merits a person may have and is an outflowing of divine grace. Badiou argues that it is through his interpretation of this doctrine that St Paul liberates Christianity from its Jewish origins and gives it a universal addressee. The Jewish law, like law generally, issues to individuals the rewards and punishments that are their due. But '[g]race is the contrary of the law, because it is what comes *without being due*.' In thus detaching salvation from the particularities of individuals' situations, grace makes the Christ-Event of universal import: 'Only what is absolutely gratuitous can be addressed to all.'[71]

It is clear that Badiou is doing more here than giving a gloss on Paul's theology. He refers to 'our materialism of grace' and declares: '"Grace" names the event as condition of active thought.'[72] In principle there can be no objection to seeking to liberate concepts from their theological context and employing them for profane purposes; Benjamin, for example, sought to use Jewish Messianism to revive a Marxism sunk into evolutionism. In the case in point, one might see Rawls's insistence on disjoining justice and desert (see §2.2 above) as a secularized version of the doctrine of grace. But there is a particular aspect of this doctrine that makes Badiou's appeal to it problematic. The function of the concept of grace is to make salvation independent of the observable qualities and actions of the individual person and purely a consequence of divine benevolence. St Augustine writes of God and the saved: 'He does not now choose them for their merits, seeing that the whole mass of mankind has been condemned as it were in its infected root; he selects them by grace . . . For each person can recognize that his deliverance from evils is due to an act of kindness freely granted, not owed to him by right.'[73] Consequently, there are no objective markers of salvation (indeed, the doctrine of original sin, which holds all humankind jointly responsible for Adam's rebellion, makes damnation the default position) – given, further, that, as St Paul himself writes of God, 'how unsearchable are his judgements, and his ways past finding out', *who* is saved and *why* and the reasons why some prosper and others suffer in this life are also unknowable.[74] As Augustine puts it, 'we do not know by what decision this good man is poor, while that wicked man is rich; why this man is cheerful, though, in our opinion, his desperate moral character makes him deserve the tortures of grief, while that man, whose exemplary life convinces us he deserves to be cheerful, is full of sorrow . . .' After listing many other examples of this kind, Augustine comforts us with the reflection that on the Day of Judgement 'it will become plain that all God's judgements are perfectly just.'[75] Add divine omniscience and omnipotence, and we have the doctrine of predestination first clearly formulated by Augustine himself, according to which God created humankind foreknowing who will be damned and who will be saved, and all the psychological uncertainties so brilliantly diagnosed by Weber in *The Protestant Ethic and the Spirit of Capitalism.*

But if the event partakes of the qualities of grace, then its origins are as inscrutable as God's decisions to save some and damn others. The event no longer simply exceeds the situation but is separated from it as an absolute barrier. This means that why an event happens becomes a mystery – like the Resurrection or Christ's appearing to Paul on the road to Damascus. This mystification of the event is reinforced by a strategic weakness in Badiou's thought, namely its hostility to relationality. Badiou approvingly refers to 'the radicalism of an ontology that suppresses relation to the profit of the pure multiple'.[76] As Hallward puts it, 'the goal of truth is always a self-sufficient "purity", where "purity is the composition of an Idea such that it is no longer retained in any relation [*lien*]".'[77] As he has persuasively argued, this enormously undermines the plausibility of Badiou's ontology. It means, in the first instance, a very impoverished conception of structure as simply counting-for-one; any more articulated account of structure would have to treat it as a relation or set of relations (see chapter 6 below). Badiou may be partly motivated in his hostility to relations by his concern to distinguish his position from the *idéalinguisterie* of 1960s structuralism, but, while this may make his stance more intelligible, it doesn't thereby make it any more plausible. Secondly, the ban on relations helps to reduce the event to a mystery. Granted that every event exceeds its situation, does it follow that there is no relation between the two? If this were the case, then it is hard to see what the interpreting intervention that makes the event visible actually does. What such an interpretation surely does is to identify the sequence from which the event emerges, but this is precisely at least in part to bring *into relation with one another* elements that were previously thought to be unrelated (see also §5.2 below).

So far I have criticized Badiou's philosophy of the event without considering its political ramifications. But my third objection begins to take us on to the terrain of his politics. In his Maoist phase during the 1960s and 1970s, Badiou can be legitimately accused of politicizing ontology: at least in its earlier parts, *Théorie du sujet* is dominated by the search for the philosophical presuppositions appropriate to his highly subjectivist version of

Marxist-Leninist politics. Now, however, he seems rather to be ontologizing politics. The clearest example of this is provided by Badiou's discussion of the state through which the structure of the situation is reduplicated and thereby stabilized. As we have seen, Badiou welcomes the political resonances created by calling this metastructure the state of the situation, and cites the classic Marxist texts in which Engels and Lenin argue that the (political) state is a product of class antagonisms. He distinguishes three possible combinations of presentation (membership/belonging) and representation (inclusion), two of which we have already encountered: a normal term is both presented and represented, a singularity is presented, but not represented, and an excrescence (*excroissance*) is represented, but not presented. According to Badiou, Marx, Engels, and Lenin correctly identify excrescences in the political state – for example, in the repressive state apparatuses – but mistakenly conclude that the entire state is an excrescence that should be abolished, producing 'the end of representation, and the universality of simple presentation'. The reason why Marxism is mistaken here has to do with the fundamental findings of Badiou's ontology:

> Basically, the classical Marxist description of the state is formally correct, but not its general dialectic. The two great parameters of the state of the situation, namely the unpresentable wandering of the void and the irremediable excess of inclusion over belonging, from which it follows that it is necessary to reassure the one and structure the structure, are taken by Engels as particularities of presentation . . . The void is folded into the non-representation of the proletarians, thus the absence of presentation [*impresentation*] into the modalities of non-representation; the separate counting of the parts is folded into the non-universal character of bourgeois interests, thus into the presentative reshuffling of normality [= the bourgeoisie] and singularity [= the proletariat]; finally the machinery of counting-for-one is reduced to an excrescence [= the state], instead of recognizing fully that the excess of which it is a trait is ineluctable, because it is a theorem of Being.[78]

Badiou concludes: 'There is no antagonism at the origin of the state because one cannot think the dialectic of the void and excess as an antagonism.'[79] Now the Marxist theory of the state may well be false; there is certainly no shortage of people who think so. But there is something slightly ridiculous about the idea that it can be refuted by appeal to some alleged 'theorem of Being' according to which the danger that the void may invade any situation, whatever its precise content, whether it be natural or historical or whatever, requires its reduplication in a metastructure. It just seems like a category-mistake to imagine that debates about the nature of the political state can be settled by some finding in ontology, certainly of the abstraction (and obscurity) of Badiou's argument about the void, excess, and so on. Moreover, in his feisty Maoist youth he would have had no hesitation about pointing out that one of the characteristic figures of bourgeois ideology is precisely to redefine a concrete socio-historical antagonism as 'ineluctable' because a universal property of 'Being'. This form of argument is no less a figure of bourgeois ideology because Badiou himself is no longer a Marxist.

This brings us, finally, to how Badiou now conceives politics. According to Hallward, [t]hough all procedures are addressed to everyone, only in the case of politics does this universality characterize both import and operation.'[80] But the universal is another point of difficulty for Badiou. This can be brought out by returning to his account of the event. We have seen the importance of fidelity in characterizing the subject that an event may produce. Just as much as any Christian connotation, fidelity probably also carries with it an after-effect of Badiou's Maoism. There was always a strongly moralizing tendency in Maoism. Mao defined the Cultural Revolution as a struggle against 'capitalist roaders' within the Chinese Communist Party, but the division between 'bourgeois' and 'proletarian' antagonists was not based on anything resembling an attempt to identify different class locations for the two sides. Instead class differences were imputed on the basis of the politico-ideological positions taken by various actors.[81] This elision of the difference between objective class location and subjective stance necessarily put great emphasis on combating the bourgeois tendencies within oneself. This is probably one source of Badiou's concern with purification. The latter sections of *Théorie du sujet* already display an increasing preoccupation with ethics.[82]

But once one is engaged in this kind of care of the self, one problem that is likely to occur during examinations of conscience is whether or not one is being faithful to an authentic event.

Despite his break with Marxism, Badiou still includes himself among those 'faithful to the event of October 17'.[83] But of course one of the many terrible experiences during the twentieth century's 'Age of Extremes' was the conclusion that vast numbers of former communists reached that they had wasted their lives precisely because of their fidelity to the Russian Revolution and its heritage. In 1979 Badiou contemptuously dismissed those of the 1968 generation who 'renounce the revolution' as 'people of the structure': lacking in subjective strength, they had surrendered to the deadening pressures of *l'esplace*.[84] But this kind of moral judgement offers no way of addressing the problem of how to identify an authentic event. How, for example, to distinguish 25 October 1917, when the Bolsheviks seized power in Petrograd, from 30 January 1933, when Hitler was appointed Chancellor of the German Reich? Badiou's answer is that the National Socialist 'revolution' was a mere '*simulacrum of truth*' because it was 'faithful only to the supposed national substance of a people, in fact addressed itself only to those whom it determined as "Germans".' By contrast, an authentic event arises from the void inherent in any situation that makes possible its supplementation. So 'the fidelity of which an event is the origin, although it is an immanent rupture in a singular situation, is no less addressed universally.' Thus Nazism was parasitic on 'true universal events' such as the Jacobin and Bolshevik Revolutions.[85]

Authentic events thus partake of the universal. Hallward sums up Badiou's conception of the universal as follows: 'universality is a result. Every universal is exceptional, has its origins in one point, is assembled step by step, is the consequence of a decision, is a category of the subject, is a matter of being-true rather than knowing.'[86] So universality and the event are closely packed together. Universality moreover is more than a formal property of generality; it has a political content. According to Badiou, '[t]he generic is *egalitarian*, and every subject is, ultimately, called to equality.'[87] It is hard not to suspect that a vicious circularity is involved here: events are distinguished by appeal to a normatively charged conception of universality, but when we try to unpack this conception it turns out to bear all the hallmarks of the event. Hallward suggests that the only way out of this circle is, once again, a decision: 'The status of universal political principles, like the status of all forms of truth, is necessarily axiomatic or non-definitional. Because equality is subjective, justice – the political principle par excellence – can only be prescriptive. Justice cannot be defined; it is a pure affirmation without guarantee or proof.'[88]

This statement runs three different aspects of a principle of justice (or indeed any assertion) – its force, justification, and content. To say, surely correctly, that such a principle is prescriptive – loosely, that it implies that we have good reason to observe its requirements – is different from establishing whether or not we also have good reason to accept the principle itself. And neither of these formal properties of an assertion tells us anything about its content – what it actually says. It is very plausible that no principle of justice can be proven in the way that a logical truth is, but it doesn't follow that it is indefinable in the sense of having no definite content. No one, and certainly not Rawls himself, imagines that there is some proof that would decisively determine the truth of his principles of justice, but they certainly have a content – roughly speaking, the equal distribution of liberties and socio-economic equality unless inequality favours the worst-off – that has been explored over thousands of pages of print. These conceptual elisions aren't just philosophically problematic; they serve to legitimize what Bensaïd calls 'politics without politics, a negative theology. The preoccupation with its purity reduces politics to a great refusal and forbids it from producing durable effects.'[89] In his post-Marxist phase, Badiou has, through his 'Organisation politique' (OP), preserved much of the style of Maoist political activism – keeping a state that he no longer believes can be abolished at arm's length, relentlessly denouncing the trade unions, and disdainfully dismissing the *altermondialiste* movement as reformist (symptomatically, the OP's bulletin is called *La Distance politique*) – without anything resembling the analysis, strategy, or programme that Marxism-Leninism, for all its follies, once provided. The following remark by Terry Eagleton, made with poststructuralism in mind, seems very apposite to the case of Badiou: 'The most we can muster is a Marxism without a name, absolved from the crimes of its political forbears only at the cost of being politically and doctrinally vacuous, as free from such complicity as the blank page of the ideal *symboliste* poem' – or, to use an example that Badiou employs to illustrate his own project of subtraction, as Malevich's masterpiece of abstract art *White on White*.[90]

3.3   Unreal: Slavoj Žižek and the proletariat

For all its weaknesses, Badiou's philosophical project has exerted an increasing gravitational pull on radical thought as it begins to reconstitute itself in the context of the revival of social critique that I have documented in earlier chapters. More than anything else it is his conceptualization of the event that has been influential, since it seems to offer an approach to history that avoids both the determinism and evolutionism associated with orthodox Marxism and postmodernist relativism. One might even say that a kind of left decisionism has become visible in contemporary French philosophy, a constellation that stretches from Derrida in his later, 'ethical' phase to figures firmly within the Marxist camp – for example, Stathis Kouvelakis in *Philosophy and Revolution*, an important recent study of the young Marx and Engels. Occupying a pivotal position in this realignment is Slavoj Žižek. The extraordinary intelligence, energy, and wit with which Žižek has over the past two decades brought together Lacanian psychoanalysis, German classical idealism, and cultural criticism in a veritable torrent of books have earned him star billing in the American academic world. But in recent years his writing has developed a much harder edged Marxist political definition that has introduced a significant distance between his thought and the post-Marxism of Ernesto Laclau, with which it had been previously closely aligned. As a result, Žižek has emerged as the premier contemporary practitioner of *Ideologiekritik*, a champion in what Althusser used to call the class struggle in theory.[91]

This politico-intellectual shift has been accompanied by what seems like a closer – or at least certainly a more visible – alignment between Žižek and Badiou. Žižek has, for example, associated himself with the kind of critical appropriation of Deleuze's vitalist ontology attempted by Badiou.[92] In one sense, there is nothing particularly surprising about this alignment, given that both are strongly influenced by Lacan, and indeed by the 'second Lacan', the theorist of the Real. But there are also important differences: as we shall see, Žižek believes the Lacanian Real is an alternative to Badiou's ontology; moreover, the fact that he now tends to describe himself as a dialectical materialist (though one has to be careful with Žižek since one can never be sure he's not joking) differentiates him from Badiou, who has unambiguously bid Marxism farewell. These intersecting affinities and differences suggest that it might be worthwhile to round off our assessment of Badiou's contribution to contemporary critical thought by taking a brief look at a couple of closely related themes in Žižek's writing.

In the first place, how does Žižek situate himself with respect to Badiou's philosophy of Being and the event? At one level, he is a remarkably eloquent and subtle propagandist for this philosophy. *The Ticklish Subject*, Žižek's most important philosophical book, is, among other things, a sustained argument for left decisionism. But Žižek takes his description (cited in §3.2 above) of Badiou as a practitioner of Catholic dogmatics seriously. Badiou is right to say that miracles do happen but wrong to seek to ground them ontologically through a 'materialism of grace': 'Here, Lacan parts company with St Paul and Badiou: God not only is but always-already was dead – that is to say, after Freud, one cannot directly have faith in a Truth-Event; every such Event ultimately remains a semblance obfuscating a preceding void whose Freudian name is *death drive*.' Žižek is a bit ambivalent about whether or not events are mere semblances; elsewhere in the book he seeks, like Badiou, to distinguish authentic events from pseudo-events. A few pages on from the sentence just cited, he corrects, but reaffirms, the relationship between events and the death drive: 'Lacan is not a postmodernist cultural relativist: there definitely *is* a difference between an authentic Truth-Event and its semblance, and this difference lies in the fact that in a Truth-Event the void of the death drive, of radical negativity, a gap that momentarily suspends the Order of Being, continues to resonate.'[93] To evoke the nature of the death drive Žižek tends to quote a remarkable passage in Hegel's *Jenaer Realphilosophie* on 'the night of the world':

> The human being is this night, this empty nothing, that contains everything in its simplicity – an unending wealth of many representations, images, of which none belongs to him – or which are not present. This night, the interior of nature, that exists here – pure self – in phantasmagorical representations, is night all around it, in which here shoots a bloody head – there another white ghastly apparition, suddenly here before it, and just so disappears. One catches sight of this night when one looks human beings in the eye – into a night that becomes awful.[94]

This is 'the phantasmagorical, pre-symbolic domain of partial drives' – it is, in other words, the realm of the death drive, at least as Lacan understands it.[95] For Lacan, 'the drive, the partial drive, is profoundly a death drive and represents in itself the portion of death in the sexed living being.'[96] Inasmuch as subjectivity involves this dimension of primordial chaos it cannot be fully incorporated into any system of social relations. Indeed the coherence and effectiveness of these relations requires the *exclusion* of subjectivity as absolute negativity. Moreover, for Žižek, 'the night of the world', the ground-zero dimension of subjectivity that cannot be fully captured by any positive social totality, partakes of the Real. Thus, he tells us that 'it was the great breakthrough of German Idealism to outline the precise contours of this pre-ontological dimension of the spectral Real, which precedes and eludes the ontological constitution of reality.'[97]

For Lacan, the subject is caught up in three orders – the Imaginary, the Symbolic, and the Real. In the Imaginary the subject misrecognizes itself as unitary and coherent when it is in fact divided and dependent. In the Symbolic the subject participates, through the signifying process, in the social reality constitutive of intersubjectivity (this is the realm of what Lacan calls the big Other whose recognition we seek in desiring): the endless substitutions and displacements of signifiers articulate the lack, the impossibility of fulfilment, inherent in desire. The Real is the limit of symbolization: as Eagleton puts it, it is 'our primordial wound we incurred by our fall from the pre-Oedipal Eden, the gash in our being where we were torn loose from Nature. Though we repress this trauma, it persists within us as the hard core of the self.'[98] 'The Real is an entity which must be constructed afterwards so that we can account for the distortions of the symbolic structure', Žižek writes.[99] The Real is thus nothing like an external reality existing independently of discourse. It cannot be discursively represented because it is nothing but the limit of such representation, discernible only through its effects on the Symbolic and posited as an explanation of these effects. Thus 'the Lacanian Real is strictly *internal* to the Symbolic: it is nothing but its inherent limitation, the impossibility of the Symbolic fully to "become itself".' Or again, 'what eludes symbolization is precisely the Real as the *inherent point of failure* of symbolization.'[100]

It is hard to imagine that the Real thus understood can provide the basis of a more successful theorization of events than Badiou's ontology. The main reason for this resistance is quite simply the speculative character of the entire Lacanian construction. There is to my mind no doubt of the profound reconfiguration of thought effected by Freud. It is, however, one thing to treat psychoanalysis as a fundamental reference point, quite another to swallow hook, line, and sinker Lacan's complex, changing, and contested reinterpretation of Freud, however suggestive it may often be. But this is what Žižek expects us to do. His writing simply takes the truth of at least the later Lacan's thought for granted and then seeks to explore its implications for our understanding of the contemporary world. This is a perfectly legitimate exercise, and the wealth of Žižek 's writings bears witness to the productive consequences that can flow from such a strategy. But there is no getting round the fact that there is a certain repetitive quality to these writings. Again and again, amid an incredible diversity of political and cultural phenomena, Žižek leads us to back to the Real. Here his work compares unfavourably with that of Badiou. When the latter writes about figures as different as St Paul and Deleuze, of course he finds in them confirmations of his own philosophy, but he also engages with the specificities of their own writing and resituates them in a new and illuminating perspective. Žižek can also produce work of comparable quality – *The Ticklish Subject* is one of the most important contributions to contemporary critical thought – but all too often, after all the fun of reading him, we are left with the eternal recurrence, not of the same, but of the Real.

The Lacanian Real also figures in the second intersection between Žižek and Badiou that I consider here. The Real is where the incoherence of the Symbolic becomes visible: bear in mind, however, that both Lacan and Žižek equate the Symbolic and the social. The implication that society itself is impossible has been most influentially developed by Ernesto Laclau and Chantal Mouffe when offering a distinctively Lacanian conception of antagonism:

> Antagonism, far from being an objective relation, is a relation wherein the limits of every objectivity are *shown* – in the sense in which Wittgenstein used to say that what cannot be *said* can be

shown. But if . . . the social only exists as a partial effort for constructing society – that is, an objective and closed system of differences – antagonism, as a witness of the impossibility of a final suture, is the 'experience' of the limit of the social. Strictly speaking, antagonisms are not *internal* but *external* to society; or rather, they constitute the limits of society, the latter's impossibility of fully constituting itself.[101]

For Laclau and Mouffe the idea of antagonism as evoking the impossibility of the social is shown as part of a larger poststructuralist project heavily influenced by Derrida that sees attempts to suture social relations into a closed totality constantly subverted by the inherent tendency of signification to exceed itself and thereby to escape all attempts to limit it (see also §6.2 below). One of the main aims of this project was to deconstruct classical Marxism in particular by detaching Gramsci's theory of hegemony from historical materialism and what they call 'classism'. But Žižek has sought to give the same Lacanian concept of antagonism a completely different theoretical and political meaning. Thus he writes that

> there is no class struggle 'in reality': 'class struggle' designates the very antagonism that prevents the objective social reality from constituting itself as a self-enclosed whole . . . In other words, class struggle is 'real' in the strict Lacanian sense: a 'hitch', an impediment which gives rise to ever-new symbolizations by which one endeavours to integrate and domesticate it . . . , but which simultaneously condemns these endeavours to ultimate failure. Class struggle is none other than the name for the unfathomable limit which prevents us from conceiving society as a closed totality.[102]

Interestingly, this Lacanian reinterpretation of class struggle seems to have been made first by Badiou: in 1977 he declared that, 'if the real of psychoanalysis is the impossibility of the sexual as a relationship, the real of Marxism affirms: "There is no class relationship" . . . The antagonism bourgeoisie/proletariat designates the relationship as impossible, discerning thus the real of Marxism.'[103] Žižek has certainly brilliantly developed the thought that ideological symbolizations are displaced forms of class struggle – for example, he has used it to explain the hold of the conservative populism of the Republican right on many working-class Americans.[104] But is this insight really dependent on the idea that class struggle is 'the unfathomable limit which prevents us from conceiving society as a closed totality'? If we take seriously the interpretation of the class-relation as the Real of Marxism, then this antagonism must be conceived not simply as discernible only in its effects, but as beyond conceptualization altogether. But then how can we say that the modern class antagonism is one between capital and labour rather than, say, one between masters and slaves? It's true that Marxism doesn't treat classes as directly visible entities, but this is because, in the normal realist mode of the sciences, it seeks theoretically to reconstruct structures and relations whose reality can be inferred from their perceptible effects (see chapters 5 and 6 below). Žižek's conceptualization of class antagonism as a case of the Lacanian Real may seem very close to this: he says that we would treat every social phenomenon as '(an)other attempt to conceal and "patch up" the rift of class antagonism, to efface its traces. What we have here is the structural-dialectical paradox of *an effect that exists only in order to efface the causes of its existence*, an effect that in a way resists its own cause.'[105] That's fine, so long as the resisted cause – the class antagonism – is not regarded as ineffable and unknowable, but this is what treating it as Real in a Lacanian sense seems to require us to do.

The difficulties involved in this approach become clearer when we consider its application to the case of the proletariat. In a discussion of Marx's 1843 Introduction (see §2.2 above), Žižek writes:

> The claim that the proletariat is the 'universal class' is thus ultimately equivalent to the claim that, within the existing global order, the proletariat is the class that is radically dislocated . . . with regard to the social body: while other classes can still maintain the illusion that 'society exists', and that they have their specific place within the global social body, the very existence of the proletariat repudiates the claim that 'Society exists'.[106]

Kouvelakis endorses the same Lacanian interpretation of the proletariat as 'an embodiment of the impossibility of full totality':

> The crux may well reside in the fact that the proletariat of the 1844 Introduction [*sic*], in its alliance with practical criticism, is not so

much a pre-existing reality that subsequently goes into action to 'make the revolution', assert its leadership of it, affirm its hegemony, and so on, as in a certain sense, *the revolution itself*, the power of rupture that comes into being in and through the revolutionary process.[107]

Once again, Badiou got there first with the distinction he first draws in his Maoist phase between the proletariat as revolutionary subject and the empirical working class (see §3.2 above). Indeed, in *L'Etre et l'événement* he argues that Marxism was destroyed by its confusion of the two: 'Of this coincidence, which it sought to assume within itself, since it declared itself simultaneously political truth – militant, faithful – and knowledge (*savoir*) of History, or of Society, Marxism ended up dying, because it followed the fluctuations of the encyclopaedia' – that is, of empirical knowledge that merely ordered visible elements of the situation and did not orient it towards the event through which it could sustain a subject.[108] But completely to disjoin proletariat and working class in the way Badiou, Žižek, and Kouvelakis would have us do involves many serious difficulties. Purely from an interpretive point of view, it cuts across a very important strand in Marx's thought that emerges in texts such as *The Class Struggles in France* and *The Eighteenth Brumaire of Louis Bonaparte*, namely the critique of the autonomization of politics from any anchorage in social reality that is so powerfully articulated in his polemics with the radical bourgeois democrats during the 1848 Revolutions and their aftermath. Consider, for example, this passage from the *Eighteenth Brumaire*, where Marx traces the practical ineffectiveness of the neo-Jacobin Montagne in the face of Bonaparte's developing dictatorship to its failure to grasp the material – above all, class – context in which the intense struggles among French political elites unfolded:

> But the democrat, because he represents the petty bourgeoisie, that is, a *transition class*, in which the interests of two classes are simultaneously mutually blunted, imagines himself elevated above class antagonism generally. The democrats concede that a privileged class confronts them, but they, along with all the rest of the nation, form the *people*. What they represent is the *people's rights*; what interests them is the *people's interests*. Accordingly, when a struggle is impending, they do not need to examine the interests

and positions of the different classes. They do not need to weigh their own resources too critically. They have merely to give the signal and the *people*, with all its inexhaustible resources, will fall upon the *oppressors*.[109]

Marx's aim is thus precisely to rescue the idea of revolution from this inflated, ultimately vacuous political phraseology by giving it a definite location in the class map of modern society. The alternative approach proposed by Badiou and his co-thinkers legitimizes groups assuming the proletariat's role on a completely arbitrary basis. Badiou brought this danger out very well when he wrote in 1976: 'As to the proletariat, it is the name as subject of the new of our times. If the working class is its place in the structure, the essential is that it gets rid of the old, which explains why the proletariat can be, in the China of 1966, the movement of young school students today, in Portugal today, the Southern peasantry.'[110] Surely Marxism got into such a mess more than anything else because of what Trotsky called substitutionism – the activities of self-proclaimed vanguards purporting to act in the name of the working class and oppressing the actual, empirical members of that class (remember Brecht's poem after the 1953 Berlin rising that famously asked: 'Why doesn't the government dissolve the people and elect a new one?'). Either one takes the idea of class politics seriously – which means pursuing the connections between social classes, political institutions, and ideological representations – or one should give up on the idea altogether. It is one of Badiou's merits that he eventually recognized this dilemma, even if (in my view) he took the wrong horn.

4

The Generosity of Being:
Antonio Negri

4.1 All is grace

Seeking to summarize his differences with Gilles Deleuze after the latter's death, Alain Badiou recalls the last words of the protagonist of Georges Bernanos's novel *The Diary of a Country Priest*, who, when told that a priest may not arrive in time for him to receive the last sacraments, replies: 'What does it matter? All is grace.' This, for Badiou, is the core of Deleuze's position: 'it is always what is that is right . . . For what is, is nothing other than the grace of the All.' For Badiou, by contrast, 'to say that all is grace means precisely that we are never accorded any grace. But this is not correct. It does *occur*, by interruption or by supplement, and however rare or transitory it may be, we are forced to be *lastingly* faithful to it.'[1] Graham Greene, writing only three years after Bernanos's novel was first published in 1936, expresses a very different kind of Catholic sensibility when he refers to 'the horrifying abundance of just life'.[2] Badiou probably wouldn't go this far, but he certainly thinks of nature as something to be subtracted from rather than worshipped. Here, then, we have the contrast between two ontologies, one for which transcendence is routine, a product of the constant overflowing of Being, the other for which events and the subjects constituted through fidelity to them are rare.

Antonio Negri is the most important contemporary figure to take Deleuze's side in this philosophical debate. Derrida accuses Negri of being 'confined, out-of-in-it, within the walled perimeter of a new ontological fatherland, a liberated ontology, an ontology of self-liberation. In, for example, a Spinozist sense of the word "liberty".'[3] It isn't obvious how damaging a charge this is. Many would say that an ontology, in the sense of a philosophical conception of the structure of the world, is unavoidable: indeed, the founding assumption of Derrida's practice of deconstruction is that it is simultaneously both impossible to escape the metaphysics of presence and necessary to employ various devices aimed at keeping it at arm's length. What is perhaps more interesting to explore is the nature of a particular theorist's ontological commitments. Contrary to what Derrida suggests, central to Negri's ontology is not liberty, but Life. He writes, with Michael Hardt:

> From one perspective Empire stands clearly over the multitude and subjects it to the rule of its overarching machine, as a new Leviathan. At the same time, however, from the ontological perspective, the hierarchy is reversed. The multitude is the real productive force of our social world, whereas Empire is a mere apparatus of capture that lives off the vitality of the multitude – as Marx would say, a vampire regime of accumulated dead labour that survives only by sucking off the blood of the living.[4]

A little later on in *Empire*, discussing the anti-humanism of Althusser and Foucault, Hardt and Negri write: 'Anti-humanism, then, conceived as a refusal of transcendence, should in no way be confused with the negation of the *vis viva*, the creative life force that animates the revolutionary stream of the modern tradition.'[5] The revolutionary version of modernity – the Renaissance humanism that culminated in Spinoza – is the subject of Negri's best book, *Le Pouvoir constituant*. In *Empire* Hardt and Negri return to the subject of ontology in the key late chapter 'Generation and Corruption'. Here they criticize both the apologetic affirmation that capitalism is natural and the 'mysticism of the limit' that, denying the possibility of revolt, 'leads merely to a cynical attitude and quietistic practices' for having 'lost track of the fundamental productivity of being'. This productivity is realized in living labour, which is conceived in Deleuzian terms: 'Desiring production is generation, or rather the excess of labour and the accumulation of a power incorporated into the collective movement of its singular essences, both its cause and its completion.' Indeed, say Hardt and Negri, generation thus understood is the 'first fact of metaphysics, ontology, and anthropology'. Corruption, by contrast, 'is not an ontological motor but simply the lack of ontological foundation of the biopolitical practices of being.' It is 'the substance and totality of Empire. Corruption is the pure exercise of command without any proportionate or adequate reference to the world of life.'[6]

Here we have outlined the key concepts that constantly recur in Negri's recent writings – productivity, creativity, life, labour, desire, and the multitude. I shall have some critical reflections to offer about them in §4.3, but I want to concentrate first on how they came to occupy the prominence they currently enjoy. Even more than Badiou, Negri was an important figure on the Marxist left in the 1960s and 1970s. Rereading Negri's writings of this period, when he was one of the leading influences on the Italian far left current known as *operaismo* (workerism), one is struck by the extent to which some at least of these themes are already present if only in embryo.[7] From this perspective, *Marx Beyond Marx* (1979), Negri's commentary on Marx's *Grundrisse*, is an emblematic text, one that points both back towards his more avowedly orthodox writings of the 1970s and to the later work, in which Marx is more and more read through Foucault and Deleuze.

In considering this book I take two reference points: first, some themes in some of Negri's writings of the 1970s, and, second, Marx's critique of political economy. Though my own position is much closer to the classical Marxist tradition than Negri's, my purpose in using this second reference point is not to put him on trial for heresy. Even if that were ever an interesting exercise, Negri has suffered too many trials as it is. But there is something very striking about the way in which he invokes the authority of one of Marx's key economic texts, the *Grundrisse*, to offer a reading of Marx that it is fairly easy to show is quite at odds with the latter's central theoretical claims. This discrepancy may tell us something about the driving forces of Negri's thought, or at least about themes, that has become ever more powerfully articulated in recent years.[8]

4.2 Negri's *Grundrisse*: revolutionary subjectivity versus Marxist 'objectivism'

The significance of the *Grundrisse* for Negri is that it allows us to conceptualize the capitalist mode of production primarily as a power-relation constituted by the irreducible antagonism between labour and capital: 'We thus see, throughout the *Grundrisse*, a *forward movement in the theory*, a more and more constraining movement constituted by the *antagonism between the collective worker and the collective capitalist*.' Indeed: 'The *Grundrisse* represents the summit of Marx's revolutionary thought.' That this is so is indicated by the fact that it starts, unlike *Capital*, not with the commodity, but with money:

> Money has the advantage of presenting me immediately with the lurid face of the social relation of value; it shows me value right away as exchange, commanded and organized for exploitation. I do not need to plunge into Hegelianism in order to discover the double face of the commodity, of value: money has only one face, that of the boss.[9]

Or, as Negri puts it more succinctly, 'in this Marx, money is a *tautology for power*.' The merit of starting with money is closely related to another, that in the *Grundrisse* the theory of surplus-value is not presented as it is in *Capital*, on the basis of an initial discussion of the theory of value (to which the first chapter of *Capital*, volume 1, 'The Commodity', is devoted):

> The difference between the *Grundrisse* and the later works of Marx resides in the fact that, in the first, *the law of value is presented not only mediatedly, but also immediately as the law of exploitation*. There is no logical way which leads from the analysis of commodities to that of value, to that of surplus-value: the middle term does not exist; it is – that, yes – a literary fiction, a mystification, pure and simple which contains not a word of truth.[10]

Negri thus explicitly thematizes the discrepancy between the *Grundrisse* and *Capital*: 'Marx beyond Marx? The *Grundrisse* beyond *Capital*? Maybe. What is certain is that the central character of the theory of surplus-value puts an end to every scientific pretension to derive any centralization and domination from the theory of value. The theory of surplus-value breaks down the antagonism into a microphysics of power.' This latter reference to 'a micro-physics of power' indicates that here already Foucault has become an important reference point for Negri. But he appropriates poststructuralism in his own way. In an interesting passage that foreshadows the discussion of anti-humanism in *Empire*, Negri praises Althusser for attacking '[t]he orgy of totality, rebirth, and plenitude to which we gave ourselves over', but continues:

> In avoiding humanism, some would also seek to avoid the theoretical areas of subjectivity. They are wrong. The path of materialism lies precisely through subjectivity. The path of subjectivity is the one that gives materiality to communism. The working class is subjectivity, separated subjectivity, which animates development, crises, transition and communism.[11]

This privileging of subjectivity forms the basis of the opposition that Negri draws between the *Grundrisse* and *Capital*:

> it is not a question of an abstract polemic against *Capital*: each of us was born in the reflection and the theoretical consciousness of the class hate which we experience in studying *Capital*. But *Capital* is also that text which served to reduce critique to economic theory, to annihilate subjectivity in objectivity, to subject the subversive capacity of the proletariat to the reorganizing and repressive intelligence of capitalist power. We can only reconquer a correct reading of *Capital* (not for the painstaking conscience of the intellectual, but for the revolutionary conscience of the masses) if we subject it to the critique of the *Grundrisse*, if we reread it through the categorical apparatus of the *Grundrisse*, which is traversed throughout by an absolutely insurmountable antagonism led by the capacity of the proletariat.[12]

So, on the one hand, *Capital* is the privileged site of an 'objectivist' understanding of capitalism, but, on the other, it can be read 'correctly' (i.e., presumably in a way that follows 'the path of subjectivity') with the help of the *Grundrisse*. This passage reminds us of the extent to which the interpretation of *Capital* was a central feature of the intellectual revival of Marxism in the 1960s and 1970s, most famously in the form of *Reading Capital* in

France, but in Germany through the study circles and discussions that gave rise to the capital-logic school, and in Italy under the aegis of *operaismo*. Already in 1955 Mario Tronti, one of the latter's founders, could write: 'One returns to *Capital* each time one starts from capitalism and vice versa: one cannot speak of the method of *Capital* without transferring and translating this method into the *analysis* of capitalism.'[13]

Marx Beyond Marx is a contribution to this discourse that constantly moves between *Capital* and capitalism, a contribution that operates at the limits of this discourse by summoning up the *Grundrisse* to correct the defects of Marx's later 'objectivism'. An example of this procedure is Negri's discussion of the tendency of the rate of profit to fall (TRPF), which

> bespeaks the *revolt of living labour* against the power of profit and its very separate constitution; a revolt against the theft and its fixation into a productive force for the capitalist against the productive force of the worker, into the power of social capital against the vitality of social labour: because of this *living labour reveals itself as destructive.*[14]

Thus necessary labour – that is, the portion of the working day devoted to the reproduction of labour-power – is *'a rigid quantity'* that constitutes

> a limit to valorization. A limit increasing to the extent that any increase in productivity and in the sum of profit is faced with a force less and less willing to be subjected, less and less available for compression. Such rigidity imparts its primary sense to the law of the tendency of the rate of profit to decline. In this law we must read what Marx had acknowledged in the *Grundrisse* immediately before the first formulation of the law, that is, the radical estrangement, *the autonomy of the working class from the development of capital.*[15]

The rate of profit falls, therefore, because of capitalists' inability, thanks to working-class resistance, to increase the rate of surplus-value (the ratio between surplus and necessary labour) or perhaps even to maintain it at its previous level. This is an interpretation of the TRPF that in effect displaces the explanation that Marx gives in *Capital*, volume 3, where the main mechanism responsible for the falling rate of profit is the tendency for the organic composition of capital – the value-ratio that reflects the growing role of dead labour relative to living labour in capitalist production – to rise, something that can in principle take place even if the rate of surplus-value also rises. Negri dismisses this as so much 'economism' and 'objectivism':

> The law of the tendency to decline represents, therefore, one of the most lucid Marxist intuitions of the intensification *of the class struggle* in the course of capitalist development. The confusions on the subject will emerge later on when Marx, *reformulating the law*, instead of proposing the ratio between necessary labour and surplus labour, proposes the formula of *the organic composition of capital* – or that of the ratio between profit and wage. These two formulae are obviously present in the *Grundrisse* as well, but here they are subordinated to the quantities defined by the law of surplus-value. Whenever, on the contrary, they become prominent or exclusive, the entire relation will be dislocated on an economistic level and objectified improperly.[16]

Consistent with his view of capitalism as a pure power-relation, Negri thus attributes to the Marx of the *Grundrisse* a view of crises as a consequence of 'the working class struggling against work under capitalism and for its own self-valorization'.[17] This is precisely the view that Negri had developed in his earlier writings. Thus he wrote in 1968 that the Marxist theory of the business cycle conceptualizes 'this cycle-form as the form of a power-relation between classes in struggle (a power-relation which was originally described by Marx in a context where capital was extremely powerful, but which can be and has been overthrown by the course of working-class struggle).' This same text articulates another long-standing theme of Negri's writing, namely that the progressive socialization of both capital and labour reduces the relation between classes to one of open and unmediated political violence:

> The new state-form corresponding to the socialization of capital does not succeed in reactivating mechanisms that the class struggle had closed off; rather it plays a (necessary and exclusive) role of political repression, and does so in ways functional to the new situation of a levelling out of the rate of profit. The antagonistic stance that capital always assumes when faced by the emergence of

the working class as a productive social force here reaches maximum proportions. 'Political violence' has always been 'the vehicle of capital's economic process' [Luxemburg], but here the ideal notion of capital as a social mediating force becomes pure abstraction: it is now represented as a pure repressive force.[18]

Another text, this time dating from 1981, at once radicalizes and reaffirms the idea that capitalist economic relations are becoming comprehensively politicized: '*The conditions for the extraction of surplus-value now exist only in the form of a general social relation*. Profit and the wage become forms of the division of a value content which no longer relates to any specific mechanisms of exploitation, other than the specific asymmetry of command within society.' Indeed, '[e]xploitation consists in command. It is violence against the antagonism of social subjects that are fighting for liberation.'[19] This last passage resonates with Hardt's and Negri's portrayal of the corruption of Empire as the pure exercise of command.

The significance of the *Grundrisse* for Negri is that it is the text of Marx's that, on his view, anticipates the formation of social capital: 'while in *Capital* the categories are generally modelled on private and competitive capital, in the *Grundrisse* they are modelled on a tendential scheme of *social capital*.' Marx's analysis of the monetary crisis of 1857–8 provided him with a lens through which to survey the future evolution of capitalism:

> As if in an enormous effort of anticipation, the crisis comes to figure the historical tendency of capitalist development. And it is in this historical projection that the crisis becomes a crisis of the law of value. Within the historical projection of a form of production which becomes increasingly more social, in which the modern function of value is transformed into a function of command, of domination, and of intervention on the social fractions of necessary labour and accumulation. The state is here the 'synthesis of civil society'.[20]

This process culminates in the fusion of an increasingly socialized capital and the state:

> Marx indicated, and often too frequently, especially in the *Grundrisse*, that to say State is only another way of saying capital. The

development of the mode of production leads us to recognize that to say State is the *only* way to say capital: a socialized capital, a capital whose accumulation is done in terms of power, a transformation of the theory of value into a theory of command, the launching into circuit and the development of the state of the multinationals.[21]

The theory of capitalist development outlined in *Marx Beyond Marx* is in many ways a familiar one, in which what Negri calls 'private and competitive capital' is progressively transformed, as a result of processes of centralization and concentration, into a single collective entity that comprises both capital and the state. In a celebrated early essay he had developed a reading of Keynes as an entry point for analysing this transformation.[22] In *Marx Beyond Marx* he cites Hilferding and Lenin, but there are plenty of others who argue something similar, from Bukharin to Castoriadis.[23] Negri's conclusion that the socialization of capital has rendered the law of value inoperative is also far from unique: 'The Law of Value dies . . . Once capital and global labour power have completely become global social classes – each independent and capable of self-valorizing activity – then the Law of Value can only represent the power (*potenza*) and violence of the relationship. It is the synthesis of the relations of force.'[24]

There are two distinctive features of Negri's version of this theory. First, the progressive socialization of capital is often seen as a relatively benign process: for Hilferding, for example, a more organized capitalism could both avoid economic crises and admit its gradual and negotiated reform. As the passage just cited indicates, this not Negri's view. The politicization and socialization of the relations of production imply their reduction to straightforward relations of force, and capitalist domination is reduced to 'pure command'. This development is both stimulated by and helps to promote the constitution of the working class as a revolutionary subject that, refusing work, practises 'self-valorization', appropriating the resources required to meet its own independently determined needs.[25]

Second, Negri, as we have seen, uses the *Grundrisse* in order to legitimize his version of the theory. He reads the manuscript as a prophetic text, one that somehow succeeds, against the grain of Marx's own later economic writings, in summing up the subsequent course of capitalist development. There is a sense in which this utilization of the *Grundrisse* is perfectly intelligible. The socialization of capital involves, according to Negri, the latter's transformation into a collective subject:

> 'Social capital' is the form in which the expansive power of capital is consolidated through and upon circulation. An expansive power, which, as we have seen, is also and above all a collective power. In this relationship *social capital is the subject of development.* In operating circulation, capital posits itself as sociality, as the capacity to engulf within its own development, in an ever more determined manner, every socially productive force. The subjectivity that this synthesis confers on capital represents what capital itself has achieved through the process of subsumption, through the ever more coherent and exhaustive acts of subjugation of society. *The very mode of production is modified.*[26]

What is interesting about this stress on the subjectivity of social capital is that it connects up with a point that commentators have often made, usually as a criticism, about the *Grundrisse*, namely that Marx tends there to hypostatize capital as a collective subject that automatically produces its own conditions of existence. Consider, for example, the following passage:

> Thus e.g. while the process in which money or value-for-itself originally becomes capital presupposes on the part of the capitalist an accumulation – perhaps by means of savings garnered from products and values created by his own labour etc., which he has undertaken as a *not-capitalist*, i.e. while the presuppositions under which money becomes capital appear as given, *external presuppositions* for the arising of capital – [nevertheless,] as soon as capital has become capital as such, it creates its own presuppositions, i.e. the possession of the real conditions of the creation of new values *without exchange* – by means of its own production process. These presuppositions, which originally appeared as conditions of its own becoming – and hence could not spring from its *action as capital* – now appear as results of its own realization, reality, *as posited by it – not as conditions of its arising, but as results of its presence.*[27]

Edward Thompson calls this 'an extraordinary mode of thought to find in a materialist, for capital has become Idea, which unfolds itself in history', a case of *'unreconstructed* Hegelianism' on

Marx's part.[28] Other critics have pointed to a tendency by Marx to rely, notably in his discussion in the *Grundrisse* of the crucial transition from money to capital, on a speculative dialectic that seeks to deduce the self-expansion of value from the concept of money itself.[29] It is in part for this reason that many commentators see Marx's economic thought undergoing between the *Grundrisse* and *Capital* a process of what Jacques Bidet calls '*rectification*' that involves the progressive (though incomplete) liberation of Marx's discourse from, as Bidet puts it, 'the Hegelian heritage of a dialectical form of exposition'.[30]

Negri himself is dismissive of the problem of Marx's relation to Hegel: 'That Marx was Hegelian has never seemed to me to be the case: on the sole condition of reading Marx and Hegel.' But he has, tacitly at least, a response to the question posed above about Marx's tendency in the *Grundrisse* to hypostatize capital: '*If capital is a subject on one side, on the other labour must be a subject as well.*' In the era of social capital the relations of production are reduced to the struggle between two autonomous and antagonistic collective subjects: 'The relation of capital is a relation of force that tends toward the separate and independent existence of the enemy: the process of workers' self-valorization, the dynamic of communism. Antagonism is no longer a form of the dialectic, it is its negation.'[31]

One might wonder how satisfactory it is to replace one hypostasis positing its own presuppositions with two conjoined in endless conflict. To begin to bring out the difficulties with both Negri's interpretation of Marx and his analysis of capitalism in *Marx Beyond Marx* let us consider the significance of the process of conceptual 'rectification' that culminates in *Capital*. Why then does Marx start with the commodity rather than money in *Capital*, volume I?[32] The short answer is because doing so allows him to conceptualize two central features of the capitalist mode of production, *exploitation* and *competition*.

In the *Grundrisse* Marx draws a celebrated distinction. On the one hand, '[c]*apital in general*, as distinct from the particular capitals', consists in 'the specific characteristics which distinguish capital from all other forms of wealth – or modes in which (social) production develops'. On the other hand, '[c]apital exists and can only exist as many capitals, and its self-determination therefore appears as their reciprocal interaction with one another', that is, in competition.[33] To put it another way (borrowed from Robert Brenner), capitalist relations of production involve both the 'vertical' antagonism between capital and wage-labour that is constitutive of 'capital in general' and the 'horizontal' conflicts among competing capitals.[34] A proper understanding of these two dimensions of the capitalist mode of production and of their interrelationship presupposes an analysis of their structural conditions of possibility.

This analysis is provided by the treatment of the commodity in *Capital*, volume 1, chapter 1.[35] Here Marx presents the labour theory of value by constructing the model of a system of generalized commodity production, in which the mass of products of labour take the form of commodities exchanged on the market. Autonomous but interdependent producers are compelled to exchange the products of their labour in order to meet their needs. As a result of the competitive interaction of rival producers on the market, these products tend to be sold at prices that oscillate around a level that reflects the socially necessary labour-time required to produce them. Hence the dual nature of the commodity: every product both is a use-value representing the human need that it meets, and has a value, the socially necessary labour-time required to produce it, whose 'form of appearance' is the price for which the commodity would be exchanged at any given moment on the market.[36]

This analysis of the commodity allows Marx to make three decisive breakthroughs in his account of capitalist exploitation once, in part 2 of *Capital*, volume 1, he extends the model of generalized commodity production to cover labour-power.[37] First, thanks to the distinction between use-value and value, and that (closely related) between labour and labour-power, he can now solve the conundrum of how to explain capital's self-expansion with which he had grappled in the *Grundrisse*. The valorization of capital is possible because labour-power, when used through the actual expenditure of labour, creates more value than the value it has as a commodity – that is, the socially necessary labour-time required to reproduce labour-power, largely (though not wholly) represented by the wages offered to workers on the market. Secondly, conceptualizing labour-power as a commodity allows Marx to formulate clearly the historical specificity of capitalist exploitation. The transformation of labour-power into a commodity implies, as its historical presupposition, the separation of the direct producers from the means of production. Consequently the extraction of surplus-labour does not, as in the case of earlier modes of production, require the direct application of political coercion: lacking direct access to the means of production, the worker finds herself without an acceptable alternative to selling her labour-power on terms that lead to her exploitation. 'The silent compulsion of economic relations sets the seal on the domination of the capitalist over the worker. Direct extra-economic coercion is still of course used, but only in exceptional cases.'[38]

Thirdly, his analysis of the commodity permits Marx to locate capitalist exploitation at its proper level, in the relations of production. One motive behind the *Grundrisse*'s initial focus on money was what he regarded as the need to develop a critique of the theory of labour-money developed by Proudhon and his followers, for whom 'the degradation of *money* and the exaltation of *commodities* was the essence of socialism'.[39] In other words, for Proudhon the problem with capitalism lay in the corruption of the commodity system introduced by money and banking. Monetary reform, including the introduction of labour-money, would help to establish a just market economy. Marx comments: 'One might just as well abolish the Pope while leaving Catholicism in existence.'[40] Exploitation for him is a consequence of the commodification of labour-power, that is, of the normal workings of a system of generalized commodity production, not that of a deformed or corrupted market economy.

At the same time, Marx's analysis of the commodity allows him to treat competition as a constitutive dimension of capitalist relations of production. Competition among decentralized but interdependent producers is an inherent feature of a system of generalized commodity production. This is the sphere of what he calls in the *Grundrisse* 'many capitals'. Coexisting in that text with the propensity noted above to hypostatize capital in general into a collective subject that produces its own conditions of existence is the idea that competition plays a critical role in bringing into operation the characteristic tendencies of the capitalist mode of production: 'The influence of individual capitals on one another has the effect precisely that they must conduct themselves as *capital*; the seemingly independent influence of the individuals, and their chaotic collisions, are precisely the positing of their general law.'[41]

Such formulations are ambiguous between the attribution of causal powers to competition among 'many capitals' and the treatment of this sphere as an external phenomenal expression of the inner tendencies of capital in general. The latter approach is evident in the following passage: 'Conceptually, *competition* is nothing other than the inner *nature of capital*, its essential character, appearing in and realized as the reciprocal interaction of many capitals with one another, the inner tendency as external necessity.'[42] The critical issue analytically here is whether the 'inner tendencies' of the capitalist mode of production can be specified independently of competition or whether the causal mechanisms responsible for these tendencies necessarily involve competition. The successive conceptual recastings that Marx's economic writings underwent in the decade between his starting the *Grundrisse* and publishing the first volume of *Capital* involve his giving increasing causal significance to competition. Bidet presents this through a contrast between the tendencies of capitalist development and the structure of class struggle and competition:

> The system only has *tendencies* (to relative surplus-value, to rising productivity, to accumulation) because of its *structure*. The latter concerns *simultaneously* the relations between classes, between the opposed elements of classes (entrepreneur/employees) and between elements within each class, here the relation of competition between capitalists. This is what is partially hidden by the theme of 'essence/surface'.
>
> The reference to the tendencies of the system and to the interests of the dominant class would be purely metaphysical if it did not refer to the question of the *interests* of the 'individuals' who compose it and of the constraints that weigh on these individuals, that is to say individual capitals 'personified', as Marx puts it, by their holders. Capitalism does not posses any general tendency except in relation to what motivates individual capitals, with this structure of interests and constraints that defines the competitive relationship.[43]

The significance of competition can be seen in Marx's explanation of the technological dynamism of capitalism. In volume 1 of *Capital*, this figures in Marx's discussion of relative surplus-value, where the rate of surplus-value is increased thanks to rising productivity of labour. Already here Marx (somewhat uneasily) introduces competition: a capitalist who introduces a new labour-saving technique can sell his products at a price somewhere between their 'individual value', that is, the actual labour-time used to produce them, and their 'social value', the socially necessary labour-time required to produce them in the sector in question, which, by definition, will be higher, allowing the innovator to make a surplus-profit. Here the differences between individual capitals competing in the same product market have become an essential dimension of the analysis.[44]

This argument is greatly extended in *Capital*, volume 3. First, in the key chapter 10 of part 2, 'The Equalization of the General Rate of Profit Through Competition', Marx greatly develops his analysis of the difference between the market-price of commodities and their market values, what in volume 1 he calls 'social value', that is, the value that reflects the average conditions of production in the relevant branch of production, and of the surplus-profits that derive from individual capitals achieving levels of productivity that are higher than the average. Then in part 3, when Marx develops the theory of the tendency of the rate of profit to fall, he makes the search for surplus-profits the mechanism responsible for the rising organic composition of capital: when other capitals copy the innovation responsible for surplus-profit, a new market value is established for that sector equivalent to the individual value of the innovator's commodities. His surplus-profit is thereby eliminated, but also, since higher productivity is bought with a higher organic composition of capital, the generalization of the innovation produces a fall in the rate of profit. That capitalism is defined by a *dual* conflictual relationship – between capital and labour and among competing capitals – is well brought out in a passage at the end of Marx's discussion of surplus-profits, which he argues offers 'a mathematically exact demonstration of why the capitalists, no matter how little love is lost among them in their mutual competition, are nevertheless united by a real freemasonry vis-à-vis the working class as a whole.'[45]

The argument of *Capital* is, of course, conducted at a very high level of abstraction. Much of the subsequent development of Marxist political economy has involved the position of more concrete levels of analysis designed, on the basis of the more abstract conceptualizations of *Capital*, to explain the course of capitalist development in the twentieth century.[46] Negri's own stance is at an oblique angle to this intellectual process. He barely adverts to the capital-in-general/many capitals distinction in *Marx Beyond Marx*: this is hardly surprising since he believes that contemporary capitalism is constituted by politicized relations of force between two antagonistic class subjects. Beyond a certain point, there is little point in simply confronting his highly selective appropriation of the *Grundrisse* with the interpretation of Marx's intellectual evolution between 1857 and 1867 briefly outlined above. I think that my interpretation is more accurate, but the history of creative misreadings of canonical texts is long and rich enough for this claim to be easily dismissed as mere pedantry. The interesting question is rather this: to what extent did *Marx Beyond Marx* capture the subsequent evolution of capitalism and the class struggle? How useful did Negri's subjectivist appropriation of the *Grundrisse* prove to be? In my view, the answer that any serious appraisal of the history of the past twenty-five years must give to these questions is: Not much.

This claim can be considered at two levels. First, is it the case that competition among capitals has been supplanted through the comprehensive politicization of the relations of production, as rival collective subjects are locked in combat? The answer, surely, must be: No. Whatever theoretical perspective one adopts, it is undeniable that economic competition, particularly at the international level, has increased very significantly over the past generation. In the face of this intensification of competition, the idea, essential to Negri's assertion that the 'Law of Value dies', that prices are no longer primarily the outcome of economic processes but are politically determined, is untenable. When competition occurs at the international level between rival capitals, no individual capital or nation-state is a position autonomously to set prices.[47] At the national level, the consequence has been to force a series of large-scale capital restructurings, which have eliminated some firms and drastically disrupted the institutionalized relations that previously existed between specific capitals that sometimes enjoyed a monopoly or semi-monopoly position within their domestic market and the nation-state.

One might indeed say that the era of neo-liberalism has seen a partial depoliticization of economic relations. Of course, these relations are still constituted by exploitation, and in that fundamental sense remain political. Moreover, the 'depoliticization' that has occurred has been in part the outcome of a series of ideologically charged political interventions at the national and international level (in the latter case, the Washington Consensus enforced by the US Treasury, the International Monetary Fund, and the World Bank) that have sought to present the economic as a neutral sphere whose mastery is purely technical and dependent on understanding the 'natural' laws of the market.[48] All the same, if we understand the politicization of economic relations in the terms in which it is presented in *Marx Beyond Marx* – that is, as a process whereby economic relations are increasingly the result of the conflict between collectively organized and politically self-conscious class subjects, then this process is less advanced than it was a generation ago. The intensification of international competition has made it harder for individual capitals to weld themselves into collective subjects at the national level, both because this competition encourages firms to invest and trade at the global level and because nation-states have to deal not just with 'native' capitals but with foreign multinational corporations that have invested in their territories. It is important not to confuse this relative disarticulation of capital at the national level with the idea that globalization has rendered the nation-state impotent. Nevertheless, a consequence of this disarticulation is that individual capitals, including the biggest multinationals, find themselves subject to processes of primarily international economic competition that they cannot control.[49]

This shift is registered by Negri in his more recent work. After all, what is Empire but 'a *decentralized* and *deterritorializing* apparatus of rule that incorporates the entire global realm within its open expanding frontiers'? The metaphor of the network that Hardt and Negri, like many other analysts of contemporary capitalism, use implies at the very least a decentralization of power, its dispersal among rival centres. Indeed, '[i]n this smooth space of Empire, there is no *place* of power – it is both everywhere and nowhere.' Such a view of capitalism seems hard to square with Negri's earlier conception of capital as a collective subject. The same would seem to be true of the '*trifunctional*' Polybian constitution of Empire involving

a functional equilibrium among three forms of power: the monarchic unity of power and its global monopoly of force [the

US and the G7 in particular]; aristocratic articulations through transnational corporations and nation-states; and democratic-representational *comitia*, presented again in the form of nation-states along with various kinds of NGOs, media organizations, and other 'popular' organisms.[50]

Yet the older idea of the state as the instrument of social capital as a collective subject continues to figure in *Empire*. Hardt and Negri interpret Marx's famous declaration in the *Manifesto* that '[t]he executive of the modern state is but a committee for managing the common affairs of the whole bourgeoisie' in precisely these terms: 'by this they mean that although the action of the state will at times contradict the immediate interests of the individual capitalists, it will always be in the long term interests of the collective capitalist, that is, the collective subject of social capital as a whole.' The form taken by this relationship varies as capitalism changes in the course of its development. As capital becomes transnational, so the functions of the state are taken over by the Polybian mixed constitution. What binds together 'the diverse functions and bodies of the hybrid constitution' is Guy Debord's 'society of the spectacle', 'an integrated and diffuse apparatus of images and ideas that produces and regulates public discourse and opinion'. In turn, however: 'The spectacle of politics functions *as if* the media, the military, the government, the transnational corporations, the global financial institutions, and so forth were all consciously and explicitly directed by a single power even though they are not.'[51]

So, despite the fact that, 'in this smooth space of Empire, there is no *place* of power', the Imperial constitution operates as if 'the collective subject of social capital as a whole' were in command. It is not clear whether we are supposed to conceive this as a paranoid collective fantasy or an objective functional relationship (or perhaps both). As is often true of authors of functionalist theories of the state, Negri easily slips into more instrumentalist formulations, for example, declaring after 9/11 that the United States was acting on behalf of 'collective capital'.[52] Alternatively one might take seriously Marx's declaration: '*Capital in general*, as distinct from the particular capitals, does indeed appear (1) *only as an abstraction*.'[53] In other words, rather than seek to hypostatize capital in general as a collective subject, 'social capital', it might be more useful to analyse the concrete forms of competition and cooperation among 'many capitals' at both the national and the international level and how these articulate with the processes of geopolitical competition constitutive of the interstate system. The outcome of such an analysis would in my view be a much more complex picture than the transfer of political power to a set of transnationally organized institutions that Hardt and Negri claim has taken place.[54]

The second level at which history has judged *Marx Beyond Marx* harshly is that of the class struggle itself. The intensification of international economic competition and the consequent disarticulation of national capitalisms involved also a number of serious defeats for the organized working class from the late 1970s onwards. If these were most severe in the United States, where the partial recovery of profitability was made possible by an unprecedented twenty-year compression of real wages, in Europe they were most spectacular in the two advanced capitalist societies where working-class combativity had been most developed in the early 1970s, Italy and Britain. It is not my purpose to explore the causes of these severe setbacks for the workers' movement here. Nevertheless, it is clear enough that they involved, on both sides of the class divide, the interrelation of objective and subjective factors.[55]

On the part of capital, the harsher competitive pressures on established industries both demanded and facilitated the dismantling or weakening of what had hitherto been strongholds of working-class organization, but the realization of such objectives required the construction of national capitalist coalitions with the ideological will and political capacity to wage the necessary class battles. On the side of the working class, the demoralizing effect of mass employment, the economic fragmentation produced by the processes of capital restructuring themselves, and the bureaucratization of workplace organization interacted with the general commitment to class collaboration of both the political and trade-union leaders of the workers' movement and the marginalization of more militant groups of workers and of the revolutionary left, partly self-induced, but partly the product of larger forces and strategies.

It would be unfair to demand of *Marx Beyond Marx* critical reflection on a defeat that took final form only after it was published in 1979. This text is an extended theoretical argument for the version of *operaismo* that Negri had developed in the course of the 1970s, one that increasingly located proletarian subjectivity outside the factory among the diverse subjects oppressed by a social capital whose politicized 'command' operated in every sphere of life. Negri himself summed this shift as reflecting the transition 'from the working class massified in direct production in the factory, to social labour-power, representing the potentiality of the new working class, now extended throughout the entire span of production and reproduction.'[56] This theme of the 'social worker' replacing the 'mass worker' is still present in *Empire*, though it is now overlaid by the new concept (taken from Spinoza) of the multitude (see §4.3 below).[57]

Neither *Empire* nor any other later texts by Negri of which I am aware develop anything that amounts to a serious critique of the positions that he took in the 1970s. He seeks to differentiate the version of autonomism that he had developed from the Red Brigades' terrorism, while insisting: 'The sharp, definitive defeat of the political organizations of the movement at the end of the 1970s by no means coincided with any defeat of the new political subjects which had emerged in the eruption of 1977.'[58] This way of putting it sidesteps the larger wave of defeats suffered by the organized working class in Italy and the rest of the advanced capitalist world that were a necessary condition for the process of capital restructuring driven through under the banner of neoliberalism. Hardt and Negri actually claim this process as a victory for the working class: 'The power of the proletariat imposes limits on capital and not only determines the crisis but also dictates the terms and nature of the transformation. *The proletariat actually invents the social and productive forms that capital will be forced to adopt for the future.*'[59] This claim is a direct echo of the primacy of proletarian subjectivity affirmed by Negri in the 1970s, for example, thus:

> The whole of capitalist development, ever since the working class reached its present high level of composition, has been nothing other than the obverse, a reaction, a following-in-the-footsteps of proletarian self-valorization – repeated operation of self-protection, of recuperation, of adjustment in relation to the effects of self-valorization, which are effects of sabotage of the capitalist

machine ... here the methodology of the *critique of political economy* has to be modified, taking as its starting point proletarian self-valorization, its separateness and the effects of sabotage that it determines.[60]

This argument is a hyped-up version of a long-standing theme of *operaismo*: Tronti also tends to portray each phase of capitalist development as a response to new forms of working-class autonomy. But the question one must ask is this: to what extent does the idea capture the tortuous – sometimes indeed tortured – reality of the kind of 'recomposition' that the working class experienced during the Great Depression of the 1930s or the long phase of economic crises that began in the early 1970s? Certainly these processes involve very powerful assertions of working-class subjectivity – sometimes full of combative self-confidence, at other times more heroic but desperate fights with backs to the wall. But it seems unconvincing to describe the outcomes of such struggles as 'invented' by workers and 'forced' on capital. What would the members of former mining communities in Britain, now often given over to drugs and despair, say if we told them that their present plight was as consequence of their own practices of 'proletarian self-valorization'? To say this is not to ignore or diminish the forms of resistance that the oppressed and exploited are able to achieve even in desperate circumstances (something well captured by Ken Loach in films such as *Raining Stones*). But it is to recognize that some circumstances are better than others, and these differences in situation are not simply a consequence of which collective subject is able to assert its class will more effectively but reflect, among other things, the structurally determined capacities that workers and capitalists can bring to bear against each other.[61]

4.3   The refusal of transcendence

Rather than reconsider the primacy that he accorded to subjectivity in his writings of the 1970s, Negri has preferred to transform it into an ontological principle. In this sense there is a parallel between his trajectory and Badiou's in that both have sought to radicalize the subjectivism that was already characteristic of their thought of the 1970s, although in doing so they have resorted to very different ontologies. Already in *Marx Beyond Marx* Negri puts forward 'the principle of constitution', which 'introduces into the methodology the dimension of the qualitative leap, a conception of history reduced to collective relations of force, thus a conception that is not sceptical, but dynamic and creative. Every constitution of a new structure is the constitution of a new antagonism.'[62] Here we have *in nuce* the idea of constituent power that plays such a central role in Negri's recent writings. His fullest development of this concept appeals to the 'second Foucault' of the *History of Sexuality*: 'Man as Foucault describes him appears as a totality of resistances that produces a capacity for absolute liberation, outside all finalism that is not the expression of life itself and of its reproduction. In man it is life itself that liberates itself, that opposes itself to all that limits and imprisons it.'[63]

Negri's account of constituent power seeks, in fact, to marry Foucault to Marx as the theorist of 'the all-expansive creativity of living labour':

> living labour incarnates constituent power and offers it the general social conditions through which it can express itself: constituent power installs itself politically on the basis of that social cooperation that is cosubstantial with living labour, as the interpretation of its productivity or better of its creativity. It is in the immediacy, in the creative spontaneity of living labour that constituent power finds how to realize its creativity in the masses. It is necessary to consider attentively this kernel of living labour, this creative tension that is simultaneously political and economic, productive of civil, social and political structures, and which is thus constituent tension. Cooperative living labour engenders a social ontology that is constitution and innovation, an interlacement of forms touching at once economics and politics; it thus engenders an indistinction of politics and economics in the figure of a creation.[64]

Here we are back in the same circle of concepts – creativity, productivity, living labour, etc. – with which this chapter began. It is not to diminish the brilliant critical history of Renaissance humanism to which the bulk of *Le Pouvoir constituant* is devoted to say that the actual theorization of constituent power in that book, notably in the concluding chapter, does little more than ring the changes on these concepts. But one doesn't have to be a card-carrying follower of Derrida to think that terms such as 'creativity' and 'productivity' that are endlessly used to specify the content of the concept of constituent power are badly in need of decon-struction. To say, for example, that '[d]ynamic creative and con-tinuous constitution of the process of power [*puissance*]: such is politics' is less the solution of any problem than an invitation criti-cally to examine the concepts in terms of which politics is being defined.[65] This observation is not intended to deny that any philo-sophical argument must find a resting point somewhere, in a set of premises whose truth is left unquestioned at least for the task in hand, or to demand that Negri pursue an infinite regress of jus-tifications, but rather to point to the fact that the particular resting point he has lighted on is particularly liable to crumble beneath him, since it consists in a set of concepts that radicalize his sub-jectivization of the social by grounding it in a subjectivized nature.

The name often given to nature so conceived is Life. It is strik-ing, for example, how the concept of social cooperation that Negri takes from Marx in order to specify the concept of living labour is itself redefined: 'Co-operation is life itself, to the extent that it produces and reproduces itself.' Negri also says that Marx is best understood from the standpoint of 'Foucault, genealogist of sub-jectivity', who must be seen, at least in retrospect, as 'a revision-ist Marxist'.[66] As we have seen, what Negri takes from Foucault is the idea that resistance is an expression of Life. This is not so much Foucault's idea as Deleuze's. The latter's *Foucault*, which Negri cites, is more reliable as an exposition of Deleuze's own views than of those of Foucault. As Badiou observes, this is a fairly typical procedure:

> in starting from innumerable and seemingly disparate cases, . . .
> Deleuze arrives at conceptual productions that I would unhesitat-ingly describe as *monotonous*, composing a very particular regime of emphasis or almost infinite repetition of a limited repertoire of concepts, as well as a virtuosic variation of names, under which what is thought remains essentially identical.[67]

Life certainly doesn't go unanalysed in Deleuze's work. *Mille plateaux* in particular is, among other things, the development of a highly distinctive ontology of Life conceived as an impersonal force that constantly outflanks and subverts the 'stratifications' and 'assemblages', the structured constellations of domination that seek to contain and control the nomadic wanderings of desire (see also §5.2 below). There is a strong case for saying that the influence of this text on *Empire* is systematic, and that the theoretical construction of Hardt's and Negri's book cannot be fully understood unless it is set alongside *Mille plateaux*. Properly to demonstrate this and to explore its implications would be a substantial study in its own right.[68] In the absence of such a work, one can still wonder whether the best strategy to rescue a version of Marxist political economy that had been found historically and politically wanting is to subsume it into the kind of vitalist ontology that, whatever its precise derivation, demonstrably organizes texts such as *Le Pouvoir constituant*, *Empire*, and the latter's sequel *Multitude*.

This last text offered Hardt and Negri an opportunity to restate and develop the themes of their earlier book.[69] Certainly with respect to the idea that provides this latest book with its title, 'multitude', what we are offered is more an exemplification of the problem I have been discussing than a successful extension of Hardt's and Negri's argument. The multitude is, on the one hand, the political subject par excellence, the bearer of constituent power. Thus: 'The multitude designates an active social subject, which acts on the basis of what singularities share in common.' By virtue of its capacity to bring about an active convergence that does not repress difference in unity or identity, '[t]he multitude is the only social subject capable of realizing democracy, that is, the rule of everyone by everyone.' On the other hand, the multitude has a specific location in the class relations of contemporary capitalism: it comprises 'all those who work under the rule of capital and thus potentially . . . the class of those who refuse the rule of capital'. Multitude is thus intended as 'a class concept', but also as an alternative to the classical Marxist concept of the working class, which is dismissed as 'an exclusive concept'.[70]

Multitude thus brings together, in the manner of Marxist class theory condemned by Badiou (see §3.3 above), subjectivity and social structure. Nevertheless, Hardt and Negri are clearly moving here well beyond Marxist orthodoxy, though they insist they are not saying 'there is no more the industrial working class' (in fact, Negri is on record that 'the struggle of the working class no longer exists').[71] The critical development they highlight here is the rise

of ' "immaterial labour", . . . labour that creates immaterial products such as knowledge, information, communication, a relationship, or an emotional response.'[72] On the face of it, it is not obvious
why this should represent the kind of transformation of class relations asserted by Hardt and Negri. Certainly the share of output
and employment devoted to the production of material goods has
fallen in the advanced capitalist economies. But Marx defines the
working class not by what they produced, but by their position in
the relations of production. His argument is that workers are compelled by their lack of direct access to the means of production to
exchange their labour-power for a wage. Their unequal bargain-
ing power leads to their being exploited in the sense of producing
surplus-value for capital irrespective of whether the commodity to
which that surplus-value is attached is a physical product or an
immaterial service. Thus an empirical study of two call centres –
surely a good case of 'immaterial labour', where employees use
information technology to interact with customers – concludes that
'the imperative of cost minimization' would lead to 'further routinization and intensification' of labour and that this 'overall tendency is likely to cast further doubt on the optimistic perspective
that call centre work, in time, will come to resemble knowledge
work' that is relatively autonomous and creative.[73]

The reason why Hardt and Negri present the idea of the multitude as an alternative to the classical Marxist conception of the
working class has, in my view, to do less with the problem in social
theory of how to interpret and explain the changes that have taken
place in class structures over the past generation than with their
vitalist philosophical commitments. They claim that what they call
'biopolitical production' is the 'nearly dominant model' as production becomes 'not merely the production of material goods but
also the production of communications, relationships, and forms
of life'. The reason why a change in the product of labour is alter-
ing the relations under which work takes place is that the distinction between life and labour is itself breaking down: 'Labour
and value have become biopolitical in the sense that living and
producing tend to be indistinguishable. Insofar as life tends to be
completely invested by acts of production and reproduction, life
itself becomes a productive machine.'[74]

The presupposition of these assertions is more clearly stated by
Hardt's and Negri's co-thinker Paulo Virno:

Labour and non-labour develop an identical form of productivity, based on the exercise of generic human faculties: language, memory, sociability, ethical and aesthetic inclinations, the capacity for abstraction and learning. From the point of view of 'what' is done and 'how' it is done, there is no substantial difference between employment and unemployment . . . The old distinction between 'labour' and 'non-labour' ends up as the distinction between remunerated life and non-remunerated life.[75]

From this perspective, then, the multitude represents, in the context of capitalist class relations, the triumph of the inherent productivity of life. But, in the first place, even if we grant Virno's premiss that the same capacities are deployed both within and beyond the contemporary forms of capitalist production, it doesn't follow that there is no difference in the kind of social relations that prevail in these two domains, or that the differences between them are growing less. Moreover there is no reason to believe that the advantages to be gained by wage-labour, in the form of both the additional resources that a worker and her dependants can gain access to thanks to her wages and the power that she may be able to exercise in common with her fellow workers through going on strike have disappeared. This power is best understood in the light of Marx's central theme that capital is a relationship: in exploiting wage-labour capital makes itself dependent on and vulnerable to labour's capacity to withdraw or take control itself of production. John Holloway criticizes Negri for his failure sufficiently to acknowledge that '[c]apital can exist only as the product of transformed doing (labour). This is the key to its weakness.'[76]

None of this is to suggest that wage-labour is any less the realm of exploitation and domination than it was in Marx's time. On the contrary, one of the objections to Hardt's and Negri's concept of biopolitical production is precisely that it tends to portray the contemporary world of work in too roseate colours. They write: 'at the high end of the labour market companies like Microsoft try to make the office more like home, offering free meals and exercise programmes to keep employees in the office as many of their waking hours as possible. At the low end of the labour market workers have to juggle several jobs to make ends meet.'[77] But this only represents the dissolution of the difference between work and life in the sense of work *qua* wage-labour absorbing life. Wage-labour is demanding more and more from people, whether they are privileged software designers or ultra-exploited migrant workers. If anything, the relationship between capital and wage-labour is becoming more pervasive economically and socially than it was in the past. Consequently the power that workers gain because capital depends on their exploitation remains of central strategic significance to anyone who wants to change the world.[78]

As we have seen, Hardt and Negri conceive the multitude as the only subject capable of realizing democracy. Democracy is a topic of pressing political importance today. The Bush administration legitimizes its proclamation of a global state of exception with the claim to be pursuing a 'democratic revolution' in the Middle East. Among supporters of this project there is an implicit rewriting of the content of democracy in which it is effectively equated with liberal capitalism. Thus Fareed Zakaria counter-poses what he calls 'illiberal democracy' – represented, for example, by President Hugo Chávez of Venezuela, who has consistently won massive popular support in challenging neo-liberalism and American hegemony – to 'constitutional liberalism', which seeks to limit the powers of government and protect individual liberties and private property. Democracy, in other words, isn't about voting or popular sovereignty, but about the institutions that allow liberal capitalism to flourish.[79] Hardt and Negri are well equipped to challenge this kind of, in reality, anti-democratic discourse. *Le Pouvoir constituant* traces from the Renaissance onwards the gradual emergence of the idea of constituent power, in which the multitude asserts its power collectively to determine its destiny. In *Multitude* Hardt and Negri affirm the idea of 'absolute democracy' that they take from Spinoza. But they make no serious attempt to spell out what this means. Instead, the democracy to come is simply folded into the mystery of the multitude. So, for example, we are told: 'The future institutional structure of the new society is embedded in the affective, cooperative, and communicative relationships of social production.'[80] What this amounts to saying is that the resistance of the multitude will develop into a constituent power essentially through the spontaneous coordination of the singularities composing it.

Interestingly Ernesto Laclau had already pointed to this weakness in *Empire* in terms that recall the contrast between Badiou and Deleuze with which this chapter began.[81] Hardt and Negri argue that European modernity is constituted by 'the uninterrupted conflict between the immanent, constructive, creative forces and transcendent power aimed at restoring order'. The first moment in the process through which modernity is constituted is through 'the revolutionary discovery of the plane of immanence' by Renaissance humanism, which they identify with the 'refusal of transcendence' by Foucault and Althusser.[82] Hardt and Negri conceive the subversion of transcendence – represented, for example, by Hobbes's theory of political sovereignty – by immanence as not simply a philosophical debate but a contemporary socio-political process: 'In contrast to the transcendental model that poses a unitary sovereign subject standing above society, biopolitical social organization begins to appear absolutely immanent, where all the elements interact on the same plane.'[83] This is one of the points where Deleuze's influence is most visible, since the plane of immanence is one of his and Félix Guattari's key concepts – a non-hierarchized matrix where differences are purely those of relative intensities spread out across the indifference of zero intensity, sustaining '[a] powerful non-organic life that escapes stratification, traverses assemblages, and traces an abstract line without contour, the line of nomad art and itinerant metallurgy.'[84]

The idea of the plane of immanence has its origins in Deleuze's interpretation of Spinoza's conception of God as a unitary divine substance expressed in its creation, the immanent cause of the profusion of beings. For Deleuze, Spinoza is radically at odds with the hierarchical conception of Being common to orthodox Christian and neo-Platonist ontologies:

> Immanence implies for its part a pure ontology, a theory of Being where the One is only the property of a substance and of what is. Moreover, immanence in the pure state demands the principle of an equality of being or the posing of a Being-equal: not only is being equal in itself, but being appears equally present in all beings. And the Cause, equally close everywhere: there is not a far removed cause. Beings are not defined by their rank in a hierarchy, are not more or less distant from the One, but each depends directly on God, participating in the equality of being, receiving immediately everything it can in receiving according to the aptitude of its essence, independently of all proximity and of all distance. Furthermore, immanence in the pure state demands a univocal Being that forms one Nature and that consists in positive forms common

to producer and product, to cause and effect . . . All is affirmation in immanence.[85]

For Laclau also, Hardt's and Negri's counter-position of transcendence and immanence recalls theological debates, in this case among mediaeval schoolmen, about the origin of evil. Is evil 'a brute and irreducible fact', as orthodox Christian theologians must assert if they are to maintain their conception of God as a transcendent and benevolent being distinct from his creation and not responsible for the evil freely chosen by mankind? Or is evil an illusion, as those from Scotus Erigena and Duns Scotus to Spinoza and Hegel who conceive God as immanent in the world have claimed, arguing that 'things we call evil are necessary stages that God has to pass through in order to reach his divine perfection'? Laclau himself conceives evil as the theological ancestor of the Lacanian concept of social antagonism (see §3.3 above): the impossibility of suturing together the inherently heterogeneous elements of the social into a closed totality requires a hegemonic intervention aimed at constructing a temporary and fragile unity. For Hardt and Negri, by contrast, '[t]here is an actual historical subject of what they conceive as the realization of a full immanence: it is what they call the "multitude".' Consequently, 'for them the unity of the multitude results from the spontaneous aggregation of a plurality of actions that do not need to be articulated between themselves . . . What is totally lacking in *Empire* is a theory of *articulation*, without which politics is unthinkable.'[86]

Laclau's critique is made from his own distinctive post-Marxist perspective; more broadly one can see it as consonant with the approach of philosophers of the event such as Badiou and Žižek, for whom transcendence is not the instance of some religious or social hierarchy but the insistence of an event whose effectivity cannot be taken for granted, but requires an interpreting intervention (§3.2 above). But one does not have to share these philosophical approaches to acknowledge that Hardt's and Negri's assumption that somehow the singularities composing the multitude will spontaneously converge as a subject is a serious weakness. Perhaps this helps to explain why, as Daniel Bensaïd puts it, *Empire* conceals 'a great strategic void'.[87] For strategy concerns itself with the necessarily hazardous calculations that political actors must make as they grapple with an objective context (including the strategies and actions of others) whose current state and future course are riddled with uncertainties, in part because the interactions among the antagonists produce unexpected transformations.[88]

But if, as Hardt and Negri argue, capital both 'operates on the plane of *immanence*' and tends to realize it, deterritorializing, breaking down national barriers to its free movement, producing a 'general equalization or smoothing of social space' where the division of the world between North and South disappears, then strategy is beside the point.[89] In this non-hierarchical 'smooth world', where the 'equality of being' is increasingly realized, there is no longer any unevenness, any 'weak links', any specific points where contradictions accumulate and capital is particularly vulnerable. Consequently, strategy no longer has any leverage. The reason why this doesn't matter too much is that liberation is always-already here. 'All is affirmation in immanence', as Deleuze puts it. This helps to explain one of the most puzzling features of *Multitude*, namely the way in which it simply juxtaposes Empire as a transnational 'network power' with contemporary realities – for example, the existence of strategic competitors to the United States and the nationalist global policy of the Bush administration – that apparently contradict the idea of Empire. The contradiction is resolved because the logic of both production and war today implies a 'distributed network structure' whose 'guiding principles' require 'an absolutely democratic organization that corresponds to the dominant forms of economic and social production and that is also the most powerful weapon against the ruling power structure.' The evidence to the contrary, most obviously the global state of war proclaimed by the Bush administration, isn't a mere illusion, but is a secondary and waning phenomenon relative to the dominant tendency towards 'absolute democracy' striving to assert itself in the shape of the multitude:

In the era of imperial sovereignty and biopolitical production, the balance has tipped such that the ruled now tend to be the exclusive producers of social organization. This does not mean that sovereignty immediately crumbles and the rulers lose all their power. It does mean that the rulers become ever more parasitical and that sovereignty becomes increasingly unnecessary. Correspondingly, the ruled become increasingly autonomous.[90]

Or, as Negri puts it elsewhere, 'the great mass of people, the multitude that is free to move about anywhere in the world, that circulates in culture, that hybridizes itself – this mass is walking away.'[91] The theme we found already in *Marx Beyond Marx* of the progressive autonomization of labour from capital that takes the form of the 'refusal of work' is now overlaid with the metaphor of flight: 'Democracy takes the form of a subtraction, a flight, an exodus from sovereignty.'[92] It is hard to know how literally to take all this. Are 'the great mass of people' really 'free to move about anywhere in the world'? Granted the importance of migrant labour in contemporary capitalism (see §2.1 above), the story of many individual workers is that of a forced flight from poverty, oppression, and persecution at home, not to freedom, but to yet more poverty, oppression, and persecution. And the vast majority of workers remain relatively immobile, tied down by bonds of economic dependence, family, and community: migrants make up 3 per cent of the world's population – even in the rich countries where they gravitate only one in twelve is an immigrant.[93] Moreover, the Book of Exodus tells us that the pharaoh pursued the fleeing children of Israel with his army. How are those walking away from sovereignty today to beat off this pursuit, in the absence of divine intervention to part the waters and confronted with a modern pharaoh armed with enormous economic and military resources? Though Holloway also thinks of resistance to capital in terms of flight – 'in the first place . . . , the refusal of domination, the destruction and sabotage of the instruments of domination (machinery, for instance), a running away from domination, nomadism, exodus, desertion' – he is nonetheless more realistic than Hardt and Negri, acknowledging that, '[t]o break from capital, it is not enough to flee', because, '[a]s long as the means of doing are in the hands of capital, then doing will be ruptured and turned against itself. The expropriator must indeed be expropriated.'[94]

Towards the end of *Multitude*, Hardt and Negri do briefly gesture towards a more strategic and interventionist approach: 'What we need to bring the multitude into being is a form of grand politics that has been called *Realpolitik*, or political realism.' And they characterize *Realpolitik*, in terms that acknowledge the problem of strategy, as including 'the capacity to separate oneself from the immediate situation and tirelessly construct mediations, feigning (if necessary) coherence, and playing different tactical games into the continuity of strategy.' But the book ends by conjuring up the prospect of 'a strong event, a radical insurrectional demand. We can already recognize that today time is split between a present that is already dead and a future that is already living ... In time, an event will thrust us like an arrow into that living future. Thus will be the real political act of love.'[95] This 'strong event' is not the same as the kind of event that Badiou thematizes: rather than being a chance occurrence emerging from the void of the situation, it fulfils the promise expressed by the plenitude of Being. But, as in the case of Badiou, the conditions from which this 'act of love' rises remain a mystery. And, since it is before us, we are left to await it, relying on the spontaneous productivity of Life. This is a posture that it is hard not to think of as passive, even fatalistic.

Part II

Three Dimensions of Progress

5

A Critical Realist Ontology

5.1 The story so far

The survey of contemporary critical thought in part I has left us with an agenda of problems to pursue. Before I attempt to sketch out a way forward, it may be helpful to set out what seem to be the main issues to be addressed.

- **Ontology:** In the first place, the nature of the ontological commitments made by critical theory has been a recurring theme. This is particularly true of the two most radical thinkers discussed in this book, Alain Badiou and Antonio Negri. Badiou's philosophy of the event is developed from a complex ontological argument based on the concepts of multiplicity and the void. As we have seen, Hardt's and Negri's theory of Empire is organized conceptually by the ontology of Life that they derive from Deleuze. I have offered reasons for rejecting both these ontologies, but this then poses the question of what philosophical conception of the nature of being should replace them.

- **Realism:** A more specific metaphysical issue has also recurred, particularly in chapters 1 and 2. One factor tending to subvert Jürgen Habermas's philosophy of law and democracy is, I argued in §1.1, his anti-realist theory of truth. Similarly, Luc Boltanski's and Eve Chiapello's attempt to renovate social critique relies on a contextualist and pluralist theory of justice that tends gravely to limit the scope of the challenge to capitalism they pose (§2.1). Pierre Bourdieu is committed to a realist understanding of science, but his analysis of the scientific field in *Pascalian Meditations* seems to flirt with anti-realism (§2.2). The undertow of my argument has been in a realist direction, but this requires explicit statement and defence.

• **Structure and contradiction:** The nature of social structure has also been a recurring theme. Habermas's account of modernity centres on the differentiation from the lifeworld of autonomous subsystems (§1.1). For Jacques Bidet, this is far too apologetic a view of a world dominated by capitalism, and he develops an elaborate, if philosophically under-argued hierarchy of metastructure, structure, and system (§1.2). Boltanski's and Chiapello's anti-realism prompts them towards the view that social structures cannot be specified independently of agents' conceptions of them (§2.1). Bourdieu and Badiou both have much more robust conceptions of, respectively, the field (§2.2) and the situation (§3.2): as a consequence, interventions by agents that transcend their context become a rarity, as Badiou explicitly argues in his theory of the event. Finally, Hardt and Negri smooth out social structures into the Deleuzian plane of immanence that Empire is realizing (§4.3). So, how best to understand structures and subject? And, more specifically, can we formulate a robust conception of structural contradictions? Should the contradictions of capitalism be reduced, as Boltanski and Chiapello suggest, to the dialectic between the spirit of capitalism and its critiques? Or do the Lacanian notion of antagonism as the limit of the social (§3.3) or Negri's notion in his writings of the 1960s and 1970s of the clash of rival class subjectivities (§4.2) offer a better way of conceptualizing contradictions?

• **Justice and universality:** Running through all the critical theories discussed in part I is a persistent tendency to conflate normative and factual considerations. I have documented this in most detail in chapters 1 and 2: Boltanski and Chiapello (§2.1) as well as Habermas (§1.1) constrain principles of justice by the function they perform in sustaining social integration; Bidet seeks to infer modernity's promise of liberty, equality, and rationality from the structural presuppositions of such societies (§1.2); Bourdieu tries to justify the political role of intellectuals by portraying them as defenders of a universality in which scientific objectivity and normative principles are tacitly confused (§2.2). But we can see the same tendency in both Badiou and Negri. Badiou reserves the term 'event' for those occurrences that he considers worthy of fidelity – the French and Russian Revolutions, Marx and Freud, Cézanne and Schoenberg, Cantor and Einstein – and dismisses as unworthy of nomination as events what one might call diabolical interventions such as National Socialism or 9/11. But this is achieved through simply stipulating that events involve a moment of universality and, indeed, egalitarianism; here philosophy helps itself to a normative programme without taking the trouble to argue for it. Hardt's and Negri's reliance on Gilles Deleuze's vitalism means that the ontological and the ethical are always-already folded together on the plane of immanence. As Deleuze puts it, '[a]ll is affirmation in immanence.'[1] All is – tendentially at least – for the best in what is, thanks to 'the joy of being', this best of all possible worlds.[2] Instead of all these different illicit fusions of the normative and the explanatory, the ethical and the ontological, critical theory requires free-standing principles of justice capable of supporting the idea of *égaliberté* that, as Etienne Balibar rightly argues (see §1.2 above), is at the heart of the great revolutions of modern times.

This is an enormous programme whose implementation could take up many lifetimes of philosophers with much greater talents than mine. All that I attempt in part II is to sketch out important elements of what seem to me to be the answers to the questions that have emerged from part I. In the rest of this chapter I address the first two themes, ontology and realism; chapter 6 outlines a Marxist theory of structural contradiction; and chapter 7 explores how egalitarian liberalism can help us address the question of justice and universality.

In the title of this chapter I describe the ontology that I present as an alternative as 'critical realist'. In doing so I wish to acknowledge my debt to the philosophical writings of Roy Bhaskar. As the name – 'critical realism' – given to his approach indicates, Bhaskar has been particularly influential among left-wing social scientists looking for a philosophy of science that will, among other things, ground an orientation towards emancipation. This is not the focus that I take here. I am more interested in the ontology that Bhaskar and other critical realists (notably, in the case of the social sciences, Margaret Archer) expound: among other virtues, this ontology allows us to escape from many of the difficulties we have discovered in the critical theorists discussed in earlier chapters. I should, however, make it clear that, while in the course of time I have become increasingly persuaded of the importance of Bhaskar's work, on which I draw especially in the next section, my espousal of critical realism does not imply that I have signed up to all the specific propositions and arguments that he has advanced. Thus I remain wholly unconvinced by Bhaskar's claim to have established the truth of many of his metaphysical doctrines by what he calls transcendental arguments on the model of Kant's attempt to show that the categories required for consciousness to arrive at an objective, causally ordered physical world can be deduced from an analysis of the conditions of possible experience. Moreover, even books as suggestive and full of brilliant flashes of insight as *Dialectic* already show signs of the intellectual decline that has, alas, been fully realized with Bhaskar's espousal of New Age spiritualism.[3]

The sense in which 'realism' is understood here, and in Bhaskar's writings before they took a spiritualist turn, is not idiosyncratic. At its core is the metaphysical doctrine that, as Michael Devitt puts it, 'the world exists *independently of the mental*.' What makes this an ontology is that it involves claims about what exists. Devitt distinguishes between two species of realism according to the kinds of entities whose existence they assert. 'Common-Sense Realism' asserts 'the existence of common-sense physical entities' that are accessible to observation; 'Scientific Realism' is committed also to the existence of 'further entities, those apparently posited by our scientific beliefs', especially '*unobservable* entities'. Accordingly, for Devitt, a full-blooded realist affirms the following: 'Tokens of most current common-sense, and scientific physical types objectively exist independently of the mental.'[4] For this doctrine to become *critical* realism it has to be extended to a third kind of entity, namely social structures conceived as the emergent properties of social interactions.[5] As we shall see in §5.2 below, the concept of emergence plays a strategic role in critical realism, which conceives the real that exists independently of the mental as *stratified*.

If critical realism cannot be grounded by a transcendental argument, what reason do we have for accepting it? W. V. Quine argued for a naturalized epistemology and metaphysics in which ontology simply comprises those entities whose existence we must presuppose for our beliefs – including the scientific theories we accept – to be true.[6] Bhaskar loosens, but does not break, the connection between ontology and what we hold true: 'A philosophical ontology is developed by reflection upon what must be the case for science to be possible, and this is independent of any actual scientific knowledge.'[7] The trouble lies with the second half of this sentence. Both Quine and Bhaskar in effect relativize ontology to the sciences. Quine's approach is, in my view, too narrow, inasmuch as he restricts ontology to those entities over which the sentences – and in particular the theories of the physical sciences – we hold true range, and does not therefore offer a place for reflection on the nature of the world that these theories jointly reveal.

Bhaskar, by contrast, seeks to establish an account of the structure of the world based on an interpretation, not (explicitly, at least) of the *content* of scientific theories, but on an interpretation of scientists' practice: thus his transcendental argument moves from the claim that scientific experimentation involves the creation of 'closed systems' in which events form a uniform sequence to the inference that the mechanisms that are thereby revealed exist independently of human activity and, further, that, in their 'natural' state, they form, with other mechanisms, an 'open system' where the result of their interactions produce perceptible effects very different from those isolated in experiment. The nature of scientific practice thus presupposes a complex, structured reality that exists independently, not just of this practice, but of human thought and life generally. The difficulty with this is that the starting point of this argument is precisely an *interpretation* of what scientists do: it is open to others to contest this account of scientific practice and to offer their own rival interpretations. It would seem better to strip away the transcendental superstructure that obscures what is interesting and original in Bhaskar's work and offer it simply as a philosophical presentation of the world as revealed to us by the sciences. Like his account of scientific practice this is a fallible interpretation that can be (and is) contested by critics and the authors of rival metaphysical doctrines. The difference is that, without the distraction offered by Bhaskar's account of scientific practice (which arguably presupposes the distinction that he is seeking to establish), we can directly consider the strengths and weaknesses of his ontology compared to those offered by others. If the result of this comparison is not conclusive, surely we gave up imagining that philosophical argument is anything but interminable a long time ago?[8]

One final point concerns whether or not ontology is itself a kind of philosophy that it would be better to eschew. Daniel Bensaïd, the contemporary Marxist philosopher with whom I feel the closest affinity, sometimes says things that imply this. For example he declares that 'Heidegger ontologizes and resacralizes; Marx secularizes and deontologizes.'[9] As a contrast between the two thinkers this statement is indisputable. Heidegger, particularly in his later thought, seeks to respond to the agonies of capitalist modernity through a poetics of Being; Marx instead seeks to confront these agonies directly through an empirically based critical theory that grounds a political project of human emancipation. But it doesn't follow that this theory makes no ontological commitments. If Quine is right, all theories do. Moreover, as we have seen, the different critical theories discussed in part I raise ontological questions. The issue between Marx and Heidegger concerns partly where we draw the boundary line between ontology and scientific inquiry: Heidegger offers an account of the world based on metaphysically distilled ideological ruminations, whereas Marx's theory of the capitalist mode of production is a scientific research programme subject to the same protocols as any such programme.[10] We should try to find as great a scope as possible for revisable empirical inquiry rather than metaphysically freeze our detailed conception of what exists. Badiou's generalization of the Marxist theory of the state to make the state a feature of every situation is an example of such unwelcome ontologization (§3.2 above). But this raises the question of how the content of ontology is derived. For Heidegger, as for much of the Western philosophical tradition, our conception of what exists is arrived at by a priori reflection distinct from and – in his case – in opposition to the sciences. The conception of ontology sketched out above is, by contrast, permeable by the sciences. Critical realism, like any metaphysics, is an a priori theory, but its content is arrived at by reflection on the results of scientific inquiry.

5.2   Dimensions of realism

Imagine the world as nested clusters of interacting generative mechanisms and the events that these interactions produce, all existing (largely) independently of human thought and activity, which must themselves be included among or understood as arising from these mechanisms. This is how the world is, according to critical realism. The best way to bring out the entailments – and the attractions – of this ontology is to unpack the opening sentence of this section piece by piece. In doing so, I try to show how critical realism can throw light on, and help to overcome, the philosophical difficulties faced by the theorists surveyed in part I.

(i)   Generative mechanisms

'A generative mechanism is nothing other than the way of acting of a thing', writes Bhaskar.[11] The world must be conceived as composed of things – 'powerful particulars', as Rom Harré and Edward Madden call them – that have causal powers, that is, the capacity to initiate sequences of events.[12] What a scientific law does is to identify the mechanism responsible for certain sets of events. The philosophical bite in this analysis is that it implies that the conventional empiricist conception of causality (attributed, rightly or not, to Hume) as a constant conjunction of events of certain kinds is mistaken. A distinction of principle must be drawn between events that may be accessible to observation and the mechanisms responsible for those events. Scientific laws are therefore *not* about the relations between or patterns among events. Rather, they ascribe powers to particulars to produce sequences of events in the appropriate initial conditions.

(ii)   Pluralism

But there is a plurality of different generative mechanisms. They interact with each other, and in so acting affect each other's operations. The mutual interference of the mechanisms means that there is no a priori answer to the question of whether any given mechanism will actually operate, either at all or purely. This is for two reasons: first, the initial conditions on which the exercise of a power may not be met, and, second, the interference of other mechanisms may impede, distort, or altogether prevent the mechanism in question from producing the effects that it would produce if no such interference took place (and the initial conditions were therefore met). Consequently, Bhaskar argues, scientific laws are best understood as tendencies. Law-like statements,

> when their initial conditions are satisfied, make a claim about the activity of a tendency, i.e. about the operation of the generative mechanism that would, if undisturbed, result in the tendency's manifestation, but not about the conditions in which the tendency is exercised, and hence not about whether it will be realized or prevented.[13]

It is against this background that the pertinence of the distinction between open and closed systems should become clear. The world is an open system, in which numerous mechanisms interact, and 'causal laws [are therefore] *out of phase* with patterns of events and experiences.'[14] The occurrence of a closed system – in which one mechanism is allowed to operate as far as possible in isolation, producing its effects unhindered by other mechanisms – typically requires the creation of an artificial situation. This is what happens when physical scientists conduct experiments: by ensuring that (what they believe to be) the initial conditions of some mechanism are met, they can test a theory stating that this mechanism will produce a certain sequence of events. As Andrew Collier puts it, '[e]xperiments are windows on to the world of underlying mechanisms that usually operate unactualized.'[15] Humean constant conjunctions of events are thus rare in nature, since it requires human intervention to isolate the mechanisms productive of them. This analysis highlights what Bhaskar believes to be one of the main differences between the social and the physical sciences: since social mechanisms are dependent on the activities of human agents, it is much harder to create closed systems in the social than in the physical world.[16]

Table 5.1   Bhaskar's three domains

	Domain of Real	Domain of Actual	Domain of Empirical
Mechanisms	X		
Events	X	X	
Experiences	X	X	X

Source: R. Bhaskar, A Realist Theory of Science, Table 0.1/1.1, pp. 13, 56.

(iii)   The real and the actual

Collier characterizes Bhaskar's version of realism as 'depth realism', which 'asserts that various kinds of entity – molecules, trees, people, societies – have just those properties that they do, and not others, because of their respective inner structures. Hence these powers can often be ascribed, on the basis of knowledge of structures, whether or not the powers have been exercised.'[17] This idea that reality has depth manifests itself in various ways in Bhaskar's philosophy. In the first place, he distinguishes between three domains of reality – the real, the actual, and the empirical (see table 5.1). Generative mechanisms belong solely to the real; they are distinct from the events that their interactions produce, which belong also to the actual, and also from the experiences through which humans register the occurrence of some of the events (the empirical). Bhaskar argues that the tendency to collapse these distinct levels together is fruitful of philosophical error. Thus he attaches the label 'actualism' to 'the idea that laws and relations are relations between events or states of affairs (which are thought to constitute the objects of actual or possible experiences)', and that thereby denies the existence of generative mechanisms that underlie and produce these events.[18]

The thought that reality has depth and indeed is, as we shall see shortly, stratified sharply differentiates critical realism from either of the two ontologies that we have encountered in previous chapters. For Badiou, both situations and events are a-relational, the first the result of an operation of counting-as-one, the second emerging from the void of the situation, and both of these originating activities (the count and the occurrence of the event) are themselves unknowable and can only be established inferentially.

For Deleuze and his follower Negri, the plane of immanence distributes singularities differentiated according to their intensity
across a neutral surface. But neither of these ontologies can account
for transcendence. As we have seen (§3.2 above), Badiou's treatment of Being as closure makes the event a mystery. As for Deleuze,
he faces, according to Peter Hallward, the following dilemma:

> to the degree that he insists on the radical univocity of being as
> continuous with 'what happens', he is forced to abandon any viable
> concept of the event as rupture. Or, insofar as he wants to retain
> a concept of the event as rupture, he is forced to introduce a notion
> of discontinuity into the fabric of being itself (virtual as distinct
> from actual, relations as distinct from terms, intensity as opposed
> to extension).[19]

The idea of the univocity of Being is closely related to that of the
'equality of Being' that we have seen Deleuze develop in his interpretation of Spinoza (see §4.3 above). The thought is that the
essence of Being is to express itself in the infinite diversity of beings
without the variations among beings representing any alteration
in the character of Being itself or constituting a hierarchy of
beings:

> the essential of univocity isn't that Being is said in one and the same
> sense. It is that it is said in one and the same sense, of all its indi-
> viduating differences or intrinsic modalities. Being is the same for
> all these modalities but these modalities are not the same. It is
> 'equal' for all, but they are not equal. It is said in one sense alone
> of all, but they don't have the same sense. It is of the essence of
> univocal being to relate to these individuating differences, but these
> differences do not have the same essence, and don't alter the essence
> of being – just as white relates to different intensities, but remains
> essentially the same being.[20]

This then leads to the first horn of the dilemma that Hallward
poses: if everything is an expression of Being, doesn't this mean
that all the differences of beings collapse into a single all-inclusive
identity, that multiplicity proves to be an illusion masking not the
univocity of Being, but the unity of the One? Deleuze takes from
Spinoza the idea that an infinity of formally (i.e., qualitatively) different attributes (for example, thought and extension) express a
numerically singular substance, God, while these attributes are in

turn expressed in modes – the plurality of individual beings, which are differentiated only quantitatively by the degree of intensity or power they express. Individual existence is thus a matter of purely quantitative difference. According to Deleuze's version of Spinoza, '[t]he power of God expresses or explicates itself modally, but only by and in this quantitative differentiation.'[21] But then, as Badiou puts it,

> given that the multiple (of beings, of significations) is arrayed in the universe by way of a numerical difference that is purely formal as regards the form of being to which it refers (thought, extension, time, etc.) and purely modal as regards its individuation, it follows that, ultimately, this multiple can only be of the order of simulacra. And if one classes – as one should – every difference without a real status, every multiplicity whose ontological status is that of the One, as a simulacrum, then the world of beings is the theatre of the simulacra of Being . . . It is as though the paradoxical or super-eminent One immanently engenders a procession of beings whose univocal status it distributes, while they refer to its power and have only a semblance of being.[22]

The Many – the multiplicities that are so eloquently celebrated by Deleuze – thus collapse into the One. This takes us then to the second horn of Hallward's dilemma, Deleuze's introduction of 'discontinuity into the fabric of being'. The key concept here is that of the virtual. Deleuze's discussion of the virtual in some respects parallels the distinction that Bhaskar draws between the real and the actual. In the first place, the virtual is opposed to the actual. Deleuze writes: 'The structure is the reality of the virtual. We must at the same time avoid giving the elements and relations that form a structure an actuality that they don't have and taking away from them the reality that they do have.' The virtual thus pertains to the real: it has a determinate structure in the way that, for example, a mathematical problem, of necessity, must be posed before it can be solved. But the virtual is also opposed to the possible: 'For the possible is opposed to the real; the process of the possible is thus a "realization". The virtual, on the contrary, is not opposed to the real; it possesses a full reality of its own. Its process is actualization.' More specifically, the barrier between the possible and the real can only be crossed by arbitrarily postulating 'a brute eruption, pure act, leap'. The same problem doesn't arise with the virtual because it belongs to the real. Moreover, 'to the extent that the possible seeks "realization", it is itself conceived as the image of the real, and the real, as the resemblance of the possible.' But 'the actualization of the virtual proceeds by difference, divergence, or differentiation. Actualization doesn't break any less with resemblance as a process than with identity as a principle . . . Actualization, differentiation, in this sense, is always a veritable creation.'[23]

Deleuze's concept of the virtual is a suggestive one, even though it suffers from serious difficulties, once again effectively diagnosed by Badiou, that arise from the idea that '[e]very object is double, without these two halves resembling each other, the one being virtual image, the other being actual image. They are unequal odd halves.'[24] More generally, there is a fundamental respect in which Deleuze's ontology is on the right track in a way in which Badiou's is not. From Deleuze's perspective, events partake of the process through which Being actualizes itself, rather than constituting a subtraction from Being.[25] As I have already suggested, counterposing Being and the event in the way that Badiou does makes the latter a mystery. His reply, implicit in the dilemma that Hallward poses to Deleuze, is essentially that to treat transcendence as an outflowing of Being is to relativize it out of existence: once events are made part of the world they no longer possess the quality of discontinuity, of the exceptional, that mark them out as events. But, at one level, this just seems to be a logical mistake. It is surely impossible to individuate anything as exceptional – as partaking in this respect of what Badiou attributes to events – except relative to whatever is counted as normal. If an event (in Badiou's sense) were really (in Daniel Bensaïd's words) a pure diamond unrelated to any context, it would be unintelligible. Thus Badiou gives as an example of fidelity 'the Cubist precipitation of the tandem Braque–Picasso in 1912–13 (effect of a retroactive intervention on the Cézanne-event)'.[26] Are we supposed to understand what makes Cézanne exceptional without exploring his relationship with the French Classical tradition and with Impressionism? Of course, one can quite understand Badiou's distaste from the banal kind of historiography that tediously reduces every irruption of the new to influences or context or whatever. But how are we to recognize it as new except against the background of the routine?

At this fundamental level, then, the dilemma that Hallward poses to Deleuze does not hold. Continuities and discontinuities must be mapped out relative to one another against the same horizon of Being. Deleuze's critical weakness lies rather in the metaphysical idea of the univocity of Being and in particular the implication that he takes from Spinoza that the differences between individual beings are purely quantitative ones, variations in intensity. *That* certainly does necessarily imply a de-differentiation of beings, their dissolution into the unity of the One. But this is in no sense required by the refusal to treat the exceptional as a subtraction from Being. Deleuze's notion of the virtual as a kind of striving towards actualization is an attempt, within an ontological framework based on this refusal, to show how innovations emerge, not as a realization of abstract possibilities, but as a process of differentiation within the real. Badiou makes the interesting observation that 'it is impossible to avoid here the metaphor of depth . . . there is a "deep" determination that concerns the expansion and differentiation of the virtualities themselves, and which thus forms, despite everything, a sort of interior of the One (or of the Whole).'[27] This is not a thought onto which Deleuze can consistently hold since he insists that Being is a surface phenomenon, associating the idea of depth with Plato's reduction of difference to the simulacra of the One. It is this that forces him into the unsustainable idea that the virtual is part of every object, which must be conceived as a disymmetric unity of the virtual and the actual. Apart from anything else, it is hard for him then to avoid the idea, which he criticizes when discussing the possible, of an isomorphism or resemblance between the virtual and the actual.

The alternative that critical realism offers is to take seriously the depth metaphor, as, for example, the triadic distinction between the real, the actual, and the empirical requires us to do. Bhaskar's real bears a certain analogy to the Deleuzian virtual. The structure of the real is given by the set of interacting generative mechanisms; there is an inherent, ontological difference between the real thus understood and the actual, which Bhaskar conceives as the events (normal and exceptional) produced by the interactions among powerful particulars. There is no reason why these two domains of reality should resemble one another. For one thing, mechanisms and events are different kinds of being: in what way, for example, does a falling leaf resemble gravitation? For another, events are the products of the *interactions* among mechanisms: the mutual interferences of mechanisms mean that the direct mapping of a sequence of events onto a single mechanism that solely gave rise to them will be a relatively unusual occurrence. Nevertheless, even when a mechanism is blocked from operating, it still pertains to the real and has actual effects. As Bhaskar puts it,

> when a tendency is exercised unfulfilled two things are not in doubt: (a) that something actually happens, towards explaining which the exercise of the tendency goes some way; and (b) that something is really going on, i.e. there is a real generative mechanism at work, which accounts for the factor the tendency represents in the generation of the event.[28]

This real, where unfulfilled tendencies have actual effects, though not the ones they would have if fulfilled (that is, if the mechanism in question operated unimpeded), has something of Deleuze's virtual about it. It is, moreover, clearly different from the possible, if the latter is restricted to the logically possible. The laws of nature – that is, according to Bhaskar, the tendencies of the various generative mechanisms making up the real – delimit a narrower domain than that of whatever is permitted by the laws of logic. Nevertheless, the real does seem equivalent to the narrower conception of the possible used in possible world semantics and causal theories of reference, where a possible world is one generally consistent with the laws of nature.[29] The actual world is then the outcome of a particular set of interactions between generative mechanisms. Other interactions consistent with the laws of nature would have produced other worlds. This kind of integration of the real and the possible doesn't seem vulnerable to Deleuze's objections, noted above. As we have seen, the real and the actual don't resemble one another. Moreover, the movement from the possible (*qua* consistent with the laws of nature) to the actual isn't an arbitrary leap, but the explicable outcome of the actions and interactions of a plurality of generative mechanisms.

From the standpoint of the kind of subtractive ontology developed by Badiou, critical realism no doubt seems just like a different way of banning transcendence from Deleuze's. For events, normal and exceptional, unfold within the limits set by the possible in the sense just discussed of consistency with the laws of nature. But *any* ontology is going to constrain our sense of what is possible and of the exceptional. Badiou's ontology of unrelated situations, the products of inaccessible though inferable operations of unification, drives us towards conceiving events as leaps out of the void. Thinking of the really possible as delimited by the laws of nature may seem to narrow down the scope of the possible. But we are constantly taken by surprise by what turns out to be possible. This may be because we discover new mechanisms that may completely change our understanding of what is possible. Consider, for example, what the world must be like for the supporters of super-string theory to be right in affirming that the ultimate constituents of matter are tiny strings vibrating in at least ten dimensions – with the extra six dimensions, too small to be accessible to observation even via a microscope, curled up in the usual four.[30] Sometimes events we thought impossible happen – thus the fall of the Soviet Union confounded the expectations of what Thomas Kuhn would call the 'normal science' prevailing among both Western political scientists and Eastern bloc exponents of Marxism-Leninism. The real seems sufficiently capacious to offer plenty of bizarre and surprising things. One of the main charms of Deleuze's philosophy is its openness to the sheer weirdness and unpredictability of the real, of the world not as a well-ordered cosmos, but as what he calls, after Joyce, a 'chaosmos'.[31]

But, from the perspective of critical realism, one of the biggest problems with Deleuze's ontology is he conceives the actualization of the virtual as a kind of constant outpouring of Being. Differences continually spread out across the plane of immanence, forming assemblages and stratifications and then outflanking and subverting them. What is completely lost here is the specificity of the different mechanisms productive of the various sequences of events that make up the actual. That actualization and differentiation occur is more important for Deleuze than the particular mechanisms and outcomes at work. He offers plenty of examples, taken from history, literature, cinema, the sciences, to show how multiplicities are formed and interlace. But their status is precisely illustrative – they demonstrate the expressive power of a Being immanent in beings. It is symptomatic, then, that Deleuze and Guattari reserve to philosophy the dignity of inventing concepts, through which events can be thought, while science concerns itself with the humbler task of identifying the functional relationships prevailing among states of things when the virtual has actualized itself.[32] It seems more plausible to reverse this surprisingly aristocratic hierarchy, and suggest that philosophers tend in fact to analyse the presuppositions of the concepts invented in the sciences. Deleuze can assume that the virtual constantly actualizes itself in the rich variety of beings, dismissing the banausic task of isolating which mechanisms produce what events to scientific under-labourers, because his affirmative conception of Being guarantees that creation, innovation, is, paradoxically, a routine feature of actualization. In doing so, he makes himself vulnerable to a version of Badiou's fundamental charge: if everything is creation, then nothing is. Hardt's and Negri's theory of Empire and multitude is a socio-political exemplification of this conception of virtuality, in which contemporary capitalism has always-already realized the tendency towards 'absolute democracy' inherent in network structures (see §4.3 above).

(iv)   Stratification and emergence

The distinctiveness of the ontology developed by Bhaskar becomes clearer when we consider a further feature of critical realism. The latter is depth realism not simply in the sense that it asserts the existence of real mechanisms responsible for events, a small sample of which are registered in human experience. The real itself has depth: it is, as Bhaskar puts it, 'a multi-dimensional structure'.[33] This structure is constituted by the relations among generative mechanisms. In Collier's formulation, 'these mechanisms are, so to speak, *layers* of nature, and are *ordered*, not jumbled up together.' Thus, 'it is *mechanisms*, not things or events, that are stratified.' The stratification of nature is revealed by the movement of explanation. Uncovering one mechanism is not the terminus of scientific inquiry: explaining this mechanism leads us to postulate other mechanisms, and so on. As a result, '[w]e are left with a permanent ordered multiplicity of sciences, a "tree" with distinct roots and branches, reflecting the real stratification of natural mechanisms, within and between the objects of the various sciences.'[34]

The movement of explanation from less to more fundamental mechanism is not, however, equivalent to the reduction of one layer of nature to another to another – say, of the mental to the biological, the biological to the chemical, and the chemical to the physical. To quote Collier again,

> Bhaskar refers to the relationship between a higher-level mechanism and the underlying one in terms of *rootedness* and *emergence*. The higher-level one is rooted in, and emergent from, the more basic one. The term 'emergence' has a philosophical history that indicates that Bhaskar does not regard rootedness as reducibility. Emergence theories are those that, while recognizing that the more complex aspects of reality (e.g. life, mind) presuppose the less complex (e.g. matter), also insist that they have features that are irreducible, e.g. cannot be thought in concepts appropriate to the less complex levels – and that not because of any subjective constraints on our thought, but because of the inherent nature of the emergent strata.[35]

Emergence is one way of thinking of the mental as part of nature – supervening on the biological, chemical, and physical – but at the same time insisting that the mental has specific properties irreducible to these other levels. It has the further advantage, much exploited by critical realists, of providing a means of thinking the autonomy of the social – in other words of refusing to reduce the latter to the mental or to treat social structures as merely the unintended consequences of individual actions. Instead, these structures can be seen as emergent properties of social interactions among human beings. I return to this topic in the next chapter. The important point at present is that critical realism conceives nature as complex and stratified, with each level being autonomous in the literal sense of being constituted by a distinct set of mechanisms irreducible to those at more basic levels.

All of this is fundamentally at odds with the two rival ontologies with which I have been comparing critical realism. For Badiou, the order of Being is that of atomic situations each governed by the same findings in set theory, so that the issue of any relationship among them, let alone that of stratification of nature according to the different mechanisms at work in them, simply does not arise. Deleuze, by contrast, admits not simply the possibility of stratification, but its reality, but sees this as highly problematic. One of his most fundamental ontological theses is the equality of Being: 'The univocity of being thus signifies also the equality of being. Univocal Being is at once nomadic distribution and anarchy enthroned [*couronnée*].'[36] The implication is not simply that reality has no necessary structure – the distribution of intensities on the plane of immanence is aleatory, wandering, shifting – but that to try to conceive whatever structure it does have through the metaphor of stratification fails to grasp its fundamental character. Thus in *Mille plateaux* Deleuze and Guattari confront the very metaphor of the tree used by Collier to evoke 'the real stratification of natural mechanisms' with that of the rhizome – in other words, instead of an ordered, hierarchical, horizontal structure, a multiplicity ramifying laterally in all directions, developing connections with other multiplicities in a decentred, anarchic fashion. It is only relative to these multiplicities that geological, organic, and social strata exist, and the latter are always vulnerable to 'the immanence of absolute deterritorialization' as the lateral movements of desire subvert ordered structures.[37]

Now Collier's formulation of 'a permanent ordered multiplicity of sciences, a "tree" with distinct roots and branches' does present an unnecessarily static picture of the sciences. Not simply does it miss out the fact that the historical movement has not necessarily been from less to more fundamental mechanisms – the seventeenth-century 'scientific revolution' took shape around the initial formation of modern physics, which surely concerns itself with some of the most basic mechanisms of all, and only much later extended to the constitution of sciences such as chemistry and biology – but it ignores the way in which conceptual reorganizations take place that change the boundaries and reorder the relations between different sciences – the contemporary power of the life sciences is a case in point. As Bourdieu notes, '[s]cientific revolutions have the effect of transforming the hierarchy of importance – things considered to be without importance can find themselves reactivated by a new way of doing science, and inversely entire sectors of science can cease to be contemporary and become outdated.'[38] In many ways the rhizome may be a better metaphor for the theoretical and institutional configuration of the sciences than Collier's tree. But this only tells us about what Bhaskar calls the 'transitive' dimension of the sciences – their conceptual structures and historical formation; it does not follow at all that it is wrong to think of 'the intransitive objects of knowledge . . . the real things and structures, mechanisms and processes, events and possibilities of the world' as being stratified in the way in which critical realism suggests that it is.[39]

At worst Deleuze's insistence on 'the equality of Being' is a kind of politicization of ontology – the assertion that conceiving Being as anything but 'anarchy enthroned' somehow amounts to supporting oppression and domination in the social world, which is just ridiculous. At best it justifies a rejection of the neo-Platonic conception of being as an emanation from God such that reality becomes progressively degraded the further the distance between it and God.[40] But it is hard to see how this is relevant to critical realism, which, like other species of realism, is quite distinct from physicalism, according to which only physical entities exist and ultimately physical laws explain everything.[41] Realism is committed to the existence of most of the entities postulated by the sciences, wherever these sciences may be placed in the 'tree' of nature. What Collier calls the 'higher-level' mechanisms – for example, those of the human and the biological – cannot be said in any meaningful sense to be 'less real' than those at the levels of the chemical and the physical. The whole point of the concept of emergence is to give these 'higher-level' mechanisms an autonomous explanatory role, which is, again, quite incompatible with an emanationist conception of Being.[42] Conceiving reality as stratified can help us to avoid the difficulties with the Deleuzian concept of the virtual discussed above. Thus we can investigate the manner in which mechanisms at a more basic level may impose constraints on the operation of those at the 'higher' levels.

(v)   *Realism and truth*

There has now surfaced, in the shape of Bhaskar's contrast between the transitive and intransitive objects of the sciences, the distinction definitive of realism between how the world is and how our theories and other beliefs assert it to be. It is time to consider this opposition more explicitly, although doing so requires us to part company with Bhaskar himself, since we will now address issues on which he is either mistaken or silent. At the heart of this discussion is the question of truth that loomed large in the earlier chapters of part I, especially §§1.1 and 2.1. There we considered, in particular, the pragmatist or contextualist conception of truth that equates it with warranted assertability: on this account, a sentence is true when it is justified. Richard Rorty, the most influential contemporary pragmatist, has himself pointed to the strategic weakness of this approach: 'such definitions always fall victim, sooner or later, to the argument that a given belief might meet any specifiable conditions, but still not be true.'[43] It is important to see that it is not only warranted assertability theories of truth that rely on what I called in §1.1 a weak conception of justification as consistency with prevailing beliefs that are vulnerable to this objection. Jürgen Habermas relies on a stronger notion of justifiability, equating truth with ideal assertability in order to defend against Rorty the idea of 'truth in a context-independent – that is, unconditional – sense':

> What we hold true has to be defendable on the basis of good reasons, not merely in a different context but in all possible contexts, at any time and against anybody. This provides the inspiration of the discourse theory of truth: a proposition is true if it withstands all attempts to refute it under the demanding conditions of rational discourse.[44]

The trouble is that it seems still perfectly coherent to ask of a sentence that has met the most demanding tests whether it is true. Habermas's crucial move is, following Peirce, to relax the spatio-temporal restraints on justification: a true sentence is one that is accepted by the ideal interpretation community that would be constituted if research were extended indefinitely into the future. But, once again, there seems nothing bizarre about saying that even a sentence accepted by this community could still turn out to be false.[45] We need a more robust conception of truth. The obvious candidate for such a role is the classical, or correspondence, theory of truth, where a sentence is true in virtue of the state of the world. As Devitt puts it, 'we can state the doctrine that a correspondence notion of truth applies to sentences of a certain type . . . as follows:

> Sentences of type x are true or false in virtue of (1) their objective structure; (2) the objective or referential relations between their parts and reality; and (3) the objective nature of that reality.[46]

Realism and the correspondence theory of truth are logically independent of one another, but there is clearly a consonance between them: realism claims that the world exists independently of the mental, while the correspondence theory makes the truth or falsehood of sentences depend on whether the world is the way they assert it to be. Taking these ideas seriously distances us from the ontologies of both Badiou and Deleuze. In conceiving the object as a unity of two *images*, actual and virtual, Deleuze rejects realism. There is indeed no difference of principle for him between the mental and the physical: all the different stratifications of reality are liable to be dissolved in the transversal movements of multiplicities. Deleuze's anti-realism no doubt reflects the influence on him of Hume and Bergson; it helps to explain why some of the best expositions of his metaphysics are to be found in his two books on cinema. Badiou criticizes Deleuze for treating the virtual as an image, but dismisses the correspondence theory as 'a dictionary convenience. To say that there is a truth when mind is in accord with things doesn't free anyone of the obligation of seeking the effective law of the accord in question.'[47]

Badiou's dismissal is a version of the standard criticism of the correspondence theory of truth, which is that it is at once trivial and absurd. The thesis that the theory is trivial typically appeals to what is often called the disquotational use of the concept of truth. Alfred Tarski's semantic definition of truth, which is, among other things, an attempt rigorously to state the correspondence theory, implies, for any sentence s, the following 'T-sentence': '"s" is true if and only if s'.[48] This takes advantage of the fact that we can both use and mention any linguistic expression: in the T-sentence 's' is first mentioned – '"s"' is the name of 's' – and then it is used. It follows from the T-sentence that if we drop the quotation marks around the first occurrence of 's' and the clause 'is true', we get 's', which is thus synonymous with – i.e., has the same truth-conditions as – '"s" is true'. This disquotational property of the semantic definition has its uses in logic, but it doesn't seem to give much content to the concept of truth. In at least some moods Rorty has appealed to what he calls 'minimalism', suggesting that 'Tarski's breezy disquotationalism may exhaust the topic of truth.'[49] The claim that the correspondence theory is simultaneously absurd focuses on the idea of sentences corresponding to the world. As Bhaskar puts it, 'propositions cannot be compared to states of affairs; their relationship cannot be described as one of correspondence . . . There is no way in which we can look at the world and then at a sentence and ask whether they fit. There is just the expression (of the world) in speech (or thought).'[50]

Bhaskar's argument here relies on the premiss that we have no access to the world unmediated by the language we use. Consequently we cannot pick out bits of the world except via the very sentences that, according to the correspondence theory, are true or false because of how the world is: how, then, can we establish whether or not they are true? Donald Davidson offers a brilliant and far-reaching critique of what is often seen as an implication of Bhaskar's premiss, namely that human beings are prisoners of culturally specific conceptual schemes. Davidson argues that this idea depends on the possibility of distinguishing between the formal framework that defines a conceptual scheme and the substantive beliefs that it permits us to hold. But this 'dualism of scheme and content' turns out to be incoherent: it is impossible to interpret another's speech unless we ascribe to her beliefs most of which are (by our lights) true, but, to determine the content of the speaker's (largely true) beliefs, we must appeal to a world common to both speaker and interpreter.[51] Thus, according to Davidson, '[t]he ultimate source of both objectivity and communication is the triangle that, by relating speaker, interpreter, and the world, determines the contents of thought and speech.'[52] As Rorty puts it, 'Davidson's point about there being no language without triangulation means that we cannot have any language, or any beliefs, without being in touch with both a human community *and* a non-human reality. There is no possibility of agreement without truth, nor of truth without agreement.'[53]

Davidson therefore uses Tarski's definition of truth in a quite different way from how its author intended, as the basis of his theory of radical interpretation, which seeks to explain how we are able to ascribe beliefs to others and meaning to their utterances. He is, however, ambivalent about whether or not this strategy commits him to the correspondence theory of truth. At times, he is highly dismissive, declaring, for example, that 'there is nothing interesting or instructive to which true sentences might correspond.'[54] But in a late text Davidson expresses a more nuanced attitude. He repeats his criticism of the correspondence theory: 'The trouble lies in the claim that the formula has explanatory power. The notion of correspondence would be a help if we were able to say, in an *instructive* way, which fact or slice of reality it is that makes a particular sentence true. No one has succeeded in doing this.' But he goes on to say: 'Correspondence, while it is empty as a definition, does capture the thought that truth depends on how the world is, and this should be enough to discredit most epistemic and pragmatic theories.'[55] This concession is crucial, and it identifies one respect in which, *pace* Davidson, the correspondence theory *is* explanatory. It explains why truth and justification are different: it is the world that makes sentences true, whereas justification reflects the necessarily fallible and contingent standards according to which, at any given time, a human community decides which sentences are true and which are false.

From this perspective, the objection that there is something incoherent or absurd about the correspondence theory because it implies that there are discrete 'slices of reality' (as Davidson puts it) that make sentences true seems deeply mistaken. The thought that the correspondence theory has this implication seems to involve a category-mistake. Sentences in some sense belong to the world, since they are uttered by human beings who are part of nature (see the discussion of naturalism below). But this in no way requires that sentences resemble or are isomorphic to any other part of nature, including whatever aspects of the world make them true: one merit of the critical realist claim that nature is ordered into levels each with their own emergent properties is to underline the disymmetries and dislocations in the real. Semantic concepts such as reference and satisfaction through which philosophers of language seek to understand the relationship between linguistic expressions and the world specify highly abstract relations with, once again, no implication that there is an identity of form or structure between word and object. The point of the correspondence theory is not, as P. F. Strawson suggests, to posit a relationship between sentences and 'sentence-like' states of affairs.[56] It is, rather, simply to state that the truth or falsehood of sentences is a matter of how the world is. This, on the one hand, explains why even our best justified beliefs may have to be abandoned: the world may turn out to be different from how they assert it is. But, on the other hand, it offers a definition of what counts as success when we seek knowledge.

Devitt argues that Scientific Realism explains what he calls 'theoretical success': 'Suppose that a theory says that S. Then it is successful if the world is as if S.' The explanation of this success is that 'the world seems that way if it *is* that way.'[57] I think that this does offer a way of showing that the correspondence theory has the explanatory power that Davidson denies to it. But the reason why it does so is because the correspondence theory gives an account of what, when it comes to knowledge, counts as success. (The qualification is important because we seek plenty of other things apart from knowledge, and these provide different standards by which to assess our utterances – for example, their beauty or effectiveness in securing the compliance of others.)[58] A pragmatist might object that justification will do just as well: does it matter whether state-of-the-art aerodynamics is true so long as it allows us to fly safely? But the goal posts may have been shifted here: the activity whose success is being assessed may now be air travel, not knowledge. So long as we are dealing with knowledge, then justification won't do as a standard of success for the familiar reason that we may end up discarding what are currently the best justified theories.

It is the correspondence theory that tells us what counts as success in knowledge. But, as Collier notes, '[i]t gives us a definition of truth, *not* a criterion of truth.'[59] In other words, the correspondence theory doesn't tell us what true theories look like. How could it, given the ontological difference between sentences and the (rest of the) world that makes them true? It is probably this aspect of the correspondence theory (along with the apparently trivial character of Tarski's semantic definition) that motivates the idea that it is empty. What's the point of a theory of truth that doesn't tell us what the true looks like? But the expectation that it should tell us this involves, once again, a misunderstanding of the content of the correspondence theory. Given that truth depends on the world, any 'criterion' of truth is simply a fallible conjecture that we (in the sense of Habermas's ideal interpretation community) will probably end up discarding. The best that we can expect is some reasonably context-independent account of the relative explanatory success of different theories. The most interesting attempt to offer such an account is, in my view, Imre Lakatos's methodology of scientific research programmes, which was developed as a means of rationally reconstructing the history of the physical sciences in which judgements of epistemic progress are based on the criteria of coherence with a set of organizing principles (the 'hard core' of a research programme), greater explanatory power than rival programmes, and a measure of empirical corroboration.[60] But, although it is a weakness of critical realism as developed by Bhaskar that it does not sufficiently address the issues raised by Lakatos's attempt to develop a philosophy of science that is at once historical and realist, these criteria are at best revisable proxies for truth, not infallible signs of its presence. That the epistemic standards through which theories are assessed, as well as the theories themselves, are fallible, and therefore open to revision, is just a consequence of the correspondence theory of truth, and of realism more broadly. If the world is largely independent of the mental, then our thinking about the world will often require correction and reform. But this seems hardly a terribly burdensome proposition for theories that challenge the prevailing ways of thinking about the social world to accept.

(vi) Naturalism

There are two respects in which critical realism as expounded here might be thought of as naturalist. The first is that Davidson's theory of radical interpretation implies that, in order to ascribe beliefs to humans and meaning to their utterances, we must place them in a world where they interact with one another and with other kinds of organism and physical object. Secondly, Bhaskar himself defends naturalism in the sense of 'an essential unity of method between the natural and the social sciences'.[61] This is motivated by the claim that social structures are emergent properties of human interactions that give rise to tendencies similar to those operative in physical mechanisms, even though in the case of the social world these tendencies are manifested through and dependent on the intentional activity of human beings. Both meanings of naturalism distinguished here are quite different from the reduction programme implied by physicalism, according to which the laws of physics ultimately explain everything. Thus Davidson seeks to offer an account of the autonomy of the mental, which he calls anomalous monism. The main thought here is that even if, under some description (say, as the firing of neurones in the brain), a mental event may be subsumed under a physical law, this is not the description that identifies it as a mental event: to do that, we need to be able to ascribe content to the mental states (beliefs and desires) of the person whose event it is, which in turn requires the concept of truth, and the rest of the apparatus of Davidson's theory of radical interpretation, and these cannot be stated in the vocabulary of physical theory.[62] More broadly, the idea of emergence through which critical realism seeks to conceptualize the stratified character of the real represents, among other things, a strategy designed to block any requirement that one level be reducible to another, since each layer of the real is constituted by a set of mechanisms with their own distinctive tendencies.[63] The upshot is a non-reductive conception of the unity of nature.

Naturalism in the second sense involves taking a realist approach to social structures: this is a subject that looms large in the following chapter. To conclude the present discussion, it seems to me that critical realism offers an ontology that avoids both the extravagant profusion of beings celebrated by Deleuze and the unnecessary austerity demanded by Badiou. This does not mean that we should prefer critical realism as a kind of common-sense 'third way' between these two apparently more exotic ontologies. What critical realism offers is an ontology that simultaneously captures the way the world is portrayed in the sciences and is open to how the real in all kinds of ways exceeds our expectations. The latter aspect is particularly important to stress because it is traditional among Marxist philosophers, despite (or maybe because of) the fact that Lenin espouses a version of realism in *Materialism and Empirio-Criticism*, to dismiss realism as 'static' and 'contemplative'.[64] This seems to me absurd, for two reasons in particular.[65] First of all, in its insistence on the duplicity of the real, its multi-layered structure, and the constitutive gap between how things appear (the empirical) and how they really are (the real and the actual), critical realism provides a philosophical motivation for precisely the kind of suspicion of appearances necessary for any social critique. One of the reasons why, for example, I argue that Boltanski and Chiapello do not provide a satisfactory framework for the critique of capitalism is that their anti-realism prevents them from establishing a sufficient distance from the discursive justifications of specific versions of capitalism (see §2.1 above). Marx famously wrote that 'all science would be superfluous if the form of appearance of things directly coincided with their essence.'[66] Social critique would not just be redundant, but impossible, if the empirical and the real coincided.

Secondly, to be effective practically social critique has to develop an understanding of the limits of the possible (in the sense used above, where a possible world is one consistent with the laws of nature). It is characteristic of ideologies that serve to legitimize the status quo that they try, in effect, to equate the real and the actual, thus circumscribing the limits of the possible so that they coincide with the structures of existing society (as portrayed in the prevailing ideology). A good example is provided by the neo-liberal *pensée unique*, which asserts, in defiance of historical experience and quite a wide range of economic theories, that the only feasible policies that can be adopted by a state are those mandated by the Washington Consensus. Hence the significance of the most famous slogan of the *altermondialiste* movement – 'Another World is Possible!' In other words, the actual doesn't exhaust the real.[67] To make this affirmation stand up, it is necessary, of course, to offer a reasonably precise and empirically corroborated account of what the limits of the possible really are.[68] But, in focusing on the underlying structural causes of existing conditions, social critique highlights the scale of the transformation required to remedy these conditions. What, then, is the best way to think about the social from a transformative perspective?

6

Structure and Contradiction

6.1 Realism about structures

It is traditional for discussion of social structures to polarize between two unappetizing positions. The first treats social structures as self-reproducing systems that constitute individual agents: this is the position associated with the normative functionalism of Durkheim, Parsons, and Habermas, with Althusser's reconstruction of Marxism, and even with the 'middle Foucault' of the writings on power-knowledge of the 1970s.[1] The other takes the opposite tack of reducing structures to the unintended consequences of individual actions: articulated in the versions of methodological individualism developed by Carl Menger, Karl Popper, and F. A. von Hayek, this is the constitutive principle in the varieties of rational-choice theory highly influential in Anglophone social science. Given the manifest weaknesses of both alternatives, there have been various attempts to displace the structure/agency opposition. Derrida in effect founded poststructuralism by dissolving the structures of signification in an endless displacement of meanings driven by the impossible but inescapable search for the 'transcendental signified'.[2] Various English-speaking social theorists and philosophers – among them Anthony Giddens, Roy Bhaskar, and myself – sought instead to rethink the opposition by rejecting any attempt to reduce one term to the other and seeking rather to conceptualize the mutual interdependence of structure and agency.[3]

This last position represents the moment of realism in social theory. If realism in general involves treating one class of entity or another as existing independently of the mental, then to be a realist in the social sciences usually means being a realist about social structures. In very different ways, both the pragmatist sociology of Boltanski and Chiapello and the post-Marxism of Ernest Laclau and Chantal Mouffe are anti-realist in the sense that they deny that social structures exist independently of the conceptions of them that are constructed in various discourses. In Boltanski's and Chapiello's case this anti-realism is implicit in the idea that business school manuals provide us with access to the nature of contemporary 'network' capitalism (§2.1). Laclau and Mouffe, heavily influenced by Derrida, are much more explicit in drawing out their philosophical agenda. Thus they make it clear that '[o]ur analysis rejects the distinction between discursive and non-discursive practice' and explain:

> The main consequence of a break with the discursive/extra-discursive dichotomy is the abandonment of the thought/reality opposition, and hence a major enlargement of the field of those categories which can account for social relations. Synonymy, metonymy, metaphor are not forms of thought for a primary constitutive literality of social relations; instead, they are part of the primary terrain in which the social itself is constituted.[4]

This is an admirably clear statement of what realism in social theory rejects. The social and the discursive are not co-extensive: rather, the social exists independently of the discursive, and more broadly of the mental.[5] Now methodological individualists don't necessarily deny this: Popper, for example, is insistent about the autonomy of the social.[6] Nevertheless, in conceiving social structures as the unintended consequences of individual actions, they tend to treat structures as of secondary importance from an explanatory point of view. Sometimes at least they explicitly commit themselves to a reduction programme of the kind demanded by G. A. Cohen when he says that 'analytical Marxists ... reject the point of view in which social formations and classes are depicted as obeying laws of behaviour that are not a function of the behaviours of their constituent parts', i.e., individual human agents.[7] Once again, it is this general reduction programme that a realist about social structures must reject (although, of course, this rejection is perfectly consistent with acknowledging that in specific cases macro-patterns are reducible to micro-behaviour).

The main thing that critical realism brings to this discussion is the idea of emergence (see §5.2 above). The thought is that social structures must be conceived as emergent properties of social interactions, arising from but irreducible to the actions and mental states of individual human beings. The most important philosophical contribution to this topic has been made by the Catholic sociologist Margaret Archer, who has pursued the implications for social theory of the metaphor of stratification that, as we saw in the previous chapter, plays a crucial role in critical realist ontology. Thus she insists on

> the *stratified nature of social reality* where different strata possess different emergent properties and powers. However, the key points in this connection are that emergent strata constitute (a) the crucial entities in need of linking by explaining how their causal powers originate and operate, but (b) that such strata do not neatly map onto empirical units of any particular magnitude.[8]

Archer's point (b) here is another version of Bhaskar's distinction between the real, the actual, and the empirical (§5.2 above). But she goes beyond Bhaskar in arguing, in effect, that structure and agency are ontologically distinct. She develops a sustained critique of Giddens's theory of structuration, which portrays structure and agency as inseparable and mutually constitutive. The danger with the position is that it is constantly liable to lapse into what Archer regards as the central philosophical error in social theory, namely 'Conflationism' – the tendency to collapse agency into structure ('Downwards Conflation', e.g., Comte and Durkheim) or structure into agency ('Upwards Conflation', e.g., Mill and Weber). For Archer, by contrast, structure and agency 'are neither co-extensive nor co-variant through time, because each possesses autonomous emergent properties which are thus capable of independent variation and therefore of being out of phase with one another in time.' This implies what she calls 'analytical dualism', identified with two main claims: first, 'an ontological view of the world as stratified, such that the emergent properties of structures and agents are irreducible to one another, meaning that they are analytically separable', and, second, the idea that 'structure and agency are also temporally distinguishable (in other words, it is justifiable and feasible to talk of pre-existence and posterity when dealing with specific instances of the two).'[9]

It is only when structure and agency are treated as ontologically distinct strata *each* – i.e., agents as well as structures – having their own emergent powers that the interaction between the two thematized by Giddens, Bhaskar, and me can be properly understood. One of Archer's most interesting arguments is that what she calls Giddens's 'central conflationism' – the claim that structure and agency are mutually constitutive – involves treating *neither* term of the relationship seriously. Giddens has a weak concept of structure as rules and resources, which in effect treats them as co-extensive with the 'praxis' they are supposed to explain. But, because of his preoccupation with social interaction, Giddens also develops an ' "over-social view" ' of the self as constituted exclusively in social practices. Archer claims that Giddens goes wrong, 'not in insisting upon mediation [between self and world], but on the *social nature* of mediation. This by fiat blocks other mediations, such as nature itself, biological needs or transcendent divinity.' But, 'contra-Giddens, the organism confronts the natural world through biological mediation', producing 'a self forced between the experiencing of its own organic needs and inner inability to satisfy them'.[10]

Despite the sudden intrusion of God into the argument, this is an important thought. Taking the naturalist dimension of critical realism seriously surely requires, as Archer suggests, the proper integration of the biological dimension of human existence into social theory. Of course, there are monsters lurking here with names such as social Darwinism and socio-biology. But the fact reductive approaches in social theory have eliminated social mechanisms in favour of (often grossly misconceived) biological mechanisms is not a reason for ignoring the various ways in which the reality of the human being as a living organism shapes and structures its social existence. Psychoanalysis interprets human mental activity at the intersection of the biological and the social: whatever we think about Lacan's concept of the Real, one of its merits is to resist any attempt to treat the subject as partaking exclusively of the Symbolic (= social), although, of course, it is of the nature of the Real not to be identifiable with any specific domain of being (see §3.3 above).

More generally, Archer offers a forceful extension and clarification of critical realism in the domain of social theory. Thus, though plainly indebted to Bhaskar, she notes his tendency to slide towards Giddens in treating structures as co-extensive with practice. While structures are dependent on activity, the actions that produced a given structure may be those of a past generation, and the actions of the present generation either reproduce or transform a structure that pre-existed them. Archer approvingly quotes Comte's 'aphorism that the majority of actors are the dead'. Once the differential temporalities of structure and agency are properly taken into account, the close bond between the two that Giddens consistently and Bhaskar in a much more vacillating way seek to secure is loosened up and social theory must attend to the discrepancies and dislocations between the two:

> it is *necessary* to separate structure and agency (a) to identify the emergent structure(s), (b) to differentiate between their causal powers and the intervening influences of people due to their quite different causal powers as human beings, and (c) to explain any outcome at all, which in any open system entails an interplay between the two. In short, separability is indispensable to realism.[11]

Archer elaborates her 'morphogenetic' version of critical realism by distinguishing different strata of emergent powers, pertaining specifically to structure, culture, and agency itself.[12] But the fundamental ontological distinction on which she relies is surely that between the two kinds of mechanisms to be found in human societies, those involving persons (or, as I also call them in a somewhat different usage from Archer's, agents) and structures. It is easy enough to outline the first kind of mechanism. Human action is to explained not by subsuming it under a covering law, but through ascribing beliefs and desires to the agent that provide her with a reason for doing the act in question. Davidson's Principle of Charity, according to which we should, when interpreting the speech and behaviour of another, ascribe to her 'a set of beliefs largely consistent and true by our own standards', is one strategy for constructing intentional explanations of this kind, though there is a strong case for the alternative strategy offered by Richard Grandy's Principle of Humanity, which requires us instead to ascribe to the other the beliefs appropriate to her place in the world and her interests.[13] It is probably worth stressing that relying on intentional explanations implies no commitment to the idea of the subject as the originary source of meaning; any unity that persons are assumed to possess when beliefs and desires are ascribed to them should be seen as itself the result of a multiplicity of external and internal forces that can as easily crack it open as fuse its constituent elements together in a tense and always provisional coherence.

What about the other kind of mechanism – structures? Archer says that social structure is '*quintessentially relational*' and defines 'structural emergent properties' as 'those internal and necessary relationships which entail material resources, whether physical or human, and which generate causal powers proper to the relation itself'.[14] This thought needs a bit of unpacking, but Archer is basically on the right track here. Conceiving social structure as relational has probably become common ground among those theorists committed to using the concept. An important point of reference here is Ferdinand de Saussure's formulation of a purely relational conception of meaning when he argued that 'in language there are only differences *without positive terms* . . . The idea or phonic substance that a sign contains is less important than the other signs that surround it.'[15] This conception of structure as a set of differential relations has been enormously influential. For example, Philippe Corcuff offers as an alternative to the Marxist concept of the social totality 'the approach of a plurality of dominations and capitalizations proposed by Pierre Bourdieu, which, if it highlights relations, even of reciprocal dependence, does not understand them necessarily and exclusively as involving some being dependent on others, even "in the last instance".'[16] It is true that Bourdieu's conceives social structures as a plurality of fields each constituted by the competition for a particular scarce resource (= capital). But if each field consists in a set of differential positions, the relationship among them is one of direct or inverted homology: thus, for example, art develops in nineteenth-century Paris as an autonomous field by creating a status hierarchy systematically opposed to the hierarchy of wealth in the economic field.[17] This is a remarkably 'structuralist' moment to Bourdieu's thought, and it is reinforced by the way in which an agent's habitus serves to adjust her expectations to her position in the field (§2.2 above). This takes us dangerously near the position rejected at the start of this section that treats structure as a self-reproducing system.[18]

William Sewell offers a less determinist theory of structure, though his attempt to rethink Giddens's conception of the duality of structure is also influenced by Bourdieu. Bourdieu's conception of the habitus as the schemes of perception and classification implicit in behaviour is visible behind Sewell's redefinition of structure as actual resources and virtual schemas, where the latter are 'intersubjectively available procedures or schemas capable of being actualized or put into practice in a range of different circumstances. Such schemas should be thought of as operating at widely different levels of depth, from Lévi-Straussian deep structures to relatively superficial rules of etiquette.' Schemas, then, are in effect mental structures. Sewell follows Giddens in insisting that structures include resources as well, as a way of acknowledging the significance of 'questions of power, domination, and social change', and posits an interaction between schemas and resources, in which the former legitimize the use of the latter, which in turn give the former an actuality they would otherwise lack.[19] In effect, this is a form of what Archer would call Conflationism, since structures are implicitly denied any reality independent of human mental activities. From a substantive point of view, this leads to two weaknesses: first, the existence of social patterns that are not legitimized by a prevailing scheme of belief is ruled out; second, the *mode of access* accorded to different categories of persons to the resources available to a given society is not included in the concept of structure. Sewell has more recently sought to develop a theory of events (understood as 'sequences of occurrences that lead to the transformation of structures') that bears some analogies to Badiou's conception of the event. It is striking that, in doing so, he modifies his conception of structure to include, alongside schemas and resources, 'modes of power as a constitutive component of structures'.[20] Something like the idea of a mode of power is indeed an essential dimension of any serious conception of social structure, but it pushes us beyond any attempt to think the latter in terms of cultural schemas.

A better strategy would be, while continuing to conceive structure as essentially relational, to focus on the manner in which an agent's position in the social structure confers on her specific powers (what I call, following Erik Olin Wright, 'structural capacities'). The basic intuition here is well expressed by Giddens when he argues that structures enable as well as constrain: '*Structure is thus not to be conceptualized as a barrier to action, but as essentially involved in its production.*'[21] This important idea should not be permitted to become lost in Giddens's unacceptably weak account of structure itself. One way of bringing out the thought here is to define a social structure as a relation connecting persons, material resources, supra-individual entities (social institutions of some kind), and/or other social structures by virtue of which persons (not necessarily those so connected) gain powers of a specific kind. This is rather a clumsy formulation but it has the following advantages. First of all, it conceives structure as a relation. Secondly, that relation is not necessarily simply an interpersonal one: if we are going to take the assertion that structures are emergent properties of social interactions seriously, then it is important that we do not portray structures as simply mimicking social interactions. Thirdly, social structures are not the same as institutions. There is a strong case for saying that corporate entities such as Microsoft or the Pentagon or the Vatican are supra-individual entities: in other words, we cannot, without loss of meaning, reduce sentences where their names occur to sentences about the individuals who belong to them.[22] The concept of structure, however, problematizes a different issue, namely that of the implicit context in which individual persons and supra-individual entities interact. Finally, structure thus defined connects up with agency, the other kind of social mechanism posited by critical realism, because structures confer powers on persons. The important point to stress here is that conceptualizing the relationship between structure and agency in this way avoids the tendency to subsume individuals under structures, to which Bourdieu, as much as those whom he criticizes such as Althusser, is liable. The reason why this is so is that to say that a person has certain powers by virtue of her position in a structure is to say nothing about how she will exercise these powers. To address this latter question we must, among other things, give proper weight to intentional explanation by seeking to reconstruct her beliefs and desires, and this bars any subsumption of agents under structures.[23]

6.2   The primacy of contradiction

One of the great merits of the critical realist conception of social structure sketched out in the previous section is thus that it avoids the problem often found with strong accounts of structure such as Bourdieu's, namely that they make transcendence – transformative action – either very difficult or impossible. Given that structures function to give persons powers, the specific use that agents make of these structural capacities is not predetermined by the nature of the structures themselves. Alternative courses are open to agents: they may simply perform the routine actions that are necessary to reproduce the existing structures, or they may seek to modify or altogether to transform these structures. Taking the second or third option is not an unbounded leap out of the void. There are three ways in which structures connect up with transformative action. First, the capacities that agents exercise when undertaking such action are themselves structurally determined: for example, should actors in the financial markets seek to replace a government whose policies they find obnoxious, the powers they will use to achieve this objective – for example, withdrawing capital from the country in question to produce a currency crisis – are likely to be the same ones that they routinely use as financial-market actors.[24]

Secondly, structures don't simply enable and constrain: they also influence action through the role played by ideologies providing agents with motivations. The conception of ideology that I invoke here is not one that asserts that all representations are structurally determined; rather, it simply conceives ideologies as sets of widely held beliefs whose acceptance is socially caused, and in that sense connected to structures.[25] Ideological representations may motivate agents to undertake actions that aren't required by their structurally determined interests. Thus, to return to the example used above, the reason why financial-market actors choose to overthrow a government might be less that its policies are causing them direct economic damage than that the rhetoric that it uses undermines the prevailing ideology of neo-liberalism: one might think of at least some of the hostility that the Chávez government in Venezuela has attracted as being so motivated. Here there is still an indirect connection with economic interests, insofar as neo-liberalism mandates the deregulation of financial markets, thereby (let's suppose) working to the advantage of the main actors in these markets. But there are cases where ideologically motivated actions hang a lot more free. To take an example I have discussed elsewhere, the Holocaust diverted resources from the German war effort, and its economic effects were too contradictory (the killing camps offered profits to firms such as I. G. Farben, but destroyed scarce and often skilled labour) to be presented as unambiguously to the advantage of German capital. The driving force in the extermination of European Jewry was the racist ideology shared by the Nazi elite and the SS, which led them to seek to 'solve the Jewish question' amid the disruptions – and opportunities – offered by a global war of unparalleled savagery (although the path they followed was notoriously crooked, as contingencies constantly intervened in the struggle among rival bureaucracies themselves subject to conflicting economic, military, and ideological pressures). The place for structural explanation here would come further back, in (to use Žižek's metaphor: see §3.3 above) the displacement of class antagonisms that made possible the formation of and seizure of power by a movement capable of pursuing a war of racial extermination.[26]

Reference to 'antagonism' highlights a third way in which structures may help to explain transformative action: strains within and between them may destabilize existing social relations and, directly and/or as result of this destabilization, motivate actors to seek change. Archer acknowledges the importance of structural contradictions, citing the famous distinction drawn by David Lockwood between social integration and system integration: the first pertains to the value consensus (or dissensus) that preoccupies normative functionalists such as Parsons and Habermas but that, Lockwood insists, does not alone determine the degree of stability or conflict within a given society, since the social system may itself be well or badly integrated: 'Whereas the problem of social integration focuses attention upon the orderly or conflictual relationships between the *actors*, the problem of system integration focuses on the orderly or conflictual relations between the *parts* of a social system.' He gives the contradiction between the forces and relations of production in historical materialism as an example of '*system* conflict'.[27] Archer suggests that this argument implies the ontological distinction between structure and agency definitive of critical realism in social theory, and goes on to make the further point that 'structures themselves contain non-observable emergent powers whose combination (relations between relations) generate the further emergent properties which Lockwood addressed – in particular those of contradiction and complementarity.'[28]

On this account, structural or systemic contradictions are properties of structures themselves – 'relations between relations'. This certainly fits the example that Lockwood gives of the contradiction between the forces and relations of production. The social relations of production plainly are structures in the sense given in the previous section, since they are, as G. A. Cohen puts it, 'relations of effective power over persons and productive forces'.[29] In my view, the productive forces also involve a structure, inasmuch as they consist not just in labour-power and means of production as elements of production, but in the combination of these elements in a technologically determined form of productive cooperation – what Marx calls the labour-process and Cohen the 'material relations of production'.[30] So here we certainly have a case of a contradiction between structures. But the philosophical starting point for such discussions of contradiction is provided by Hegel, for whom both Being itself and every specific form of being is *constituted* by an internal contradiction that both defines its nature and drives the movement from one determination to another. This would imply that contradictions may exist not just between structures but within them. This Hegelian ancestry is, of course, highly problematic. Hegel's doctrine of determinate negation asserts that the contradiction inherent in every concept, when developed, introduces new content that articulates an increasingly differentiated though internally unified structure of reality, and that this process finds its justification in its goal, the self-realization of Absolute Spirit. Each step in this dialectic thus has three moments – immediate and therefore unconscious identity; the disruption and differentiation of this identity by the emergence of negation; and the restoration of identity enriched and rendered self-conscious thanks to the negation of the original negation in the reconciliation of the opposites that the latter brought forth. The great Marxist debate on the dialectic is driven by the effort to dissociate the concept of internal contradiction from this idealist teleology.[31]

One of the difficulties in this debate is that Hegel's concept of internal contradiction originates in logic, where a contradictory sentence – formally, $p.\sim p$ – violates the law of non-contradiction. This doesn't represent a problem for Hegel, whose absolute idealism implies that the development of contradictions in determinate concepts constitutes the realization of the Idea in the world. But Marxists who have concerned themselves with this topic have typically sought to retain the idea that contradictions occur in reality while disagreeing with Hegel that the dialectic is essentially conceptual. Bhaskar puts the problem in an interesting way:

> The driving force (in principle) of Hegelian dialectic is the transition . . . from positive contraries simultaneously present and actual (thereby continually violating the principle of non-contradiction, as Hegel both does and says he does) into negative sub-contraries now simultaneously actual and absent, but retained as negative presences in a cumulative memory store, as the dialectical reader's consciousness or the path of history moves on to a new level of speculative reason. At this stage they are now retrospectively redescribed as moments of a transcending totality. Contradiction thus cancels itself.[32]

For Hegel, then, contradictions are thus posited only to be overcome and the content they introduce absorbed into the reconciling self-identity of the Absolute: as he puts it, 'contradiction is not the end of the matter, but cancels itself.'[33] The law of non-contradiction is, according to Bhaskar, 'a norm that he covertly accepts, while seeing it ubiquitously violated as the mechanism that powers his dialectic to its final glaciating repose.' Thus 'Hegelian dialectic . . . is never simultaneously dialectical and contradictory. The materialist dialectic is.'[34] In other words, what interests Marxists in the dialectic is not the reabsorption of contradictions back into the Absolute, but the destabilizing and dynamizing role that they play in the movement of history. But how to formulate a defensible theory of internal contradiction that is not dependent on Hegel's absolute idealism? One really bad move that Marxists sometimes make is to attack the law of non-contradiction as static and stultifying. The trouble is that *any* sentence whatsoever may be validly inferred from a contradictory sentence, which therefore, in saying or implying everything, succeeds in saying nothing at all. For Lucio Colletti by contrast, the law of non-contradiction is a prerequisite of any serious materialism. He draws on Kant to distinguish between 'real opposition', where two positive, independently existing forces are in conflict with one another (for example the mutual repulsion of two forces), and logical contradiction, where the law of non-contradiction is violated. According to Colletti, the idea of dialectical contradiction illicitly conflates these two concepts, in the process reducing the real to the conceptual.[35]

Although Ernesto Laclau is committed to a form of discursive idealism that conceives society on the model of language, he uses the distinction Colletti draws when explicating his Lacanian conception of antagonism (see also §3.3 above):

> So how are we to explain antagonism? We might begin to rethink the question by asking what the categories of real opposition and logical contradiction have in common. The answer is that both are objective relations; they both produce their effects within a system of differences. Alternatively, I want to argue that antagonistic relations are not objective relations at all but involve the collapse of any possible objectivity . . . antagonism is neither a real opposition nor a logical contradiction. A real opposition is an objective relation among things; a logical contradiction is an equally objective relation between concepts. An antagonism is the experience of the limits of any possible objectivity, the way in which any objectivity reveals the partial and arbitrary character of its own objectification. To use a simile from linguistics, if the langue is a system of difference, then antagonism is the failure of difference. And in this sense antagonism locates itself in the limits of language and can only exist as a disruption of language, that is, as metaphor.[36]

Laclau relies here on Derrida's subversion of Saussure's conception of language as a system of differences (see §6.1 above). Just as signification is an infinite process driven by the endless substitutions of signifiers ('the primacy of the signifier should be asserted', Laclau writes, 'but with the proviso that signifiers, signifieds, and signs should all be conceived as signifiers'),[37] so the social is constitutively open and incomplete. Indeed, the two are the same: 'Society never manages to be identical to itself, as every nodal point is constituted within an intertextuality that overflows it.'[38] Creative political interventions take the form of a hegemonic articulation through which an empty signifier gives a universal significance to some particular content, disrupting existing relations of difference by establishing a chain of equivalences between previously unrelated elements. Laclau gives the example of feminism:

> Consider the signifier 'woman': what is its meaning? Taken in isolation it has no meaning. But, on the one hand, 'woman' can enter into a relation of equivalence with family, subordination to men, and so on; and, on the other hand, 'woman' can enter into discursive relations with 'oppression', 'black people', 'gay people', and so on. The signifier 'woman' in itself has no meaning. Consequently, its meaning in society is going to be given only by a hegemonic articulation.[39]

Given *'the constant overflowing of every discourse by the infinitude of the field of discursivity'*, any such hegemonic articulation can only partially fix meanings constantly liable to slide into other, incompatible relations.[40] The inherently arbitrary and provisional character of any articulation is expressed in Laclau's conception of the universal as *'an empty place, a void which can be filled only by the particular, but which, through its very emptiness, produces a series of crucial effects in the structuration/destructuration of social relations.'* Consequently there is an inherent gap between the 'always open intertextuality [that] is the ultimately undecidable terrain in which hegemonic logics operate' and the decision to undertake a specific hegemonic intervention: 'the Subject is the distance between the undecidability of the structure and the decision.'[41] Although Badiou would no doubt dismiss Laclau's textualist ontology as a form of *idéalinguisterie*, there are parallels between the two forms of decisionism that they offer. For Laclau the decision is ungrounded because everything is: the void that is the universal is inherent in the signifying process itself. Badiou also rejects the idea that Being is grounded; moreover, the decision is to be faithful to an event whose site in a situation is on the edge of the void (see §3.2 above). It is hard not to see here the underlying idea that being is pure positivity, what Sartre in his Marxist phase called the 'practico-inert', filling up space and time with material objects and social institutions that block any transcending movement. One of the merits of Bhaskar's critical realist ontology is that it can liberate us from such concerns. The distinction that he draws between the real and the actual is an innovation of great strategic significance because it allows us to conceptualize the world of events that we experience as dependent on the inter-actions of underlying generative mechanisms whose tendencies, even if in many cases currently unactualized, delimit a far wider horizon of possibilities than the merely actual (§5.2 above). Tran-scendence – going beyond the actual – is, from this perspective, not a pure leap out of nothingness, but the activation of some of these possibilities. The source of transcendence is not indetermi-nation – for example, the indifferent and ineffable Being as incon-sistent multiplicity posited by Badiou – but the determinate structure of a real that necessarily differs from the actual. One might therefore say that, when Laclau counterposes antagonism, the experience of the limits of objectivity, to the objective rela-tionships of logical contradiction and real opposition, he is relying on too narrow a conception of objectivity.

It is interesting that Bhaskar, in his later attempt to develop his philosophy into 'dialectical critical realism', should target what he calls 'the doctrine of *ontological monovalence*' that he attributes to Parmenides – 'a purely positive . . . conception of reality', whereas Bhaskar wants us 'to see the positive as a tiny, but impor-tant ripple on the surface of a sea of negativity'. 'There are inter-vals, voids and pauses, desire, lack and need within being; and such absences and their tendential and actual absenting are . . . transcendentally and dialectically necessary for any intelligible being at all.' Bhaskar's attempts to make out this assertion, and the stronger thesis that 'the negative has ontological primacy', while suggestive, are highly problematic: in particular, the prior-ity of negation or absence or not-being over the positive or the presence or being (the terms are used equivalently) is established by an appeal to the role of human agency in absent*ing* things that, since the thesis is meant to apply to the physical as well as the social world, points towards Bhaskar's later lapse into spiritualism.[42] Presumably, however, these are claims about the nature of the real, and therefore, even if not tenable in the form in which Bhaskar makes them, they do underline how the real exceeds the positivity of what merely exists. Locating contra-dictions in reality is then to locate them in the *real* in this sense, in the strata of generative mechanisms underlying events and experiences.

Bhaskar offers the following account of real contradictions:

dialectical connections ... are connections between entities or aspects of a totality such that they are in principle *distinct* but *inseparable*, in the sense that they are synchronically or conjuncturally internally related, i.e. both (some, all) or one existentially presuppose the others ... Real dialectical contradictions possess all these features of dialectical connections. But their elements are also *opposed*, in the sense that (at least) one of their aspects negates (at least) one of the other's [*sic*], or their common ground or the whole, and perhaps vice versa, so that they are *tendentially mutually exclusive*, and potentially or actually tendentially transformative.[43]

In substance Bhaskar's account broadly corresponds to a definition of structural contradiction that I first put forward in 1987. A structural contradiction exists if and only if

(1) a relationship exists between two or more social entities;
(2) the social entities are constituted by virtue of their being terms of the relationship;
(3) the entities are mutually interdependent by virtue of the relationship;
(4) the entities are potentially in conflict by virtue of the relationship.[44]

The main difference between the two conceptions is that Bhaskar leaves open whether real contradictions are restricted to the social world, as my definition requires them to be: this raises issues that I discuss in the next section. Another difference is the connection that Bhaskar posits between contradiction and transformation. This suggests the addition of another clause to the definition above:

(5) where this conflict develops, the relationship is liable either to collapse or to be transformed.

What is to be said for this conception of real, or structural, contradiction? In the first place, to assert that contradictions of this nature exist is not to deny the law of non-contradiction. The latter is a requirement of coherent and determinate thought; structural contradictions are located in the real, and there is no reason in principle why conceptualizing them should generate logical contradictions (though, of course, any particular case of dialectical thinking might, like any case of thinking in general, prove to be incoherent). What connects the conceptions of logical and real contradiction is, I think, the idea of an *intrinsic* conflict. A sentence is contradictory by virtue of its logical form: this contradiction can be removed only by changing its logical form, that is, by replacing the defective sentence with a different one. Similarly, a structural contradiction is not, like Kant's and Colletti's notion of real opposition, an actual or potential conflict between two independently constituted entities. On the contrary, the terms to the relationship are constituted *by* that relationship, and it is this relationship that brings them into conflict with one another. Bhaskar refers to this feature of real contradiction when he makes the latter a case of dialectical connections, which involve internal relationships between 'distinct but inseparable' entities or aspects of a totality. The idea of internal relations has an idealist history, originating in the Hegelian doctrine of determinate negation, according to which the contradictions discovered in concepts render explicit new content, and the totality of these connections articulate the structure of Absolute Spirit as it comes progressively to full self-consciousness in philosophy. But in the Harré–Bhaskar account of causality, phenomena are internally connected when they belong to the nature of the same thing – i.e., to a generative mechanism and the events that it will, when unimpeded, produce. Internal relations, in other words, arise from the natural necessity manifested in causal interactions that scientific inquiry seeks to uncover; any logical entailments that hold between different aspects of our conception of a thing are the result of the theories we formulate a posteriori, through empirical investigation into the real nature of the thing, rather than being deduced or developed a priori from the Absolute Idea.[45]

There is, then, no inconsistency in asserting that the terms of a structural contradiction are internally related while conducting a scientific inquiry into the nature of the social world. This is, of course, what Marx does in *Capital*, and I shall use his theory of the capitalist mode of production, which has already figured in chapters 1 and 4, as a template for the rest of this discussion of structural contradiction. It is perhaps first worth stressing that this exercise has nothing to do with what is sometimes called the 'new dialectic', developed by, among others, Chris Arthur and Tony Smith, which interprets the conceptual construction of *Capital* as an instance of Hegelian dialectical logic. Not only does this interpretation in crucial respects misrepresent Marx's discourse in *Capital*, but it leads to serious philosophical difficulties inherent in the nature of Hegel's dialectic – namely that he conceives contradictions as generating new content in a pattern that is retrospectively validated by the ultimate goal of the process, the self-consciousness of Absolute Spirit. No work of empirical science could rely on such assumptions, and *Capital*, despite Marx's occasional flirtations with Hegel (especially the *Grundrisse*: see §4.2 above), certainly does not do so.[46]

Having made this clarification, let me make explicit one feature of the definition offered above. It leaves open the nature of the entities that are related in a structural contradiction. There is, then, no reason why these could not be structures. We have already seen such a 'relation between relations' in the case of the contradiction between the forces and relations of production: here the potentially conflictual relationship binds together two interdependent structures. Of course, to say that a structural contradiction exists between the forces and relations is not of itself to explain why this contradiction holds. The best answer that the Marxist theory of history has come up with is that the relationship between the forces and relations is an asymmetric one: the productive forces tend to develop, both because humans have a general interest in raising the productivity of their labour and because the prevailing relations of production remain in place insofar as they tend to promote the development of the productive forces; when the relations cease to play this role (as they predictably will, since they are consistent only with a limited range of levels of economic development), then, in Marx's famous metaphor, they become a fetter on the further growth of the productive forces and the mode of production enters what Gramsci calls an 'organic crisis'.[47]

This general model raises, of course, many questions: here I concentrate on the relationship between this transhistorical pattern of contradiction and transformation and Marx's more specific account of how this pattern manifests itself in the capitalist mode of production. His theory of the tendency of the rate of profit to fall (TRPF) in *Capital*, volume III, part 3, is among other things an explanation of the form taken by the contradiction between the forces and relations of production in the capitalist mode. As

we saw in §4.2 above, the TRPF is, counter-intuitively, a consequence not of declining but of rising labour productivity, since
higher productivity tends to involve a rise in the organic composition of capital (the ratio between value invested in the means of
production and value invested in labour-power) and hence a fall
in the rate of profit. Hence: 'The progressive tendency for the
general rate of profit to fall is thus simply *the expression, peculiar to the capitalist mode of production*, of the progressive development of the social productivity of labour.'[48] Recurrent economic
crises arise from the interaction between the TRPF and the various
counter-tendencies to its operation; these are symptoms of how
capitalist relations of production fetter the development of the
productive forces, a process that need not take the form of the
absolute stagnation or decline in output, but instead may be manifested in the chronic waste of productive resources, both human
and material, represented by recessions.[49]

The TRPF and, more broadly, the contradiction between the
forces and relations of production of which it is an instance thus
constitute a case of structural contradiction as a contradiction
between structures. But Marx's procedure in *Capital* involves conceptualizing contradictions *in* structures as well, and may be more
important to his argument. We saw in §4.2 above that Marx contends that the capitalist mode of production is constituted by two
relations, what Robert Brenner calls the 'vertical' relationship
between capital and wage-labour and the 'horizontal' relations
among 'many capitals'. Both these are cases of structural contradictions. One of Marx's most fundamental theses is that
capital is a relation: the very possibility of the valorization, or self-
expansion, of capital as a free-standing economic process rather
than a form parasitic on non-capitalist relations such as feudalism
or slavery is dependent on the exploitation of wage-labour. At
the same time, however, wage-labour itself presupposes capital
because, for wage-labour to exist, the direct producers must be
separated from the means of production and left with only their
labour-power to sell to capitalists who collectively control the
means of production. Not only are conditions (1) to (3) of my definition of structural contradiction thus met, but the capital-
relation is also an inherently conflictual one, since it is constituted
by the exploitation of wage-labour, which both presupposes
and reproduces the mutual interdependence of capital and wage-

labour.[50] But the capital-relation also necessarily includes 'many capitals' because it is through the competitive struggle among rival firms that the characteristic tendencies of the capitalist mode become operative. This relationship, too, seems like a case of a structural contradiction. Individual capitals, as participants in a market economy involving a complex division of labour, are interrelated and interdependent; moreover, were one capital to take control of the entire (global) economy it would, by virtue of this very success, cease to be capital, since the disappearance of competition would remove the pressure to make technological innovations increasing labour productivity and thereby reducing costs that gives to capitalism its unique economic dynamic.[51] But the horizontal relation among capitals is no less a case of conflict: even if individual firms derive their profits from the surplus-value extracted from workers, they nonetheless fiercely struggle against each other to maximize their share of the loot.

So the capitalist mode of production isn't simply liable to a structural contradiction, in the shape of the TRPF: this tendency is in turn explained by the vertical and horizontal contradictions constitutive of the capital-relation, respectively those between capital and wage-labour and among capitals themselves. This suggests that what *Capital* involves is an *ordering* of determinations through the construction of distinct but related levels of analysis, some of which posit the existence of real contradictions. This is expressed in Marx's famous description of his 'method of rising from the abstract to the concrete', beginning with 'the simplest determinations' in order to reconstruct the capitalist mode of production conceptually as 'a rich totality of many determinations and relations'.[52] The starting point is provided by Marx's analysis of the commodity, which gives us the labour theory of value, which must be understood as a theory of the allocation of social labour in an economy of autonomous but interdependent commodity producers (§§1.2 and 4.2 above). This then makes possible the conceptualization of the capital-relation itself: here the capital–wage–labour relationship takes priority because, without the production of surplus-value, capital as a free-standing economic relation cannot exist, but the analysis of this relation requires also an analysis of the competitive struggles on which the tendencies of the capitalist mode depend. The most important of these tendencies, the TRPF, itself involves a contradiction, this time between structures. One point that is worth making here is that the ordering of determinations does not require us to conceive every determination as involving a real contradiction: one of the *ennuis* of Hegelian interpretations of *Capital* is that they tend to give rise to a game of Hunt the Contradiction because, if Marx's analysis is to be a genuine instance of dialectical logic, each determination must contain a contradiction that then forces the argument on. But if such an exercise is both theoretically unnecessary and productive of interpretive distortions, nevertheless it does seem important that Marx conceives capitalism as a *totality constituted* by the contradictions that define the capital-relation and are manifested in the TRPF. To put it in the terms used by John Rees in his outstanding account of the Marxist dialectic, the capitalist mode is to be understood as 'an internally contradictory totality in a constant process of change'.[53]

The very idea of a totality has, of course, come under steady attack from poststructuralists and postmodernists since the 1960s. It is, for example, the idea of society as a totality that Laclau is targeting when he declares society impossible:

> Society as a sutured space, as the underlying mechanism that gives reasons for or explains its own partial processes, does not exist, because, if it did, meaning would be fixed in a variety of ways. Society is an ultimate impossibility, an impossible object, and it exists only as that attempt to constitute that impossible object or order. That is to say, the order of society is the unstable order of a system of differences which is always threatened from the outside. Neither the difference nor the space can be ultimately sutured.[54]

A hegemonic articulation sutures previously discrete 'elements' of difference, transforming them into 'moments' of a structured totality. But such an articulation is an intervention that constructs a totality where it previously did not exist; moreover, it is necessarily partial and provisional because of the inherent potential of differences to overcome any limits: 'A *totally* sutured society ... would have ... managed to identify itself with the transparency of a closed symbolic order. Such a closure of the social is ... impossible.'[55] The critical move here is the equation of totality and closure. Here again we encounter what Bhaskar calls ontological monovalence: the only form in which beings can be said to have a determinate structure is where they form actually, positively existing things that crowd creative transformation out of the space of the possible – or, rather, would do so were it not for the inherent slipperiness of meaning. But there seems no reason to accept the equation of totality with closure, except in the trivial sense that, because everything isn't possible, any determinate reality represents a limitation of the possible (*omnis determinatio negatio est*, as Spinoza put it). Once again, the Bhaskarian conception of the real is helpful here: the capitalist mode of production as a structured and contradictory totality pertains to the real. It is a differentiated structure of generative mechanisms that give rise to various tendencies, but the extent to which these tendencies are actualized depends on the outcome of the interaction of these mechanisms and on other conditions external to the capitalist mode. Thus, in the definition I gave of structural contradiction, the related entities are *potentially* in conflict: conceptualizing society as a contradictory totality involves a constant movement away from the actual in two directions – downwards to identify the underlying mechanisms that at once produce but are liable to subvert the actual, forwards to track the effects of the tendencies that threaten to break the actual up.[56]

The distinctive feature of the Marxist conception of totality is the central role played in it by contradiction: it is the structural contradictions that Marx identifies that order and unify the capitalist mode of production. This is the respect in which the idea of contradiction offers 'value-added' from an explanatory point of view. In the case of each contradiction a mechanism responsible for the conflictual relationship in question is given: for example, the TRPF is explained by the way in which individual capitals are motivated to seek super-profits by introducing cost-cutting innovations that, when generalized, reduce the general rate of profit (see §4.2 above). A sceptic might argue that the explanatory work is done by mechanisms like this one, and that talk of contradiction is merely a rhetorical Hegelian façade. There are certainly versions of Marxism where contradictions are thrown around freely, getting in the way instead of facilitating genuine analysis: this was partly what Edward Thompson had in mind when he denounced Diabolical and Hysterical Materialism. But the idea that contradiction is *constitutive*, when grounded in the kind of theory of the capitalist mode of production that Marx inaugurated in *Capital* and that the tradition of Marxist political economy has sought to continue, seems really to go beyond the specific mechanisms postulated at different levels of determination. Two thoughts are involved here. First, the most important relationships – for example, the two dimensions of the capital-relation discussed earlier (capital vs. wage labour and many capitals) – involve structural contradictions. Second, it is these relationships, and the contradiction between the forces and relations of production to which they give rise, that give to the capitalist mode its overall form. Consequently, the conflicts that develop from these relations are not secondary features of the social world that can be removed through a judicious mixture of reform and statecraft: contradiction does not efface itself in a Hegelian moment of reconciliation where the opposites recognize their shared identity. Structural contradictions can be overcome only through the transformation of the existing totality that abolishes them.

In a crucial passage in *Theories of Surplus-Value* Marx attacks John Stuart Mill for assuming the identity of supply and demand, production and consumption, and therefore asserting the impossibility of crises. 'Here . . . the *unity* of these two phases, which does exist and which forcibly asserts itself in crises, must be seen as opposed to their *separation* and *antagonism* of these two phases, separation and antagonism which exist just as much, and are moreover typical of bourgeois production.' In fact, however, 'the unity of the two phases . . . is essentially just as much separation of these two phases, their becoming independent of each other. Since, however, they belong together the independence of the two correlated aspects can only *show itself*, forcibly, as a destructive process. It is just the *crisis* in which they assert their unity, the unity of different aspects.'[57] In other words, production and consumption are not immediately identical with one another, as mainstream economists claim when they assert that supply generates its own demand. They are 'different aspects' of a contradictory whole. The 'unity' of production and consumption finds expression in their antagonism, the fact that commodity producers cannot automatically find markets for their goods, and therefore the real interdependence of production and consumption 'forcibly asserts itself in crises', when commodities go unsold in huge numbers.

Marx sums up his methodological difference with Mill thus: 'Where the economic relation – and therefore the categories expressing it – includes contradictions, opposites and likewise the unity of opposites, he emphasizes the aspect of the *unity* of the contradictions and denies the *contradictions*. He transforms the unity of opposites into the direct identity of opposites.'[58] One might then say that Hegel's idealism, for all the richness of the specific analyses he offers and the suggestive character of many of his general formulations, finds expression in a tendency to resolve contradictions into 'the direct identity of opposites'. The *Philosophy of Right* displays a realistic understanding of the social conflict and economic instability inherent in modern 'civil society', but Hegel thinks that they can be harmonized, in the first instance through the structures of the liberal state, but ultimately in the self-knowledge of Absolute Spirit: 'contradiction . . . cancels itself'.[59] For Marx, however, the opposites are different from each other, even if they are caught up together, and indeed defined by their conflictual unity. Capital and labour are not the same, even if neither could exist without the other: their contradictory relationship can only be overcome through a social transformation whose tendency is to abolish this relationship, not to transfigure it intellectually. Marx famously left *Capital* unfinished, but he planned that it would conclude with 'the *class struggle*, into which the movement and the smash-up of the whole business would revolve itself'.[60]

The location here of class struggle within the larger conflicts of the capitalist mode of production underlines that this account of structural contradiction does not equate it with the kind of collision of class subjectivities at the centre of the otherwise very different versions of Marxism embraced by Badiou and Negri during the 1970s (§§3.2 and 4.2). Reducing contradiction to class conflict may seem like a way of correcting the determinism and objectivism of the Marxisms of the Second and Third Internationals (though in fact there is a strong voluntarist strain in Stalinist ideology that Maoism radicalized during the Cultural Revolution). But the effect is often, as we saw in the case of Negri's reinterpretation of the *Grundrisse*, to reduce history to a clash of antagonistic collective wills and thereby – even when the focus is directly on the capital–labour relationship itself – to make its vicissitudes, the advances made by one side, the retreats and setbacks suffered by another, unintelligible, since the structural context, from which one of the antagonists might gain additional resources, while the other is placed at as disadvantage, ceases to be visible. Hardt's and Negri's solution in *Empire* and *Multitude* is, in effect, to deny the possibility of labour being defeated and make every restructuring of capitalism a victory, an affirmation of the creativity of the multitude, but this is tenable neither intellectually nor ethico-politically. It is hardly surprising that Negri, having disengaged class conflict from the structures of the modes of production, should have been so receptive to Foucault's rehabilitation of a Nietzschean vision of history as an unending struggle for power. John Holloway, the other leading contemporary theorist of autonomist Marxism, espouses a similarly subjectivist theory of history (though one indebted to the early Frankfurt School rather than Foucault and Deleuze), summed up by the slogan: 'in the beginning is not the word, but the scream' – the protest of a human subjectivity dominated by the fetishized products of its own doing.[61] The extreme polarization, here not of antagonistic subjectivities but of subject and object – of the labouring human and an eternized capital – once again reduces historical variation, and therefore social transformation, to a mystery.[62]

The relationship between contradiction and transformation must in any case be specified carefully. The existence of a contra-dictory social relationship will not of itself inevitably lead to the transformation of this relationship, for two reasons. The first is just a restatement of one of the general principles of critical realism, namely that what actually happens is usually a result of no one generative mechanism, but of the interaction of a plural-ity of different mechanisms. The general Marxist theory of history and the special theory of the capitalist mode of production require a certain ordering among the relevant social mechanisms, but this does not imply that the mechanisms postulated in the earlier stages of the analysis short-circuit those introduced later on. Secondly, the stratification specific to the social involves agency as well as structure(s). Organic crises don't predetermine outcomes but pose alternatives (in the broadest terms collapse or transformation, but other options may exist as well, for example, stagnation): the nature of the actual outcome will depend on the subjective responses of the human actors affected by the crisis. It is on this terrain than Laclau's hegemonic articulations become pertinent, as different groups of actors weld themselves into collectivities whose self-identity depends on a particular set of ideological representations that give them a degree of cohesion, an interpretation of the crisis, and a programme for resolving it. Laclau's and Mouffe's complaint against classical Marxism is precisely that its most politically creative exponents – Lenin, Trotsky, and especially Gramsci – pursue a dualistic approach that seeks to combine a set of 'essential' relations given in the mode of production – the constitution of classes in the relations of production, etc. – with the indispensable 'supplement' provided by hegemonic relations that permit the construction of practically effective alliances amid all the contingencies of everyday politics.[63] Their solution is to let the indeterminacy of hegemonic relations spread downwards to infect the social as a whole.

But this isn't the only strategy mandated by the problem Laclau and Mouffe identify. On the one hand, acknowledging the reality of the relatively deep-seated structures of modes of production that (to borrow a famous metaphor of Weber's) switch the tracks along which history runs implies no commitment to any doctrine of historical inevitability, which then requires some account of the 'secondary' circumstances that have temporarily delayed the inevitable. On the other hand, politics is undoubtedly a realm of irreducible contingency, where subjective qualities of calculation and leadership, courage and cruelty – everything that Machiavelli tries to sum up in the idea of *virtù* – as well as sheer luck – *fortuna* – are indispensable in accounting for the success or failure of specific projects. This is what Daniel Bensaïd calls '[t]he broken time of politics and strategy'. But to recognize all this does not mean that the political field is entirely indeterminate: the capacity of different collectivities to realize their particular projects will depend in part on their access to various kinds of material and ideological resources. The victory of capital over labour in the 1970s and 1980s no doubt had something to do with the relative qualities of leadership on the two sides, but the kind of hegemonic articulation that, for example, Thatcherism represented in Britain possessed structural advantages deriving from the global restructuring of economic relations that began in the second half of the 1970s and from the profound ideological malaise of the left produced by the collapse of post-1968 militancy, the crisis of the Keynesian welfare state, and the death agony of 'existing socialism'. The indeterminacies inherent in ideological and political struggles don't require us to say that it's indeterminacy all the way down.

Rather every level of determination, from the deepest structures to the most aleatory movements of subjectivities, involves a particular blend of determinacy and indeterminacy, of closure and openness, each requiring analysis in its own terms. As Bensaïd puts it, '[d]eterminate historical development remains full of junctions and bifurcations, forks and points.'[64]

It is against this background that we should approach the whole problematic of decisionism that so preoccupies contemporary left-liberal thought. It was Kant who in *The Critique of Judgement* points to the inherent gap that separates a universal from the particular cases that are held to exemplify it. There can be no principle determining the application of universal to particular: to posit such a principle would merely generate an infinite regress, since a further principle would be required to determine the application of *that* principle, and so on *ad infinitum*.[65] Very similar reasoning is involved in Wittgenstein's remarks on rule-following.[66] The upshot is that there is always a gap between a universal principle and its particular applications. In that sense decisions are necessarily ungrounded, since no principle can uniquely determine them: applying a principle is an inherently creative act that necessarily goes beyond (and may significantly change the content of) this principle. But it doesn't follow that political judgements are completely disjoined from an at least implicit theoretical context (both normative and explanatory) that identifies a range of relevant considerations. It is in fact hard to see how a determinate set of alternatives between which to choose could even be identified without some such context. Principles, in the sense of both explanatory theories and normative conceptions, still serve to orient judgements and the actions they entail. Indeed, one of the main dimensions of any difficult judgement is likely to be the task of identifying what principles are relevant to the decision under consideration. Once again, there is no set of meta-principles that can make this task the mechanical application of a rule; moreover, when it has been performed, the actor still has to work out the weight to assign to the different principles she has concluded are relevant, as well their precise application to the situation she is confronting. But the picture that emerges is one of a constant to-ing and fro-ing between considerations of principle and the features of the situation that the actor deems relevant to her decision, rather than an abyssal leap.

6.3   A dialectic of nature?

The broad thrust of this chapter and its predecessor has been, first, to vindicate a critical realist ontology that is naturalistic in the sense of conceiving the world (*including* the social and the mental) as strata of interacting generative mechanisms, and to outline a Marxist theory of social contradiction. This invites the question, which I left hanging in the preceding section, whether or not contradictions exist in nature as well as society. Anyone answering this question in the affirmative could appeal to the explicit authority of leading figures in the Marxist tradition – most notably, Engels, Lenin, and Trotsky. But the idea of a dialectic of nature has been strongly resisted by many Marxists, particularly since the Second World War. Such opposition is, for example, one of the few things that that would have united Sartre in his Marxist phase with Althusser. Colletti contemptuously dismissed dialectical materialism as practised in the orthodox communist movement as 'an evening class philosophical pastiche'.[67] John Roemer probably spoke for analytical Marxists generally when he called the dialectic 'the yoga of Marxism'.[68] Colletti's and Roemer's formulations probably capture the principal reason why many contemporary radical theorists have rejected a broadly dialectical conception of nature as a whole – that it amounts to a kind of intellectual faddism out of keeping with the state of the art in the physical and the social sciences. But, when closer attention is paid to developments particularly in the physical sciences, the grounds for this attitude are not as self-evidently valid as is often thought. It is interesting that Bhaskar, although ambivalent about whether his chief dialectical category of real negation extended beyond the social world, is remarkably sympathetic to Engels's famous three 'laws of the dialectic'.[69] The issues involved have to be approached with some care before a conclusion can be reached.

It is certainly true that the dialectic as it was developed by Hegel and Marx is primarily one of human history. *The Science of Logic*, which unfolds the structure of the process of self-development of the Absolute Idea, is universally operative, but the dialectical process only comes to life when it becomes self-conscious in the minds of individual persons – what Hegel calls finite spirit. *The*

Phenomenology of Spirit traces the succession of different historical shapes of consciousness from which 'absolute knowledge'
finally emerges in European modernity after the French Revolution.[70] For Hegel nature is undialectical because it is the Other
of Spirit, the stage at which the Absolute Idea is alienated
from itself, unconscious and objectified, before it attains self-
consciousness in the finite forms of human subjectivity: 'Nature is
Spirit estranged from itself; in Nature, Spirit lets itself go (*ausge-
lassen*), a Bacchic god unrestrained and unmindful of itself; in
Nature the unity of the Notion is concealed.'[71] Nature only begins
to become interesting insofar as we see gradually the emergence
of living forms that anticipate self-conscious mind. Marx focuses
more or less exclusively on human history. The contradictions
in which he is interested are those discussed in the preceding
section – above all, those that constitute the capitalist mode of
production.

It is, of course, Engels who develops the idea of a dialectic specific to nature, first in *Anti-Dühring* and especially in *Dialectics
of Nature*. It is important to appreciate the intellectual context
that confronted him. Engels sees discussion of the physical sciences
as polarized between two plainly mistaken positions. On one
hand, there is the rejection of the modern sciences expressed
notably by Romantic *Naturphilosophie* with its speculative search
for analogies between the mind and nature. On the other hand,
the contemporary sciences are defended by reductive materialists
such as Büchner, Moleschott, and Vogt in Germany and Spencer
in Britain. Both these currents fail to register what Engels regards
as the transformation occurring within the physical sciences themselves. He argues that the seventeenth-century scientific revolution
assumed '*the absolute immutability of nature*': classical mechan-
ics, for instance, takes no account of time – its equations are
reversible. But, in the late eighteenth century, we see 'the dawning
conception that nature does not just *exist*, but *comes into being*
and *passes away*.' The main examples that Engels gives are Lyell's
geological history of the earth, Darwin's theory of evolution by
natural selection, and the constitution of thermodynamics, and
especially its second law, which posits an irreversible process of
growing entropy.[72] In other words, a historical conception of
nature was emerging that is broadly consonant with the approach
that Marx adopts in *Capital*. As Bensaïd puts it,

In the mid-nineteenth century, three simultaneous but logically heterogeneous innovations helped to undermine the Newtonian paradigm: the Darwinian theory of evolution, the principles of energy conservation and loss, and the Marxian critique of political economy. These 'sciences' of transformation no longer refer to factual certainties, but to probabilities, choices, and bifurcations. They tackle instability and equilibrium, aperiodic motion and time's arrow.[73]

This is the context in which Engels advances the idea of a dialectic of nature: seeing the physical world as undergoing dialectical processes of transformation does justice to the actual development of the physical sciences while avoiding reductive materialism. This is a highly suggestive strategy that, as we shall see below, can claim support from a variety of more recent theoretical innovations. What has undermined greatly its plausibility is the claim Engels advances that there are universal dialectical laws of nature:

> It is . . . from the history of nature and human society that the laws of dialectics are abstracted. For they are nothing but the most general laws of these two aspects of historical development, as well as of thought itself. And indeed they can be reduced in the main to three:
>
> The law of the transformation of quantity into quality and vice versa;
> The law of the interpenetration of opposites;
> The law of the negation of the negation.[74]

In fact Engels culled these 'laws' from Hegel's *Logic*. But the really problematic thing about them is not their derivation or even their content – though the concept of the negation of the negation does seem hard to marry with any serious materialism since it is the category by means of which in Hegel's dialectic contradictions are cancelled by being absorbed into the reconciling self-identity of the Absolute.[75] The real trouble comes with the very idea of universal dialectical laws operative everywhere, in nature, history, and thought. As we have seen in §5.2 above, what a scientific law does is to specify the generative mechanism that, when left unimpeded, produce sequences of events. Engels's 'laws' don't do this – they don't give any mechanisms that explain what happens in the world. Arguably their very generality prevents them from doing this. This then poses the following dilemma: either the 'laws of the dialectic' aren't really laws at all – i.e., they don't explain anything – or they gain an explanatory role by constraining and directing actual scientific research. This latter outcome did, of course, actually occur, when 'dialectical materialism' was canonized as the philosophical core of the Marxist-Leninist ruling ideology in the Soviet Union and the other Stalinist regimes, most notoriously in the Lysenko affair, which had disastrous consequences for biological research in the USSR.[76]

It is this experience that first motivated many Marxists to conclude that Engels was wrong, and that real contradictions are unique to the social world. This used to be my own view, but two reasons have led me to change my mind. The first is the refinement of the dialectic of nature offered by Trotsky in his *Philosophical Notebooks*, which were written in 1933–5, but only published in 1986. Critically Trotsky reduces the three 'laws of the dialectic' to one: the transformation of quantity into quality:

> *the fundamental law of dialectics is the conversion of quantity into quality,* for it gives [us] the general formula of all evolutionary processes – of nature as well as of society ... The principle of the transformation of quantity into quality has universal significance, insofar as we view the entire universe – without any exception – as a product of formation and transformation and not as the fruit of conscious creation.[77]

Trotsky's move here is more than a tidying-up exercise. The other two 'laws' are much more problematically applicable to nature as opposed to history: in particular, few things have done more to discredit the idea of a dialectic of nature than attempts to find physical instances of the unity of opposites by, for example, postulating a 'contradiction' between an acorn and the oak that it eventually becomes. The transformation of quantity into quality does by contrast seem genuinely universal insofar as it highlights two crucial features of the world – first, the phenomenon of emergence and stratification – the existence, that is, of qualitatively different levels of physical being each governed by specific laws, including the human species, with its peculiar capacities and distinctive history (see §5.2 above), and, second, qualitative transformations from one state of being to another. Both these features are surely important to the non-reductive and historical conception of nature that Engels is seeking to promote. The transformation of quantity into quality is still, however, no law in the sense of an explanatory theory that identifies a generative mechanism. It rather generalizes the features common to physical and social processes which are produced by a wide variety of different mechanisms. This line of thought suggests that we should see the dialectic of nature as a broad philosophical conception of nature rather than a set of general laws from which more specific ones applicable to particular aspects of the world can be deduced. This way of thinking about the dialectic of nature has the advantage that it rules out the kind of dogmatic dictation to working scientists which under Stalinism gave the idea a bad name, but it implies a fairly loose and open relationship between dialectical philosophy and scientific research of the kind that Trotsky seems to have had in mind: 'The dialectic does not liberate the investigator from the painstaking study of the facts, quite the contrary: it requires it. But in return it gives investigative thought elasticity, helps it cope with ossified prejudices, arms it with invaluable analogies, and educates it in a spirit of daring, grounded in circumspection.'[78]

My second reason for becoming open to the idea of a dialectic of nature in the sense just elaborated is provided by the 'invaluable analogies' offered by the actual development of physical sciences, which strongly supports this conception of nature. Three examples may be helpful here. First, there are the debates in evolutionary biology – for example, over whether evolution consists in an accumulation of small, gradual changes, as Darwin himself believed, or occurs in sudden bursts (as Steven Jay Gould and Nils Eldredge argue when putting forward the idea of 'punctuated equilibrium') or between the 'beanbag genetics' of ultra-Darwinians such as Richard Dawkins and those such as Richard Lewontin and Steven Rose who argue for more holistic conceptions of the relations among genes or between genes and their environment.[79] Second, cosmology, which concerns itself with the study of the history of the universe, now entertains the eminently dialectical suggestion offered by super-string theory that the laws operative at one stage in this process were radically different: before the so-called Planck time of 10^{-43} seconds after the Big Bang, the universe was compressed into a tiny (10^{-33} cm in all dimensions) ultra-hot and ultra-dense nugget in which all nine spatial dimensions were symmetrical and the strong, weak, and electromagnetic forces formed a single 'grand unified' force; after the Planck time, as the universe cooled and expanded, the three forces became differentiated from one another, and only three spatial dimensions expanded.[80] Finally, chaos and complexity theory, though misleadingly used to suggest that reality is a tissue of accidents, in fact represents something quite different, namely the effort to construct mathematical models that will allow us to understand complex systems and dynamic processes that had hitherto seemed beyond scientific explanation. Once again, the results include highly dialectical conceptions – for example, dissipative structures whose behaviour is highly sensitive to their initial conditions, so that small changes in these conditions can lead to very large differences, and far-from-equilibrium situations that generate bifurcation points where the path actually taken will result from the probabilistic outcome of the system's fluctuations. Both here and more generally, we see scientists relying on the concept of phase transitions – sudden qualitative changes, for example, when a system of chemical reactions reaches a critical point where it becomes self-catalysing, and therefore capable of life.[81]

Sometimes scientists reflecting on their findings explicitly recognize how they resonate with the idea of a dialectic of nature. Ilya Prirogine and Isabelle Stengers write that chaos theory reveals 'a nature that might be called "historical" – that is, capable of development and innovation. The idea of a history of nature as an integral part of materialism was asserted by Marx and, in greater detail, by Engels.'[82] More frequently scientists are unaware of the connection, but nevertheless come to conclusions remarkably consonant with what Bhaskar calls 'dialectical critical realism'. Consider, for example, the cognitive scientist John Holland's 'recapitulation' of emergence:

> 1. *Emergence occurs in systems that are generated . . .*
> 2. *The whole is more than the sum of the parts in these generated systems . . .*
> 3. *Emergent phenomena in generated systems are, typically, persistent patterns with changing components . . .*
> 4. *The context in which a persistent emergent pattern is embedded determines its function . . .*

5. Interactions between persistent patterns add constraints and checks that provide increasing 'competence' as the number of such patterns increases . . .
6. Persistent patterns often satisfy macrolaws . . .
7. Differential persistence is a typical consequence of the laws that generate emergent phenomena . . .
8. Higher-level generating procedures can result from enhanced persistence . . .[83]

The stratified and dynamic conception of nature that emerges from such reflection supports the idea not of a single dialectic of nature, but of dialectics of nature – of a multiplicity of different logics analogous to those that Marx discovered in history. It is this kind of loosening up that Bhaskar has in mind when he advocates 'the materialist diffraction of dialectic'.[84] But a sceptic might ask: if all this is happening in the sciences anyway, what is the point of formulating and defending an explicitly dialectical conception of nature? Apart from the fact that this conception plainly has been suggestive for some working scientists, arguably the ideological conjuncture with respect to the physical sciences isn't that different from the one that Engels confronted. On the one hand, there are reductive materialists such as Dawkins, who is seriously committed to explaining everything human in terms of the purposeless combinations and recombinations of DNA ('DNA neither cares nor knows. DNA just is. And we dance to its music'), and who is in many ways a throwback to Enlightenment rationalism – for example, denouncing religion and astrology without any attempt to understand the social needs they meet.[85] On the other hand, we have the efforts to spiritualize nature, which include not merely New Agers such as Prince Charles (and now, alas, Bhaskar) but some scientists as well. One example is provided by Stuart Kauffman of the Santa Fe Institute, who uses complexity theory in order to provide sophisticated reassurance that we are at home in a fundamentally benign and orderly universe where 'organisms are not contraptions piled on contraptions all the way down, but expressions of a deeper order inherent in all life' and 'our social institutions evolve as expressions of deep natural principles'. The analogy between cosmic order and social structures is especially telling. According to Kauffman, '[t]he mutualism of the biosphere, where advantages of trade exist, finds its mirror in economic systems . . . We are all hustling our wares – bacteria, fox, CEO. Moreover, we are all creating niches for one another.'[86] For those unpersuaded that Enron was somehow mandated by the structure of a benevolent universe, there does seem to be much of value in a non-reductive materialism that recognizes complexity and qualitative differences in nature and that conceptualizes transcendence not as a miracle but as the outcome of interacting but mutually irreducible mechanisms.

7

Justice and Universality

7.1 From fact to value

In the two preceding chapters I have sought to outline a critical realist ontology that is able, unlike the theories surveyed in part I, to offer a satisfactory basis on which to understand the possibility of innovation and that, further, avoids the anti-realism that, as I tried to show with respect to Habermas and to Boltanski and Chiapello, weakens their attempts to offer a critique of existing society. But reference to the idea of critique returns us to the point that I made at the beginning of chapter 1, namely that it presupposes some moral principle or conception of the good, and to the problem that I introduced there of the relationship between explanatory social theory and normative political philosophy.[1] As I tried to show, the general tendency of all the theorists discussed in part I was to collapse the two – and more broadly the dimensions of the factual and the evaluative – together. Habermas and Boltanski and Chiapello run together justice and functionality (§§1.1 and 2.1); Bidet builds the promise of equality, liberty, and rationality into the presuppositions of modernity as a social form (§1.2); Bourdieu conflates ethico-political universality with scientific objectivity (§2.2), Badiou stipulatively makes universality a necessary condition of events (§3.2), and Negri derives from Deleuze an affirmative conception of Being (§4.3). The provisional conclusion that I reached at the end of chapter 1 was that social critique requires free-standing, substantive principles of justice. It's time to consider the implications of this conclusion.

To begin with, it clashes with the general drift of the tradition in social theory whose profile has been steadily been rising as the argument of this book has progressed, namely classical Marxism. In the founding texts of historical materialism, notably *The German Ideology*, Marx develops a withering critique of abstract philosophical speculation. One of his main targets is moral philosophy, whether in the form of Kant's categorical imperative or Bentham's utilitarianism. Normative conceptions and principles, Marx argues, are simply historically specific expressions of class interests. Their claim to universality is therefore false, and indeed ideological, since it conceals class antagonism beneath the façade of the general welfare or the moral community. The socialist movement, Marx concludes, should eschew talk of justice or rights.[2] There is no shortage of contemporary Marxist theorists who think this judgement was basically correct. Fredric Jameson, for example, dismisses passing moral judgements on post-modernism as 'a category mistake', preferring instead 'a genuinely dialectical attempt to think our present time in History'.[3] In his brilliant study of the young Marx, Stathis Kouvelakis writes about the challenge posed by the French Revolution to 'something at the heart of Kant's enterprise, the subsumption of politics under the moral law':

> As soon as morality consents to confront real situations, it splits in two, reflecting the contradictions of these situations within itself and revealing, in the process, its political overdetermination. It should now be clearer how the revolutionary event dangerously undermines Kant's construction at its nodal point – the point at which it tries to articulate the two previously distinct legal orders [i.e., those of the *ancien régime* and the revolution], positing that a gradual historical process can bring about their reunification. For the revolution suspends the existing legal order and plunges society into a legal vacuum, even if it eventually produces a new system of right in closer conformity with freedom. Right, as the form of the external intersubjective conditions of freedom, does not arrive together with the means of establishing it; politics, at its culminating point – the revolutionary event – asserts itself independently of any moral foundation; the revolution, precisely as an event, over-turns the conception of a historically homogeneous time, oriented in linear fashion, towards progress.[4]

Kouvelakis advances this argument as part of a broader attempt to underline the significance of the French Revolution, not simply for Marx and Marxism, but for the entire subsequent development of the left, as an event whose meaning is not yet exhausted. This is certainly a welcome corrective to a certain left historiography that dismisses 1789–94 as a marginal interlude in the constitution of capitalist modernity.[5] Kouvelakis is also right to insist on the specificity of the political, its unamenability, as the field where the contradictions of the social totality are concentrated and condensed but also refracted according to the peculiar imperatives of conquering or maintaining state power, to either subsumption under moral laws or reduction to the social. But to deny that the political can somehow be inferred from normative generalizations does not require us to agree that the French Revolution is a pure event that 'asserts itself independently of any moral foundation'. On the contrary, as Jacques Bidet has stressed, the great revolutions that inaugurated political modernity seek to legitimize themselves on the basis of declarations affirming universal moral principles (§1.2). Of course, in one sense revolutions are self-founding, in that, as Kouvelakis observes, they overturn 'the existing legal order' and inaugurate a new one: they are, in other words, instances of what Negri calls constituent power. Part of the difficulty here is that 'legitimacy' is ambiguous between consistency with a given constitutional order and moral justification. Kouvelakis elides these two meanings, referring to Kant's project of 'the juridico-moral subsumption of politics'.[6] Such equivocation is, of course, licensed by the fact that in many Continental languages the same term – *droit*, *Recht*, etc. – is used to refer to both positive law and natural rights.[7] But this does not justify moving from the fact that in revolutions constituent power is asserted to found new legal orders to the claim that participants are mistaken when they seek to legitimize their actions by appealing to moral principles that transcend specific political institutions and that therefore pre-exist what they are instituting. In treating revolutions as morally unfounded Kouvelakis is, I think, influenced by Badiou's conception of events as instantiating an arbitrary and empty but somehow egalitarian universality, but, as I have tried to show, Badiou fails to offer a plausible account of how these conditions could be coherently met (see §3.2 above).[8]

Though Kouvelakis draws on some of the most sophisticated contemporary critical theory, in his hostility to moral discourse he is in line with long-standing Marxist orthodoxy. But, in my view, Marxism itself suffers from an 'ethical deficit' – or indeed a flagrant contradiction. Norman Geras's minute analysis of Marx's economic writings has exposed the tension between Marx's relativist interpretation of ethical discourse and his tacit reliance on half-articulated normative concepts and principles in his critique of exploitation.[9] Consider, for example, the following passage, where Marx in effect treats collective (and inter-generational) ownership of the land as a universal moral principle:

> From the standpoint of a higher socio-economic formation, the private property of particular individuals in the earth will seem just as absurd as the private property of one man in another man. Even an entire society, a nation, or all simultaneously existing societies taken together, are not the owners of the earth. They are simply its possessors, its beneficiaries, and have to bequeath it in an improved state to succeeding generations, as *boni patres familias* [good householders].[10]

This is a remarkable passage, which shows Marx sensitive to the same kind of considerations involved in contemporary notions of sustainable development. But in criticizing existing property forms in the name of a society to come he seems very close to just the kind of appeal to transhistorical normative principles that he condemns in others. This gap between Marx's official doctrine and his implied theoretical commitments has helped to create a tendency to counterpose classical Marxism, with its emphasis on the explanation of antagonistic social structures and the struggles to which they give rise, and normative political philosophy, with the ethical ideals and conceptions to which it appeals. The thought is that one can't do both; one has to choose to work within one of these discourses. This is an attitude expressed not just by many orthodox Marxists but also by theorists who consider themselves to have transcended Marxism such as Habermas and G. A. Cohen.[11] But I see no need to choose: one can have one's cake and eat it. To put it more strongly: a theoretically consequent Marxist critique of capitalism requires the articulation of ethical principles in terms of which capitalism is condemned as unjust. How else can it succeed as *critique*? Pursuing this insight demands a genuine dialogue between classical Marxism and egalitarian liberalism – i.e., a mutual engagement that does not take the form of one discourse imperialistically absorbing the other. In other words, the pursuit of normative issues does not require one to abandon the explanatory social theory that has been Marxism's great intellectual strength. At the same time, Marxism may pose some challenging questions to egalitarian liberals about how their conceptions of justice can actually be realized.[12]

Of course, the idea of a dialogue between classical Marxism and egalitarian liberalism recalls earlier episodes – for example, those of Eduard Bernstein's revisionism and of Austro-Marxism around the beginning of the twentieth century, when neo-Kantian ethics were introduced into Marxism as part of a political attempt to deprive the latter of its revolutionary charge. Perhaps the memory of these attempts helped to motivate Daniel Bensaïd in declaring: 'Attempts to temper the critique of Marx with a theory of justice amount to a mixture of chalk and cheese.'[13] Certainly my aim here is not to water down the Marxist critique, but rather to make it more effective. In my view, taking egalitarian liberalism seriously means challenging it by showing, against its own assumptions, that its principles of justice can only be realized, not through the reform of capitalism, but its overthrow.[14] Moreover, for reasons that have been most powerfully stated by Bernard Williams, Kant does not offer to be the best model for understanding ethical and moral thought.[15] In the following section I sketch out a version of ethical naturalism whose key concept is the (ultimately Aristotelian) concept of well-being. In other words, I do not find it helpful to treat what Williams calls the 'peculiar institution' of morality as sharply differentiated from the rest of human life.

All the same, a main theme of part I was that a forced unification of explanatory social theory and normative political philosophy would be undesirable. This is not primarily because of the naturalistic fallacy, that is, the supposed impossibility of deriving 'ought' from 'is', the evaluative from the factual, but, in part, for more directly political reasons. Rawls's *Theory of Justice* has been frequently criticized for its abstraction – for its distance from the realities of contemporary social life. This criticism was initially made chiefly by Marxists, but it has been taken up and developed by communitarians such as Michael Walzer and Michael Sandel who deny the validity of any principle of justice that purports to transcend its particular social context.[16] But it seems to me that it is precisely from this abstraction, the lack of 'realism', that Rawls's theory, and indeed egalitarian liberalism more generally, derives its critical force. It is its very remoteness from what counts as feasible in the debased currency of contemporary liberal-democratic politics that makes the difference principle, according to which social and economic inequalities should only be tolerated when they benefit the worst off, a standing reproach to a world where inequalities are plainly arranged to benefit the best off.

The normative principles formulated by egalitarian liberalism are thus like the austere Modernist artefacts of Beckett and Schoenberg, which Adorno prized because in their stark abstraction they tacitly exposed the cruelty and injustice of the late capitalist world. But this comparison with Adorno highlights the difficulty with an egalitarianism that remains content merely to formulate universal principles commanding a profound reorganization of social life. For Adorno the social world was so comprehensively corrupted by commodity fetishism and instrumental reason as to deprive any agent perhaps of a material interest in transforming it, and certainly of the capacity to effect any significant change. The critical challenge and Utopian desires intimated by high Modernism were thus expressions more of despair than of resistance. The unmediated confrontation of normative critique and social reality may thus induce a sense of impotence rather than one of defiance. It is interesting that Rawls should have progressively retreated from the universalistic commitments of *A Theory of Justice* towards what Brian Barry crushingly dismisses as 'a rather muddled version of Michael Walzer's anti-Enlightenment particularism'; Rawls's later, political conception of justice aspires only to be the best articulation of the principles more or less explicitly governing the practice of liberal democratic polities.[17] The gap between philosophical theory and socio-political reality almost vanishes in his last book, *The Law of Peoples* (1999), where Rawls views the world through the categories of the State Department that counterpose liberal-democratic polities to 'failed' and 'rogue' states. The move here from abstract universalism to what the young Marx calls uncritical positivism is very striking: the attempt to free normative political theory from its confinement to philosophical abstraction ends up by transforming it into something dangerously close to a rationalization of superpower *Realpolitik*.[18]

7.2 Equality and well-being

The moral of this story is that it is necessary to establish what Marx in a very different context calls 'intermediary stages' between normative political philosophy and explanatory social theory.[19] Recent debates within egalitarian liberalism may help us to develop these connections. Perhaps the most extended and philosophically complex of these debates concerns what Cohen calls the currency of egalitarian justice.[20] When we say that persons should be treated equally, in what respect are we demanding that they be treated equally? As Amartya Sen points out, even champions of free-market liberalism such as Robert Nozick argue that *something* should be distributed equally, namely individual freedom. Forms of egalitarianism are distinguished according to how they answer the question: 'Equality of What?'[21] More specifically, granted that everyone should be allocated equal liberties, in what should *economic* equality consist? Just giving everyone the same monetary income won't do, since people have different needs and abilities. If a disabled person has the same income as an Olympic athlete then she is not being treated equally. So should society aim at equality of welfare? In other words, should we be trying to make everyone equally satisfied? This runs up against what is called the problem of expensive tastes. If I develop the desire to engage in space travel (which may become commercially available in a few years), should society pay for my trip? Most people would say 'No', but then I will be less satisfied than everyone else. This problem highlights the relationship between equality and responsibility. Ronald Dworkin in particular has argued that egalitarian justice seeks to remedy the consequences of bad 'brute luck' – that is, of the contingencies that disadvantage us through no fault of our own. The distribution of natural talents – described by Rawls as 'morally arbitrary' – is an example of brute luck. So too (though Dworkin is less clear about this) is the wealth that different individuals inherit.[22]

Dworkin's alternative is equality of resources. He imagines a hypothetical auction in which individuals, having been allocated an equal set of claims on society's resources, bid for different bundles of goods and services. The equilibrium outcome of these bids, adjusted for the insurance individuals take out to protect themselves against disadvantages that do not derive from their own choices (suffering disability, for example), constitutes equality of resources: public policy should as far as possible seek to approximate to this hypothetical state of affairs. This form of equality will produce great variety in individuals' material situations, since ambitions differ and so people will make quite different uses of their equal entitlement to resources. This is, however, no objection to equality of resources according to Dworkin, since egalitarians should seek only to remedy the consequences of bad brute luck, the unchosen natural and social contingencies that disadvantage some individuals: differences that flow from the choices individuals make on the basis of equality of resources constitute no injustice. It is then up to individuals to make whatever use they choose of those resources. If I choose to be lazy and squander my allocation, that's my problem. Or if I develop a yearning for space travel, then it is my responsibility to find a way of financing my trip out of my own share of resources.[23]

This ideal of equality of resources has been criticized for various reasons. I shall mention merely three here. First, Dworkin has been criticized for an excessively individualistic conception of justice. If I am disabled from birth, then plainly I am suffering from bad 'brute luck'. But what if, thanks to my own careless driving, I crash my car and am crippled for life? On the face of it, I am responsible for my plight. Does that mean I'm on my own?[24] In other words, Dworkin's strategy is to connect egalitarianism with an ideal that is often counterposed to it, particularly by the neo-liberal right – individual responsibility. But hasn't he made too many concessions to the right? Second, this strategy depends on drawing a distinction between choice and chance: 'We distinguish, for a thousand reasons, between what part of our fate is open to assignments of responsibility because it is the upshot of someone's choice, and what part is ineligible for any such assignment because it is the work not of people but of nature or brute luck.'[25] But individual choices and objective circumstances are not always so easy to separate. A poor and oppressed person may react to her situation by accepting it as fate. Her choices and the preferences these express may seem to reflect satisfaction with her circumstances. But one might argue that this is a case where, in the apparent absence of genuine alternatives, individual preferences have adapted to circumstances. To treat this outcome as really chosen by its victim would be to sanctify injustice.

A third problem with equality of resources is that, like equality of income, it is insensitive to differences in individual needs and capacities. If I am chronically ill, I won't benefit from the same bundle of resources as much as a healthy person. For this reason Sen has advanced a different ideal, equality of capabilities. He argues that the quality of a person's life consists in her ability to engage in as broad as possible a range of 'functionings', which range from states such as being healthy or well fed to complex activities such as those involved in the freedom reflectively to choose the life that I have reason to value. According to Sen, what we should be trying to equalize is the capability to have the widest range of functionings possible. This approach has the advantage of providing a criterion for assessing individual well-being that is more complex and subtle than the crude measures of national income favoured by conventional economic thinking. Sen has influenced the work of the United Nations Development Programme to develop a Human Development Index that provides a more accurate measure of progress.[26]

Like Dworkin, though in a different way, Sen connects equality and liberty. We should seek to equalize 'the substantive freedom to achieve alternative functioning combinations (or, less formally put, the freedom to achieve various lifestyles)'.[27] G. A. Cohen has argued that this involves a forced marriage of liberty and equality. It is, he suggests, really a misrepresentation to describe being healthy, for example, as a freedom or a capability: it is simply a condition or a state of being. Behind this criticism may be the thought that, however polemically useful it may be to appropriate the neo-liberals' favourite concept of freedom for egalitarian purposes, the effect is to efface crucial differences between distinct ideals that, though interrelated, have each their own particular content and rationale. Cohen proposes instead a broader and more neutral conception of equality, equality of access to advantage, where 'advantage' is understood as 'a heterogeneous collection of states of the person reducible neither to his resources bundle nor to his welfare bundle'.[28]

Equality of access to advantage is probably the most philosophically subtle of the different currencies of egalitarian justice, though it is hard to see in what the practical differences between its adoption and that of equality of capabilities would consist. Both conceptions of equality point us towards some broader theory of well-being conceived as an objective condition. This is a direction in which we are driven as soon as we reject the simpler forms of welfarism. Once we refuse to take preference-satisfaction at face value, then we cannot avoid distinguishing between an individual's well-being and her subjective perception of that condition. But this refusal is inherent in any serious egalitarianism. How otherwise can we deal with the case of the happy slave or contented housewife, who sincerely avows that she accepts her condition, however disadvantaged? Social critique must treat this as a case, if not of false consciousness, then of what Jon Elster calls 'adaptive preference': the housewife is content with her lot because she sees no way of changing it. But any such interpretation tacitly contrasts the housewife's actual preferences with the condition that would obtain were she to have equal access to advantage.[29]

Here larger philosophical questions emerge. The influence on Anglophone philosophy of utilitarianism is enormous. Utilitarianism defines the good we should be seeking in terms of maximizing the general welfare, where welfare is defined either as pleasurable mental states or (in modern discussion) as the satisfaction of desires. Equality of welfare as an ideal relies on the same conception of welfare. This is a subjectivist conception of individual well-being. But the Equality of What? debate highlights the limits of such a conception. As we have seen, individual preferences often adapt to circumstances. All a slave's desires may be satisfied – but only because she has renounced any desires incompatible with her wretched and oppressed situation. This suggests that properly to assess personal well-being we need to go beyond welfare conceived in subjective terms. We might, for example, make the benchmark not a person's actual desires, but the desires that she would have were she able rationally to reflect on her situation.[30] But this correction may not be sufficient. What if there is no prospect of the slave fleeing, or of a successful rebellion – let alone of the abolition of slavery as an institution: is her contentment then an accurate guide to her well-being?

These considerations seem, once again, to drive us towards a more objective conception of well-being – what Rawls calls 'perfectionism'. We could, for example, try to ground equality in the ideal of individual self-realization espoused by Aristotle, Marx, and John Stuart Mill. But such a move cuts across one of the deeper motivations for liberalism at least as it is defended by Rawls, namely that it offers a form of society which allows individuals and groups to pursue their own conceptions of the good. To justify an egalitarian distribution of resources on a perfectionist basis would seem to privilege one conception of the good – say, individual self-realization – over others. In other words, a properly worked out egalitarianism requires a theory of human flourishing, of what Aristotle called *eudaimonia* (well-being). This is a conclusion that Rawls would strongly resist. The relativist drift of his later work is in part motivated by his desire to detach his theory of justice from contamination by any conception of the good, even a liberal one. This evolution is hardly a good advertisement for anti-perfectionism. As we saw in chapters 1 and 2, substantive and universal normative principles are required to legitimize the practice of social critique, and in particular its readiness to find fault with prevailing forms.

The greater difficulty lies in how to state a defensible conception of well-being. The problem lies in the very thing that makes the idea attractive, namely that it implies that we can give some account, independently of the desires that individual humans actually have, of what will make their lives go well. In his outstanding exploration of conceptions of well-being, James Griffin draws the following contrast: 'Desire accounts focus on a person in all his individuality; objective list accounts focus on an index of goods that are good for everyone, regardless of the differences between them; perfectionist accounts focus on a species ideal.' According to Griffin, Aristotle, the acme of perfectionists, vacillates between making the ideal life consist in philosophical contemplation and developing the 'virtue version of moral perfectionism', according to which 'we should regard practical rationality, and the virtues in which it displays itself, not as a substantive account of the ideal life but a formal account of the modes of approach that will fix on the best life.' The first alternative is obviously untenable: it offers as an ideal the life of the leisured Athenian gentleman in a society based on the exclusion and exploitation of slaves and women (although this ideal has enjoyed a remarkable longevity thanks to its transformation by Christianity into the contemplation of God in Heaven by the saved). As to the second, Griffin accepts that '[t]here are prudential values that are valuable in any life' – for example, accomplishment, autonomy, liberty, understanding, enjoyment, deep personal relations, but '[t]here are not enough of them, nor is a specific balance between them prescribable universally enough, to constitute a *form of life*.'[31]

Moral perfectionism therefore cannot pick out a single form of human flourishing as the ideal towards which we should all gravitate: when it simply mandates a particular kind of life it is much too strong; when instead it offers a theory of the virtues it is too weak to specify the sort of life we should pursue. What damages these versions of perfectionism, Griffin argues, is the fact that the well-being with which we are concerned is about how well individual human lives go, and that depends on the particular perspective each of us has on the world. This is the rock on which, for example, attempts to equate well-being with the satisfaction of basic needs founder. Health is one obvious basic need – indeed, Len Doyal and Ian Gough argue that it is the most basic of human needs.[32] But Griffin points out that there are cases when health isn't that important to us. I may value other goals (my children's welfare, or pursuing a scientific project) even if the price of achieving them is to shorten my own life: 'Health, on its own, is not valuable; it is necessary to life, out of which each of us in his own case can make something valuable. But then what moral status has a necessary condition of a good life, in a case where achieving it will not allow one, and may prevent one, from having a good life?' He concludes that 'informed desires, as they figure in prudential values, go deeper than basic needs' because 'even objective universal values matter only by making individual lives better.'[33]

The idea of 'informed desire' is the basis of what Griffin self-deprecatingly calls a 'padded-out utilitarianism', according to which '[u]tility . . . is the fulfilment of desires that persons would have if they appreciated the true nature of their objects.' In fact, Griffin's account of well-being takes him well beyond any conventional utilitarianism. He is in particular concerned to go beyond what he describes as the dualisms of desire and understanding and subjective and objective: 'It is the strength of the notion of "informed desire" that it straddles – that is, does not accept – the divide between reason and desire.' Establishing the good for an individual requires

> knowledge not of a person's present, individual, perhaps idiosyncratic, tastes and preferences (these may not be for what is in his best interests) but of what in general makes life good. And if the person deviates from the norm, then we shall still need general causal knowledge about how persons of this sort work. For the most part what we need is the sort of knowledge of informed global preferences that is derivable from a general theory of prudential good and a causal theory of human nature.[34]

Thus 'the basic list of prudential values and unavoidable means provides an "objective" measure (in the sense that the measure does not depend on individual desires), which greatly eases the burden of interpersonal comparisons', though it is only a starting point because '[i]ndividuals differ in how, or even whether, they can realize some particular values.' Moreover, a theory of prudential value, on its own, gives us only a theory of the good for the individual – an account, that is, of what it is in the interest of the individual to pursue. Prudence isn't the same as morality: 'A valuable life . . . consists importantly in doing things with one's life that are themselves of sufficient value to turn back on the life itself and make it valuable. And we cannot see what we are doing in these necessary terms if we have no regard for, or if we damage, values generally, including the value of other people's lives.' The integration of the prudential and the moral requires the introduction of 'that vague but fateful notion of *equal respect*' that calls on the utilitarian goal of welfare maximization to incorporate 'a principle of equal chances of well-being', which seems close to Cohen's idea of equality of access to advantage. This requirement reflects the fact that '[e]quality is a very different kind of value from the others. Unlike autonomy and liberty, which focus in a way on one life, equality focuses on the comparison of lives. It is not a prudential value at all; it is a moral value, in a way *the* moral value.'[35]

This brief summary cannot do justice to the subtlety of Griffin's discussion of well-being, which probably provides the best basis on which to develop a defensible perfectionism. Griffin's approach invites two general reflections. First, the role played by the idea of equal respect in articulating the specifically moral dimension of well-being underlines how hard it is to escape Kant. One of the original impulses behind Rawls's political philosophy was to develop a theory of social justice that captured what he believed utilitarianism violated when setting as its goal the maximal satisfaction of the desires – somehow aggregated together – of all the persons belonging to a society, namely the intuition captured by the following version of Kant's categorical imperative: '*So act that you use humanity, whether in your own person or in the person of any other, always at the same time as an end, never merely as a means.*'[36] If the satisfaction of my desires is taken into account solely by being added, together with that of everyone else's, into an aggregate general welfare, where my interests may well turn out to be completely outweighed by those of others, surely I am being treated solely as a means rather than an end? Griffin rejects Rawls's critique of utilitarianism, but his appeal to the idea of equal respect to get us from prudence to morality seems like an acknowledgement of the Kantian thought that underlies this critique. It seems hard for modern moral philosophy to escape the space defined by Aristotle, Kant, and Bentham – with, perhaps, Nietzsche completing the square with an aristocratic critique of morality *tout court* that continues to have very powerful resonances.[37]

Secondly, though Griffin's informed-desire theory is offered as 'a natural development of classical utilitarianism', there are striking parallels between it and the more robustly perfectionist account of well-being developed by another Oxford philosopher, Joseph Raz.[38] For Raz, the concept of 'individual well-being . . . captures one crucial evaluation of a person's life: how good or successful it is from his point of view.' Well-being consists in 'the successful pursuit of valuable goals'. It is therefore irreducible to the satisfaction of a person's actual desires, and also of her biological needs. Like Griffin, Raz seeks to displace the opposition between reason and desire, and sees the concept of well-being bridging the gap between self-interest and morality. Though he argues that values depend on social forms, he highlights the value of autonomy for liberal societies, where an 'autonomous person's well-being consists in the successful pursuit of self-chosen goals and relationships.'[39] There are two main differences between these accounts of well-being. The first is that, while Griffin acknowledges that 'there are irreducibly many prudential values', he remains enough of a utilitarian to maintain that the concept of value itself is a 'quantitative value' that offers 'the ultimate scale' of 'worth to a life', allowing us to rank values and to make trade-offs between them.[40] Raz is a more radical pluralist, who asserts not simply that some goals are incommensurable, in that we cannot say either that one is better than another or that they are of equal value, but that there are 'constitutive incommensurabilities', where agents who have chosen one goal rather than the other remain steadfast in their refusal to entertain the alternative, finding the comparison between the two abhorrent, and 'the refusal to trade one option for another is a condition of the agent's ability successfully to pursue one of his goals.' Consequently, 'widespread incommensurabilities put paid to the hope of developing a general system or technology of calculation for practical reasoning.'[41]

The second difference is that, whereas, as we have seen, Griffin regards equality as perhaps '*the* moral value', Raz's liberal perfectionism is anti-egalitarian. He argues that equality is less a coherent or defensible ideal in its own right than a vehicle for other moral concerns:

> What makes us care about various inequalities is not the inequality but the concern identified by the underlying principle. It is the hunger of the hungry, the need of the needy, the suffering of the ill, and so on. The fact that they are worse off in the relevant respect than their neighbour is relevant. But it is relevant not as an independent evil of inequality. Its relevance is in showing that their hunger is greater, their need is more pressing, their suffering more hurtful, and therefore our concern for the hungry, the needy, the suffering, and not our concern for equality, makes us give them the priority.[42]

Partly for this kind of reason, a distinction has been drawn between egalitarianism and 'prioritarianism'. This latter position is concerned not with treating everyone equally, but with improving the situation of the worst off. Rawls's difference principle, which says that socio-economic inequalities are justified when they benefit the worst off, for example, might be seen as a prioritarian rather than an egalitarian ideal. One attraction of prioritarianism is that it avoids what is called the levelling-down objection to equality as an ideal. This is the ancient argument that for egalitarians any change is welcome so long as it increases equality. So, for example, if half the population has one eye, and half are completely blind, blinding those with one eye will produce a better outcome, since everyone will then be equally badly off. Much of the force of this objection is removed once one treats equality not as the sole political ideal, but as one of several interrelated but distinct ideals. If, for example, one values liberty as well as equality, then blinding the half-blind is unacceptable if for no other reason than it violates their personal autonomy.[43]

7.3 Why equality matters

Acknowledging the plurality of ideals does not itself provide a justification for the specific ideal of equality. Jeremy Waldron has set out what he calls the principle of basic equality as 'an assumption of moral and political thought', as opposed to the specification of the kind of equality that we should be seeking that is the focus of the Equality of What? debate:

> E_1: Moral argument ranges over the good of all human beings, and that range does not admit of any further fundamental human divisions (e.g. into men and women, black and white, etc.).[44]

E_1 introduces the idea of what Waldron calls 'an undifferentiated human range' as the relevant domain of moral argument. This poses the question of why all humans should be included in this range. It would plainly be a mistake to answer this question by saying all humans are equally deserving, since, on any plausible account of desert that distinguishes it from the general concept of entitlement, what a person deserves depends on what she does, introducing difference into the range that must, as Waldron suggests, be undifferentiated for the principle of basic equality to have the required content.[45] It would also be a mistake to say that E_1

is justified by the fact that humans are equal in ability, since this would be to affirm a falsehood. Rawls's argument for disjoining justice and desert expresses the thought that the differences in ability that are reflected in greater or lesser individual productivity depend on the distribution of natural talents, which is not chosen by those who benefit (or suffer) from it – in other words, which is a case of what Dworkin calls 'brute luck' whose consequences cannot be deserved by those advantaged or disadvantaged by it. Waldron suggests that the idea of an undifferentiated human range needs to be backed up by the identification of what Rawls calls a range property – roughly speaking, a property that one either has or hasn't got and that, if one has it, one does so in virtue of being within a certain range on the scale connoted by that property – common in the appropriate way to all humans. He cites as an example Colonel Rainborough's famous remark during the Putney Debates of 1647, at the height of the English Revolution 'that the poorest he that is in England has a life to lead as the greatest he':

> the implication was that even though the poorest person's life might differ in some sort of objective significance from that of the greatest person, still it mattered to the poor person as much as the greatest person's life mattered to the greatest person. *Mattering to the person who lives it* might therefore be a range property that applies to all lives, despite their different locations in a range of 'objective significance'.[46]

Rawls's own preferred range property is 'the capacity for moral personality', where '[m]oral persons are distinguished by two features: they are capable of having (and are assumed to have) a conception of the good . . . ; second they are capable of having (and are assumed to acquire) a sense of justice, a normally effective desire to apply and to act upon the principles of justice, at least to a certain minimum degree.' He insists that

> the sufficient condition for equal justice, the capacity for moral personality, is not at all stringent. When someone lacks the relevant potentiality, either from birth or accident, this is regarded as a defect or deprivation. There is no race or recognized group of human beings that lacks this attribute. Only scattered individuals are without this capacity, or its realization to the minimum degree,

and the failure to realize it is a consequence of unjust or impoverished social circumstances, or fortuitous contingencies. Furthermore, while individuals presumably have varying capacities for a sense of justice, this fact is not a reason for depriving those with a lesser capacity of the full protection of justice. Once a certain minimum is met, a person is entitled to equal justice on a par with everyone else.[47]

As Waldron notes, 'Rawls's position is avowedly Kantian . . . Kant too emphasized the common human capacity to grasp and respond to the moral law.'[48] Once again we see that articulating and defending equality as an ideal drives us back to Kant. My guess is that ultimately the source of any such justification must derive from his demand that humans are treated as ends and not merely as means. Raz dismisses appeal to such considerations: 'principles of equal respect or concern, etc., amount to little more than an assertion that all human beings are moral subjects, to an assertion of humanism.'[49] But it doesn't seem as if the thought is quite as wishy-washy as all that. Not everyone would accept the idea of equal respect. Waldron cites this remarkable passage from a major work on moral philosophy, first published in 1907, by Hastings Rashdall, Fellow and Tutor at New College, Oxford:

> It is becoming tolerably obvious at the present day that all improvement in the social condition of the higher races of mankind postulates the exclusion of competition with the lower races. This means that, sooner or later, the lower Well-being – it may ultimately be the very existence – of countless Chinamen or negroes must be sacrificed that a higher life may be possible for a much smaller number of white men. It is impossible to defend the morality of such a policy upon the principle of equal consideration taken by itself and in the most obvious sense of the word . . . Individuals, or races, with higher capacities (i.e. capacities for a higher sort of Well-being) have a right to more than equal consideration as compared to those of lower capacities. Hence the formula, 'Everyone to count for one, nobody for more than one,' must be interpreted to mean 'everyone's good to count for as much as the like good of any one else'.[50]

Here, then, is a formidably anti-egalitarian perfectionism: this underlines the importance of conceptualizing well-being as a means of focusing on how well a person's life goes *for that person,* rather than ranking 'higher' and 'lower' kinds of well-being and hence of persons. But, quite aside from the conceptual issues that Rashdall's remarks raise, the fact that a highly respected Oxford philosopher could write what he did a hundred years ago helps us to understand why the twentieth century was one of racial exterminations – exterminations, for the Holocaust was only the worst of these. Of course, precisely because of Auschwitz, hardly anyone would openly affirm anything resembling Rashdall's view today. But even if denying equal human worth has gone out of fashion in public discourse, that doesn't mean it has disappeared from social practice. Indeed, one might say that one of the particular obscenities of our own age is that, while enormous lip-service is paid to the *idea* of equal respect, that idea is systematically violated as a routine feature of the social world.

A couple of examples may help to bring the moral issues into focus. First of all, one of the many controversies provoked by the war in Iraq has concerned the number of Iraqis killed by the Anglo-American occupation forces. One difficulty in resolving this argument is that, while the occupiers keep a scrupulously presented (if carefully managed) record of their own casualties, they refuse as a matter of principle to count the number of Iraqi dead. This task has been left to unofficial investigators – for example, a team of public health experts who estimated in October 2004 that 100,000 Iraqi civilians had died as a result of their country's invasion by the United States and Britain, primarily in air attacks.[51] The Pentagon, which disputes such estimates, justifies its own refusal to keep figures of the Iraqi dead primarily by appeal to the example of the Vietnam War, when the obsession of the White House and senior US commanders with enemy body counts helped to produce both military defeat and a human catastrophe. But it's hard not to see the refusal to count Iraqis as implying that they don't count in another sense – that is, in the sense in which Rashdall suggests the utilitarian principle that 'Everyone to count for one, nobody for more than one' should, in effect, be reinterpreted so that some people – members of the 'lower races' – count for less than one.

To believe that, in practice, US policy in Iraq implicitly treats Iraqis as not counting as much as Americans doesn't require one to believe that this policy is directed by consciously racist attitudes towards Iraqis (or to Arabs in general or to Muslims). It is more a matter of tracking the regular, and predictable, effects of the policy. This is brought out by a closely related issue. The study of Iraqi deaths cited above reminds us that, in Iraq as elsewhere, the most important single way in which US military power is projected is through the use of bombers and missiles. Of course, air strikes predictably kill many civilians. These deaths are placed by the Pentagon in a different category from those killed in combat, and labelled 'collateral damage'. This neutralizing vocabulary is presumably meant to convey the thought that the killing of civilians by American air strikes is an unintended, and unwelcome, side-effect of US forces pursuing their main task by conducting military operations against armed enemies. But it's not obvious that this thought is sufficient to absolve US military personnel (and their civilian chiefs) from responsibility for 'collateral damage'. After all, the crime of manslaughter is designed specifically to address cases of unintentional killing where the perpetrator can be shown to have been negligent in a relevant way. Moreover, killing civilians in air strikes isn't just a one-off accident, but a regular and predictable consequence of the use of air power. So even if US pilots and their commanders, civilian and military, don't set out with the aim of killing civilians, they know that they probably will. They cannot therefore disclaim responsibility for this outcome of their actions.

Of course, this isn't enough to say that they shouldn't carry out the air strikes. Even if we leave aside the controversy over the saturation bombing of Germany and Japan during the Second World War, allied air attacks on transport links in the run up to D-Day killed 12,000 French and Belgian civilians.[52] One might still want to say that these attacks were nevertheless justified by the aim of defeating Nazi Germany – balancing up the civilian deaths predictably caused by bombing France and Belgium against all the gains implied by ridding the world of the National Socialist regime might be a case of the kind of trade-off that Griffin argues we must make and doesn't in any obvious way violate the principle of basic equality. Of course, defenders of the Iraq War would argue that the felicific calculus would reach the same conclusion in this case – the civilian death toll in Iraq is counterbalanced by the benefits produced by getting rid of Saddam Hussein and bringing liberal democracy to Iraq. But, in the first place, even if the war could be so justified (which I don't believe it can), this would not absolve the perpetrators of air strikes of responsibility for the civilian deaths they cause – something that American and British political and military leaders regularly deny. Secondly, quite aside from the question of the real motives for the war, the kind of contrast we see in Iraq – the care taken to avoid US and British casualties with the regular and predictable killing of large numbers of Iraqi civilians by American air power – does look like a violation of basic equality, particularly since the two are connected: one of the main attractions of using air power is that it reduces the extent to which your own troops are put in harm's way. Of course, it would be silly to demand that today's generals should return to the practices of their predecessors during the First World War and positively seek casualties, but the pattern in which the great military powers can inflict large-scale death with a high degree of impunity does make many people feel morally queasy. One way of articulating the reasons for this queasiness would be to contend that this pattern violates the principle of basic equality.

The trouble is that the Anglo-American way of waging war from the air isn't the only case in the contemporary world where avoidable deaths are regularly and predictably caused, although not directly aimed at. Indeed, poverty and inequality kill in this way on a far larger scale than the Pentagon. Thomas Pogge has assembled a set of stomach-turning turning statistics: in 1998 1,214 million out of the 5,820 million human beings then alive had an income of less than 1 US dollar a day; 2.8 billion were living on less than $2 a day, the poverty line set by the World Bank; 18 million people die prematurely each year from poverty-related causes, one-third of all human deaths. Pogge estimates that 250 million people died of starvation and preventable diseases in the fourteen years following the end of the Cold War: 'The names of these people, if listed in the style of the Vietnam War Memorial, would cover a wall 350 miles long.'[53]

Mass poverty persists in the context of growing global inequality: the ratio of the income of the richest fifth of the world's population to that of the poorest fifth has risen from 30:1 in 1960 to 60:1 in 1990 and 74:1 in 1997.[54] Pogge calculates that inequality – particularly between North and South – is now so great that a mere 1 per cent of aggregate global income, equivalent to $312 billion a year, would be sufficient to eradicate severe poverty world-wide.[55] Therefore, '[f]or the first time in human history, it is quite feasible, economically, to wipe out hunger and preventable diseases without real inconvenience to anyone.'[56] It is worth reflecting that this sum is significantly less than the US defence budget: the Bush administration requested no less than \$419.3 billion for the fiscal year 2006.[57] One does not have to be an egalitarian to support such a transfer: it could be justified on quite conservative grounds of charity, or by the imperative to reduce suffering invoked, for example, by Raz. Pogge argues that failure to do so leaves the rich countries of the North responsible for those 18 million deaths a year, even if no one in those countries positively seeks them:

> there are at least three morally significant connections between us and the global poor. First, their social starting positions and ours have emerged from a single historical process that was pervaded by massive grievous wrongs. The same historical injustices, involving genocide, colonialism, and slavery, play a role in explaining both their poverty and our affluence. Second, they and we depend on a single natural resource base, from the benefits of which they are largely, and without compensation, excluded. The affluent countries and the elites of the developing world divide these resources on mutually agreeable terms without 'leaving enough and as good' for the remaining majority of mankind. Third, they and we coexist within a single global economic order that has a strong tendency to perpetuate and even to aggravate global economic inequality.
>
> Given these connections, our failure to make a serious effort toward poverty reduction may constitute not merely a lack of beneficence, but our active impoverishing, starving, and killing of millions of people by economic means.[58]

Pogge goes astray here in treating North and South as largely undifferentiated entities (he makes an exception for elites in poor countries who benefit from 'the privileges freely to borrow in the country's name . . . and freely to dispose of the country's natural resources').[59] There are enormous inequalities in wealth, income, and access to resources and to political power in the North as well: how much control over the policies of their rulers and the great transnational corporations do most citizens of the US or the European Union have?[60] But Pogge's basic point is surely right. The prevailing inequalities in the world today lead to millions of avoidable deaths. These deaths – and all the other forms of suffering that go along with them – are systemically caused: they are a predictable result of the routine operation of existing social and economic structures. But the fact that no one may intend these deaths does not mean that no one is responsible for them happening, just as American commanders and aircrew cannot disclaim responsibility for the civilian deaths that they regularly and predictably cause. This analysis raises all kinds of questions, but the one on which I want to focus is of how precisely to characterize what is going wrong here. Pogge argues that tolerating deaths caused by poverty violates the overriding negative duty we all have 'not to wrong (unduly harm) others': 'By continuing to support the global order and the national policies that shape and sustain it without taking compensating action toward institutional reform or shielding its victims, we share a negative responsibility for the undue harms they foreseeably produce.'[61] But of course this begs the question of the range governed by such duties: who counts as an other whom we must not harm? Here again the idea of basic equality plays a role by requiring that any human count as much as any other. More generally, when trying to spell out what is so morally awful about the way in which the accident of birth condemns millions to either an early death or a short and miserable life, it seems to me that it isn't just a matter of the suffering involved, but also the fact that, thanks to the impersonal mechanisms of the capitalist world economy, so many people are counted as less than one, as worthy of less attention and care than those fortunate enough – in Dworkin's sense of brute luck – to be born into more favoured circumstances. So equality as an ideal has some bite: it isn't the kind of vague humanist waffle that Raz dismisses it as.

How would one give this ideal more content? An egalitarian perfectionist might, for example, say that each person should be provided with resources that will give her an equal opportunity to achieve well-being (where well-being, as we have seen, cannot be reduced to the satisfaction of a person's actual preferences). As a conception of justice this is broadly consonant with the realist social ontology defended in the previous two chapters. Building the concept of well-being into the idea of egalitarian justice doesn't commit one to moral realism strictly defined, i.e., to the idea that evaluative sentences are true or false in the same way as any other class of assertoric sentences is.[62] (Although, as a matter of fact, I do accept moral realism.) But, in relating our moral judgements to how well a person's life goes – and, once equality comes into the picture, to how others' lives go – it does require us to attend closely to what human beings are like, both in general and in specific societies, and to the circumstances likely to promote their flourishing in these different contexts – in other words, to the subject matter of what Griffin calls 'a causal theory of human nature'. This provides a possible junction point between normative political philosophy and explanatory social theory. To see how this might work, consider the concept of equal opportunity just outlined. It is important to see that 'opportunity' must be understood here as objective – that is, a person's access to advantage doesn't depend on her beliefs about what access she has, but on the opportunities, i.e., the set of choices, really provided her by the prevailing social mechanisms.[63] Now any social theory must have a theory of social structure. But, as I argue in §6.1 above, precisely what structure does is to endow persons with specific powers to realize their ends.[64] This is true, for example, of the Marxist theory of the forces and relations of production, which comprise, respectively, human productive capacities and the modes of effective control of these capacities. But it is also true of Weberian conceptions of social structure, for example, Michael Mann's theory of power networks.[65]

On this account, then, egalitarian perfectionism would state principles of justice, while explanatory social theory identifies the social mechanisms that to a greater or lesser extent confer on individuals the opportunities required by these principles. More concretely, given the scale of the global inequalities discussed above, the particular importance of explanatory social theory for normative political philosophy is that it provides the basis of a realistic account of the sources of social injustice. Jacques Bidet in his study of Rawls notes the latter's failure to thematize the problem of *in*justice and the ethics and politics of overcoming it.[66] This failure became even starker with the passage of time. Rawls in *The Law of Peoples* refuses to give the difference principle a cosmopolitan extension by applying it to the world as a whole. He contends that 'the crucial element in how a country fares is its political culture – its members' political and civic virtues – and not the level of its resources.'[67] The implication is that societies are poor not, for example, because of their position in the global economy, but because of their domestic political culture, which, in effect, they have chosen. Their plight is not a matter of brute bad luck but of the choices embodied in their social and political institutions. All this is particularly odd because, when discussing justice within nation-states, Rawls takes precisely the contrary position, famously insisting:

> We do not deserve our place in the distribution of natural endowments, any more than we deserve our initial starting place in society. That we deserve the superior character that enables us to make the effort to cultivate our abilities is also problematic; for such character depends in good part upon fortunate family and social circumstances in early life for which we can claim no credit.[68]

So individual persons don't deserve their characters and therefore aren't entitled materially to benefit from what they allow us to do (unless this also benefits the worst off), but societies deserve their political cultures and hence the wealth or poverty to which these may condemn them. Quite aside from the inconsistency involved, the result is a conception of global justice that closely accords with the Washington Consensus, according to which societies are poor because of their failure to adopt the appropriate norms of 'good governance', which mandate them to embrace neo-liberalism and open their markets to the transnational corporations. An alternative approach, in line with the strategy sketched out above, would involve two distinct, though mutually interdependent, elements. First, it would explicitly integrate into its conception of justice cosmopolitanism, which Barry defines as 'a moral stance consisting of three elements: individualism, equality, and universality. Its unit of value is individual human beings; it does not recognize any categories of people as having less or more moral weight; and it includes all human beings.'[69] One might think of cosmopolitanism in this sense as a kind of geographical specification of Waldron's concept of an undifferentiated human range – but it has the radical implication that principles of justice apply globally. It differs from the cosmopolitanism of Jacques Bidet because Bidet relies on a combination of assertion – that the social contract necessarily has a planetary extension – and the loosely Hegelian idea that politics is assuming a cosmopolitan form thanks to the tendential emergence of a global state to regulate the capitalist world system (see

§1.2 above). What is missing is any attempt to develop a properly *normative* conception of cosmopolitan justice, some of whose prerequisites have emerged in this chapter.

But any conception is necessarily incomplete without the contribution, secondly, of a realistic political economy of poverty and inequality. This would start off by filling out the structural context that endows actors with the capacities to pursue their goals. The assessment by one leading Marxist political economist, Giovanni Arrighi, of the plight of sub-Saharan Africa, the poorest of the world's regions, is in this respect exemplary, contrasting dramatically with Rawls's effort apparently to blame the victims: it reconstructs the constellation of circumstances – the impact of the global crisis of the 1970s and 1980s, the consequent recentralization of financial and military power in the United States, the comparative historical and economic disadvantages from which Africa suffered in responding (compared above all to East Asia), and the political failure of African elites – that have condemned so many of the continent's inhabitants to misery. Arrighi is careful not to absolve these elites of their share of responsibility for this situation:

> while there may be little that most states can do to upgrade their national economies in the global hierarchy of wealth, there is always something they can do to increase (or decrease) the well-being of its citizenry at any level of poverty or wealth . . . From this standpoint, most African ruling groups have probably done far less than was in their power to do.[70]

This kind of analysis invites us to probe the complex interplay between structure and agency in the making of global poverty and inequality. More broadly, through a process of mutual interrogation and cooperation, egalitarian normative philosophy and Marxist political economy could provide a formidable intellectual frame in which to throw into sharp relief the nature and causes of the injustices that still dominate our world.

8

Conclusion

The argument of this book has described two movements. First, in part I, I developed what amounted to an immanent critique of a series of contemporary theorists – Jürgen Habermas, Jacques Bidet, Luc Boltanski, Eve Chiapello, Pierre Bourdieu, Alain Badiou, Slavoj Žižek, and Antonio Negri. This was an immanent critique to the extent that, rather than find them wanting according to a set of independently established standards, I sought to show how these different theorists had failed in their own terms to provide a sound philosophical basis for social critique and, more broadly, for transcendence, understood as our ability to go beyond the limits set by existing beliefs and practices. The argument developed on to an ever broader terrain, concluding as it did by focusing on two of the most philosophically ambitious of today's radical thinkers, Badiou and Negri. In part II, I have tried to outline some elements of an alternative approach that would allow us more effectively to conceptualize transcendence. Here I went beyond a purely immanent critique, which is supposed to arrive at positive results solely from the content generated from the theories criticized. The three main themes of part II – a realist ontology, a Marxist theory of structural contradiction, and a free-standing normative conception of egalitarian justice – cannot be found in any of the theorists discussed in part I; their pertinence lies in the fact that they are necessary to overcome the weaknesses and limitations exposed by my critique.[1]

In this concluding chapter I want to bring together the arguments of parts I and II by highlighting what seem to me some of their main implications. In doing so I sometimes repeat, but also sometimes extend, points that have already been established.

(1) **Ontology matters** This is the result that has most surprised me personally. Despite (or sometimes because of) Heidegger's attempt to revive the thinking of Being as such, a main thrust of twentieth-century philosophy has been to liberate itself from ontology, for example, in the form of the primarily epistemological, methodological, and increasingly historical focus of much philosophy of science and in that of the deconstruction of the metaphysics of presence practised by Derrida. I have personally been much influenced by Gaston Bachelard's critique of ontology as a means whereby idealist philosophers seek to control and direct scientific research. But it is, in principle, impossible to separate epistemology and ontology: realism, for example, in offering a particular picture of the relationship of thought and the world, carries implications about how that world is. Paul Feyerabend once highlighted the interdependence of epistemological criteria and cosmological theories by arguing that the formulation of what is now a commonplace, the idea of the sciences as engaged in a potentially infinite progress, was dependent on acceptance, consequent on the Copernican revolution, of the proposition that the universe itself is infinite:

> The idea that nature is infinitely rich both qualitatively and quantitatively leads to the desire to make new discoveries and thus to a principle of content increase which gives us another standard to judge theories by: theories that have excess content over what is already known are preferable to theories that have not . . . The demand has no point in a finite world that is composed of a finite number of basic qualities.[2]

The boundaries between ontology, epistemology, and empirical science are thus highly porous. While aware of this general truth, I did not expect ontology to loom so large when it came to contemporary critical theory. But, as it turns out, for example, Boltanski's and Chiapello's anti-realism proved to have greatly limited the critical scope of their account of the rise of the new spirit of capitalism. Two very different, indeed in some ways directly opposed, ontologies, moreover, inform Badiou's and Negri's thought. Hence in chapter 5 I took the trouble to spell out how the kind of critical realist ontology developed by Roy Bhaskar could accommodate the strengths and overcome the weaknesses of these metaphysical accounts. I must confess some vestigial wariness about the whole subject. Because any ontology is an a priori theory it is enormously open to arbitrariness and the extravagances of the imagination. The example that Feyerabend gives of how the new cosmology that emerged from the scientific revolution made possible changes in ontology and epistemology gives an illustration of how things should work, with breakthroughs in explanatory theory forcing rethinking of philosophical presuppositions, but this immensely simplified picture of a very complex historical process is at best only indicative of how things go in these matters when they go well.[3]

(2) **The centrality of the Marxist critique of political economy**
There might seem to be a big jump from the preceding rarefied reflections on ontology to Marx's *Capital*, but the move is less arbitrary than it seems. In chapter 6 I sought to cash in the critical realist ontology previously sketched out by developing a Marxist theory of social contradiction. Such a theory can pull in different directions – towards a dialectic of nature (§6.3), towards Marx's general theory of history, towards his special theory of the capitalist mode of production. It is consonant with Marx's own abiding preoccupations, but also, more important, the most appropriate response to our current predicament to take the third path. For a dominating fact about that predicament is that the world is increasingly shaped by a rather pure version of the logic of capital, embodied in the policy prescriptions of neo-liberalism and the Washington Consensus. One good reason for having a strong theory of social structure is the better to understand the very powerful structures on which our capacities to live our lives, and perhaps to change our world, currently depend.

The fact that the interpretation of Marx's *Capital* has repeatedly figured in the course of this book is not simply a consequence of the biographies of various of the thinkers discussed here (or indeed of the author). Any critical theory worth the name today has to situate itself with respect to capitalism and that means with respect to the most consequent body of writing about that economic system, namely the Marxist critique of political economy. It is an abiding weakness of Badiou's thought that even in his Marxist days he had no time for that critique, of Habermas's that in the theory of communicative action the capitalist mode of production vanishes beneath the functionalist logic of social integration, of Boltanski's and Chapiello's that we have in principle no access to capitalism outside the ideal political communities from which its spirit is formed, and of Hardt's and Negri's that in *Empire* and *Multitude* the logic of capital gives way before the immanent triumph of productive Life. In a world ruled so comprehensively by capital, we need still to read *Capital*.

It should be clear enough that I am not commending a pious reading that seeks to extract and reaffirm lessons for the faithful. Our discussions of Bidet and Negri in particular highlighted important ambiguities in Marx's discourse: like any complex theoretical work *Capital* demands critical interrogation. More than that, Marx's critique of political economy needs to be continued in new original work. For all their limitations, the Marxisms of the Second and Third International did extend Marx's own analysis, in particular by seeking to conceptualize the specific phase of capitalist development that they called finance capital or (under Lenin's influence) imperialism.[4] Subsequently, Marxist political economy has developed in various directions, many of them productive. But the political conjuncture since 11 September 2001 commands a renewed focus on the problem of imperialism. Here the direction taken by David Harvey seems exemplary. Author of *The Limits to Capital* (1982), a work that combined a rigorous critical reading of Marx's concepts with an attempt to open them up to help analyse in particular the process of 'time–space compression' that he argues is distinctive to capitalism, Harvey has more recently sought to reformulate the Marxist theory of capitalist imperialism. Imperialism, he argues, must be seen as the 'contradictory fusion' of two logics of power, which he calls, following Giovanni Arrighi, the capitalist and the territorial: 'The relation between these two logics should be seen, therefore, as problematic and often contradictory (that is, dialectical) rather than as functional or one-sided.'[5] This kind of Marxist approach to imperialism, which conceptualizes it non-reductively as the intersection of two distinct forms of competition, economic and geopolitical, permits us to analyse the global strategy of the Bush administration as a response to both the long-term general crisis of over-accumulation and profitability and the shifting distribution of economic and political power among the leading states.[6] An analysis of this kind is essential to a critical theory capable of confronting what Giorgio Agamben calls the global state of exception in whose shadow we now all live.

(3) **The status of critique** Marx's ambition was to develop a theory that was simultaneously explanatory and critical. In order to highlight this I have tended to use the title, or subtitle, of all his major economic texts – the critique of political economy – when referring to this theory.[7] Marx tried to develop an explanatory theory that exposed the mechanisms of capitalist exploitation and crisis without appealing to normative conceptions and ideals. This was, in my view, simply a mistake induced in particular by the influence of Hegel's critique of Kant. But different versions of the same mistake also appear in the critical theories discussed in part I. It would be a worthwhile investigation in its own right to consider why radical thought has been so preoccupied with avoiding giving itself some kind of moral reference. Perhaps there is a common fear of trapping critique in an ineffectual condemnation of the present, an abstract ethical 'beyond' that lacks any means of effectively engaging with forces capable of bringing about change. But whatever the deeper reasons for this evasion of the normative, it remains an error. In chapter 7 I sought, by critically examining some of the philosophical issues raised by contemporary egalitarian conceptions of justice, to sketch out a strategy for beginning to remedy this weakness. Some of these issues are very difficult, and I am all too conscious of the gaps in my argument. All the same, even if this strategy proves not to be the best way to address the problem, the problem itself remains unavoidable.

It is, however, not the only one posed by the project of social critique. The very idea of a critical theory pulls away from the ideal of impartiality deeply embedded in the Western philosophical tradition. Critique arises where there is some internal conflict in the whole, when society is divided against itself.[8] The Marxist conception of social contradiction offers a way of thematizing this kind of constitutive division. But when society is thus split, surely any perspective can only be a partial and partisan one that denies us access to universality and truth. But critical thought has frequently challenged precisely the thought expressed in the last sentence. For Badiou, for example, the truth of an event emerges only from the perspective of an interpreting intervention that is faithful to it. Žižek has highlighted the parallel between this marriage of partiality and truth and a certain strand in Marxism:

> Within the Marxist tradition, this notion of partiality as not only not an obstacle to but a positive condition of Truth was most clearly articulated by Georg Lukács in his early work *History and Class Consciousness*, and in a more directly messianic, proto-religious mode by Walter Benjamin in 'Theses in the Philosophy of History': 'truth' emerges when a victim, from his present catastrophic position, gains a sudden insight into the entire past as a series of catastrophes that led to his current predicament.[9]

It is indeed Lukács in the great essay 'Reification and the Consciousness of the Proletariat' who most fully develops the 'notion of partiality as . . . a positive condition of Truth'. He argues that it is the specific position of the working class within capitalist relations of production that offers the sole perspective from which these relations can be understood as a totality:

> Above all, the worker can only become conscious of his existence in society when he becomes aware of himself as a commodity. As we have seen, his immediate existence integrates him as pure, naked object in the production process. Once this immediacy turns out to be the consequence of a multiplicity of mediations, once it becomes evident how much it presupposes, then the fetishistic forms of the commodity system begin to dissolve: in the commodity the worker recognizes himself and his own relations with capital. Inasmuch as he is incapable in practice of raising himself above the role of object his consciousness is the *self-consciousness of the commodity*; or in other words it is the self-knowledge, the self-revelation of the capitalist society founded upon the production and exchange of commodities.[10]

It is the worker's status as the 'absolute commodity', the apex of the reified relations of capitalist society, that provides the standpoint from which the nature of these relations can be properly understood as part of the process of abolishing them: 'the purely abstract negativity in the life of the worker is objectively the most typical manifestation of reification, it is the constitutive type of capitalist socialization. But for this very reason it is also *subjectively* the point at which this structure is raised to consciousness and where it can be breached in practice.' Lukács presents this argument as a development of Marx's conception in the 1843 *Introduction* of the proletariat as the universal class whose particular interests are identical to those of society as a whole.[11] As we have seen, Bourdieu's theory of the intellectual is another variant of the same conception, in which the particular properties of the scientific field generate an interest in the universal (§2.2 above). Despite its interesting qualities, Bourdieu's argument doesn't stand up, if only because of the ambiguity in his conception of universality between scientific objectivity and the irreducibly normative claims of equality and liberty. But his attempt to breathe life into the idea that a partial perspective offers access to the universal indicates that its suggestive power is far from exhausted.

Badiou, Žižek, and Stathis Kouvelakis also draw on Marx's conception of the proletariat as the universal class (§3.3). But their treatment is less interesting because they all distinguish sharply between the proletariat as political subject and the working class as social class. The effect is to relax the tension between particularity and universality, partiality and truth, that makes the idea so powerful. If 'proletariat' is merely one of those empty signifiers that, according to Ernesto Laclau, are employed in hegemonic articulations, then it can be used to give shape to any old raw material. Its actual class referent, if any, is a matter of the kind of empirical contingency that Badiou treats with such sovereign contempt. Rejecting this kind of approach does not, however, mean simply equating working class and proletariat, so long as we see these concepts as expressing the difference between the occupants of a set of structural places and a collectivity. A class, in other words, is a set of agents who share the same structural capacities, or, to put it in more explicitly Marxist terms, who occupy the same position in the relations of production. A collectivity, on the other hand, is a group of agents who coordinate their actions because they believe themselves to share a common identity. A class (or a part of a class) may become a collectivity, but there is nothing automatic about this.[12] The ability, then, of the proletariat to act as the universal class, as a revolutionary political subject, depends on whether workers develop the necessary sense of shared identity required for them to become a collectivity.

Is there an actual or potential universal class today that can act as the bearer of social critique? I have discounted Bourdieu's claim that intellectuals can play such a role. Hardt's and Negri's conception of the multitude as the new revolutionary subject does not stand up to closer examination, both because of its inadequacies as a concept in class analysis and because of its vitalist presuppositions (§4.3). What about Lukács's original position? He takes from Hegel 'the grandiose conception that thought can only grasp what it has itself created', and accordingly conceives the proletariat as 'the identical subject-object of the social and historical processes of evolution', a kind of empirical substitute for the Absolute Spirit.[13] But there is no need to proceed on such a radically idealist basis. One of Lukács's most powerful insights was the formulation of what I have called 'a perspectival conception of ideology', according to which a person's beliefs are likely to reflect the perspective on the social totality that her own position in that totality, and more specifically in the class structure, gives her.[14] (Here again Bourdieu is remarkably close to Lukács: 'Each field is the institutionalization of a point of view in things and in habitus.')[15] The mechanisms of capitalist society can thus only be understood from the perspective of the class on whose exploitation these mechanisms depend; the perspective of the bourgeoisie within the capitalist social fields gives them, by contrast, only a limited grasp of these mechanisms. Fredric Jameson comments:

> Such an approach posits ideology in terms of *strategies of containment* . . . Lukács's achievement was to have understood such strategies of containment – which Marx himself described principally in his critiques of classical political economy and in the ingenious frames the latter constructed in order to avoid the ultimate consequences of such insights as the relationship between labour and value – can be unmasked only by confrontation with the ideal which they at once confront and repress . . . Here Marxism is no doubt implied as that thinking which knows no boundaries of this kind, and which is infinitely totalizable, but the ideological critique does not depend on some dogmatic or 'positive' conception of Marxism as a system. Rather, it is simply the place of an imperative to totalize, and the various historical forms of Marxism can themselves equally effectively be submitted to just such a critique of their own local ideological limits or strategies of containment.[16]

From the perspective of this 'imperative to totalize', the real difficulty lies with the proletariat itself. The revolutionary imagination
of the twentieth century took as its social reference point the proletarian collectivity forged from the working class that emerged
from the second Industrial Revolution, out of the great industrial
plants of Petrograd and Turin, Berlin and Glasgow, Detroit and
Billaincourt, Gdańsk and São Paulo. But we live today amid the
ruins of this working-class collectivity, which was systematically
dismantled – deconstructed, as Boltanski and Chiapello put it – in
the great neo-liberal offensive and capitalist restructuring of the
past generation. There remain, nevertheless, good reasons for
holding on to the idea of the proletariat as the universal class. I
emphasize two here. First, as I have already argued, contemporary
capitalism is tending, if anything, to generalize the socio-economic
category of wage-labour rather than to abolish it. Today's working
class is concentrated in new places – for example, in the factory
complexes of the Pearl River Delta in southern China – and in new
kinds of workplaces – hypermarkets and call-centres, for instance
– but these novelties do not mean that capital is any less dependent on its labour, even if that labour may not lead to any identifiable physical product. But what cannot be disputed is that this
working class is an aggregate of different categories of wage-
labourer scattered across a globally integrated economic system,
and not any kind of collectivity, let alone a revolutionary political
subject. On the one hand, the old forms of proletarian collectivity
– above all, the trade-union movement and social democratic
parties in the North – are in crisis, and, on the other, new forms
have yet to take shape. One reason why the movement for another
globalization is significant is that it may provide a relatively
favourable context, particularly through the transnational networks of solidarity and mobilization that it has developed, through
which these forms can begin to be imagined and constructed.

A second reason for not giving up on the idea of the proletariat
as the universal class is suggested by Žižek when he interprets
Benjamin as proposing that we view history from the standpoint
of the victims. Critique, I have suggested, implies that society is
divided against itself. At the heart of this division lies the very
stark injustice reflected in the horrifying inequalities in life-chances
that I evoked in §7.3 above. But if this structural injustice shat-
ters the world to pieces, doesn't this demand from us a certain

kind of partiality? In this riven world, isn't the appropriate stand-point to take that of the victims of injustice, those excluded and denied access to the resources to which they are entitled? Respond-ing to these questions in the affirmative involves taking a moral position rather than the kind of epistemological argument devel-oped by Lukács. It resembles the 'preferential option for the poor' proposed to the Catholic Church by the theologians of liberation in Latin America.[17] The idea of the universal class as it is devel-oped by Marx and Lukács goes further than this, because it con-ceives the proletariat not simply as victim, but also as *subject*. The liberation theologian Enrique Dussel argues that Marx conceives 'living labour' 'as *corporeality* (poor, bodily existence of the nude), . . . as not-being of capital', 'exteriority, the alterity of the Other than capital'. This interpretation is intended to affirm the radical exteriority of the poor of the Third World to capital.[18] But there is a difference between the worker being the other of capital and the worker being outside the capital-*relation*. In the famous passage from the *1861–3 Manuscript* that Dussel repeatedly cites in support of the thesis of the exteriority of the poor from capital, after calling labour-capacity both '*absolute poverty*' and 'the general possibility of wealth', Marx writes: 'This is labour, such as it is presupposed by capital as antithesis, as the objective exis-tence of capital, and as such for its own part it in turn presup-poses capital.'[19] From Marx's perspective, then, exploitation is not merely the source of suffering and evidence of injustice; it implies a relationship of mutual presupposition, and hence of interde-pendence between wage-labour and capital (see §6.2 above). It is thus a hopeful sign that the uneven development of global capital has drawn portions of the South into the productive networks of the transnational corporations. For it is the dependence of the exploiter on the labour of the exploited that endows the working class with the power to transform the world and thereby to end the suffering and injustice experienced by all those oppressed by capital.[20] Social critique must be conducted against the horizon of this kind of universal emancipation – even if we are only at the very beginning of the process through which a subject capable of carrying out this transformation is imagined and constructed.

(4) **The meanings of politics** Stating the need for a socially grounded project of universal emancipation poses the question of

the relationship between critique and politics. This is a difficult topic because politics itself seems such a thoroughly debased domain. Under the sign of the Washington Consensus, conventional politics has declined into the micro-management of the state subject to a set of neo-liberal policy prescriptions that every 'serious player' is expected simply to take for granted, even if their effect is to rule out of order most policy options. The social is thus renaturalized, and policy-making reduced to technique. Add the progressive mediatization of party politics and the centralization of power in the hands of increasingly presidential leaders and their personal staffs, and it's hardly surprising that most citizens should increasingly withdraw from public life: why should the practice of citizenship seem worthwhile when politicians and corporations alike seek to infantilize the people, reducing them to consumers confronted with the most trivial of choices? When more serious decisions cannot be excluded from the public domain, for example, over the invasion of Iraq, governments systematically sabotage the decision-making process by misrepresenting the issues and caricature the often deeply felt and well-informed opposition as reflecting differences of opinion not amenable to rational discussion. Žižek calls this 'post-politics' because it forecloses 'authentic politics', 'the art of the *impossible*', which 'changes the very parameters of what is considered "possible" in the existing constellation'.[21] This doesn't mean that politics of a more deeply felt kind simply disappears, but it tends to migrate to the margins of the conventional political system and express itself, on the one hand, in assertions of exclusive national or racial identity, directed against stigmatized minorities – refugees, Muslims, gypsies – and in different kinds of religious fundamentalism, and, on the other, in movements of a tendentially cosmopolitan character – for example, anti-globalization and anti-war protests and campaigns against global poverty.

It is little wonder, then, that when contemporary critical theorists intervene in the public sphere – as, in different ways, Bourdieu did and Badiou does – they keep conventional politics at arm's length. But there are other meanings of politics than the inexpressibly dull confrontation of rival leadership machines. Two in particular seem important. One is that implied by the classical Marxist theory of the state, where the political is the domain where the contradictions of the social totality are concentrated and condensed. This reality has not simply vanished merely because the political today is represented as 'post-politics': the fact that, under the neo-liberal hegemony, decision-making powers in key policy areas have been surrendered to the financial markets, or transferred to public institutions such as central banks that are not accountable to citizens or their elected representatives, doesn't mean that these areas are any less political. The years of crisis since 9/11 have highlighted the persisting effectivity of the political in this sense: the fracture that opened up in the state system over the Iraq War showed how, quite unexpectedly, foreign policy has emerged as the lightning conductor of deeper tensions in the global political economy.[22] Žižek therefore greatly oversimplifies when he criticizes Marxism as one of 'a series of disavowals of this political moment, of the proper logic of political conflict', more specifically as

> *meta-politics*: political conflict is fully asserted, *but* as a shadow-theatre in which events whose proper place is on Another Scene (of economic processes) are played out; the ultimate goal of 'true' politics is thus its self-cancellation, the transformation of the 'administration of people' into the 'administration of things' within a fully self-transparent rational order of collective Will.[23]

It is undeniably a serious weakness of classical Marxism that it tends to portray the management of a communist society as a purely technical problem. Thus in his 'Notes on Bakunin's *Statehood and Anarchy*', Marx says that under communism 'the distribution of general functions has become a routine matter which entails no domination.'[24] But his own conception of communism as the liberation of individuality implies that human beings are always likely to have different desires (and also, I would add, sometimes different conceptions of the good as well). As long as resources aren't infinite – namely forever – the result will be conflict among individuals or groups with different projects. What Hume and Rawls call the circumstances of justice would therefore prevail even under communism.[25] In a society where egalitarian justice prevails, which in my view could only be a communist society, one could reasonably expect conflicts to lack the intense and systemic character that they have in class societies where access to resources and hence to advantage are very unequally distributed and therefore to be relatively amenable to debate and compromise in the context of a democratic decision-making process. But they would occur and would often require collectively negotiated solutions. A conception of egalitarian justice could offer a normative framework in which to conduct such negotiations, though no doubt one source of dispute would continue to be which (if any) conception should be preferred.[26]

There is, however, a striking tension between the idea that the management of communist societies would be purely technical and the Marxist conception of politics *in capitalism*. In the first place, as Žižek himself notes, 'the very term "political economy" opens up the space for the opposite gesture of introducing politics into the very heart of the economy, that is, of denouncing the very "apolitical" character of the economic processes as the supreme ideological illusion.'[27] In particular, Marx's theory of capitalist exploitation makes the inherently political conflict between exploiters and exploited constitutive of the economic. But, secondly, the fact that Marxism treats politics as intelligible only in the context of the 'Other Scene' of the economic doesn't make politics a mere epiphenomenon of the accumulation process. On the contrary, precisely because it is in the political that the contradictions of the capitalist mode of production are condensed and concentrated, what happens there matters an enormous amount both intellectually and practically. Thus Lenin's famous dictum 'politics is the most concentrated expression of economics' is intended to highlight the necessity of focusing on the ways in which social conflicts are refracted in the political field in a specific and irreducible form governed by the logic of the struggle for state power.[28] As Daniel Bensaïd puts it, 'Lenin was one of the first to conceive the specificity of the political field as a play of transfigured powers and social antagonisms, translated into a language of its own, full of displacements, of condensations and of revealing slips of the tongue.'[29]

Contemporary radical movements tend to be ambivalent about the political. Some wish to see either the nation-state or regional groupings such as the European Union (re)endowed with the capacities required to bring the ascendant market back under control: such an approach is broadly consonant with the role accorded to social critique in renewing capitalism by Boltanski and Chiapello. Others express a deep suspicion of the state, as is summed up by John Holloway's slogan, now taken up by Hardt and Negri, 'Change the World without Taking Power'. Both these stances seem quite inadequate. The first implies that the state is a neutral instance that can be mobilized against capital, and to restrict its operations, but one thing that all the historical experience of the past generation has underlined is the strength of the connections that bind the state and capital together. The second forgets that, if we ignore the state, it doesn't follow that the state will ignore us. Resistance as exodus carries the promise that we can cultivate our own garden, that we can find a space where we can live despite capitalism. But capital today, vigorously aided by the state, is invading the gardens of the world and sowing them with genetically modified crops. The challenge that I explored above, of constructing a new proletarian collectivity, a new revolutionary subject, is precisely that of developing the capabilities required to confront and break the power of existing states and to create forms of popular power that can govern the world and its resources according to radically different priorities from those that currently reign.[30]

This directs us towards the second meaning of politics beyond 'post-politics'. This is politics as it is understood in the classical republican tradition, where freedom is the property of a collective subject that has the ultimate power to make and remake constitutional orders. This is clearly very different from the right to express one's preference between different neo-liberal packages to which citizenship is increasingly reduced under contemporary 'post-politics'. Once again, the problem is how to construct a subject capable of exercising constituent power. It is important to see that this does not require us to imagine a macro-subject into which individual identities are dissolved. Hardt and Negri see the multitude as the emergent bearer of this power. One of their merits is to insist on the singularity of individual persons: 'the challenge posed by the concept of the multitude is for a social multiplicity to manage to communicate and act in common while remaining internally different.'[31] But, as I tried to show above (§4.3), Hardt and Negri conceive this subject as tendentially already in existence, whereas I argue that it has still to be formed. Missing from the theory of the multitude is one crucial dimension of republican politics as it is understood by Machiavelli – *virtù*, the carefully calibrated creative interventions through which a political project is pursued, across and through the unexpected hazards and opportunities thrown up by *fortuna*, by the objective context that one confronts, that can steer a political project towards its goal. This kind of strategic approach to politics is very different from mere opportunist tactics, since it is distinguished by the unremitting struggle to bring strategy and circumstances into alignment, rather than seeking to harvest the moment for whatever immediate rewards it may offer. While a new political subject can never be the work of an artificer, however ingenious (perhaps like Rousseau's legislator), strategic thought of this kind is one essential ingredient in its formation. Precisely because what *fortuna* brings is unexpected – who can seriously claim to have anticipated the reconfiguration of global politics that followed 9/11? – strategic judgements cannot be deduced from more general theoretical propositions. But a suitably rich and realistic critical theory can help to map out the objective context and specify the normative principles that together determine the space within which such judgements move. In this book I have sought to explore what resources contemporary thought offers such a theory.[32]

One way of thinking about the present is as a moment of transition, in which one political subject has died and a new one has yet to emerge. One might take the different forms of anti-capitalist resistance gathered together under the banner of *alter-mondialisme* as the first stirrings of the subject to come. This makes it easier to understand the confusions and indeterminacies of the 'movement of movements', as a mixture of experimental gropings and premature attempts to give a final form to what is just beginning to emerge. Though they have developed in very different registers and temporalities both from one another and from the activist networks of the *altermondialiste* movement, the varieties of critical theory I surveyed in part I also bear the marks of this in-between time – they are all, in a certain sense, 'after' Marxism, but pointing towards new ways of resisting capitalism or reining it in. A common source of the difficulties in which these theorists have found themselves is the attempt to get beyond Marxism, for the apparent triumph of full-blooded capitalism underlines the actuality of Marx's critique of political economy. To say this is not to take refuge in a complacent orthodoxy: the version of classical Marxism that I have sought to defend in part II is undergirded by a critical realist ontology and capable of learning from egalitarian liberalism. But there is no reason to limit the dialogue to Rawls or Bhaskar. Indeed, this book is also an attempt to widen the discussion – not in a spirit of uncritical syncretism, but out of a willingness to learn from those with whom one sometimes disagrees deeply. That, at any rate, seems to me the best stand to take at a moment when, though dark storm clouds dominate the horizon, flashes of red may presage a new day's dawning.

Notes

Introduction

1 Though, as we shall see in §4.3 below, immanence – the antonym to the theological conception of transcendence, the idea that God is identical to the world, that was most influentially articulated by Spinoza – is an important theme of the version of social critique developed by Toni Negri.

2 For an exception, see W. Easterley, 'The Lost Decades: Developing Countries' Stagnation in Spite of Policy Reform', *Journal of Economic Change*, 6 (2001). Robert Pollin gives a damning survey of the economic record of neo-liberalism in *Contours of Descent* (London, 2003). In *The New Imperialism* (Oxford, 2003) David Harvey portrays the neo-conservatism so influential on the administration of George W. Bush as an authoritarian militarist radicalization of neo-liberalism that, nevertheless, 'will continue a political economy that rests on accumulation by dispossession' (pp. 201–2). Giovanni Arrighi, by contrast, argues that 'the neo-conservative imperial project constitutes a far more fundamental departure from the neo-liberalism of the 1980s and 1990s than Harvey concedes', 'Hegemony Unravelling', I, *New Left Review*, 2nd ser., 32 (2005), p. 51. See also the discussion of 'military neo-liberalism' in 'Retort' (I. Boal et al.), *Afflicted Powers* (London, 2005).

3 J.-F. Lyotard, *The Postmodern Condition* (Manchester, 1984), pp. 16–17, 10, xxv.

4 Ibid., p. 66.

5　J. Baudrillard, *The Illusion of the End* (Cambridge, 1994), pp. 81, 92, 108. See also id., *Simulations* (New York, 1983).

6　See E. Bircham and J. Charlton, eds, *Anti-Capitalism: A Guide to the Movement* (London, 2001), A. Callinicos, *An Anti-Capitalist Manifesto* (Cambridge, 2003), D. Bensaïd, *Un nouvel internationalisme* (Paris, 2003), T. Mertes, ed., *A Movement of Movements* (London, 2004), S. Tormey, *Anti-Capitalism: A Beginner's Guide* (Oxford, 2004), and H. Dee, ed., *Anti-Capitalism: Where Now?* (London, 2004).

7　L. Boltanski and E. Chiapello, *Le Nouvel Esprit du capitalisme* (Paris, 1999), esp. part III.

8　This is not by any means to diminish the significance of the work of, among others, François Chesnais, Gérard Duménil, Dominique Lévy, and Claude Serfati.

9　M. Hardt and A. Negri, *Empire* (Cambridge, MA, 2000), p. 413.

10　E. Laclau and C. Mouffe, *Hegemony and Socialist Strategy* (London, 1985), p. 4.

11　A. Callinicos, *Equality* (Cambridge, 2000), esp. ch. 3.

12　F. Jameson, *The Political Unconscious* (London, 1981), ch. 1 (quotation from p. 53). See also ch. 8 below.

Chapter 1　Modernity and its Promises

1　J. Bidet, *Théorie générale* (Paris, 1999), p. 9. Boltanski's and Chiapello's work is discussed in §2.1 below.

2　For an excellent overview, see J. Roemer, *Theories of Distributive Justice* (Cambridge, MA, 1996).

3　B. Barry, *Justice as Impartiality* (Oxford, 1995), p. 214. See also Bidet, *Théorie générale*, pp. 325, 337.

4　For a more detailed critical discussion of these texts, see A. Callinicos, *Against Postmodernism* (Cambridge, 1989), ch. 4.

5　A. Honneth, *The Critique of Power* (Cambridge, MA, 1991), p. 62; see generally ibid., part I.

6　J. Habermas, *The Theory of Communicative Action*, I (London, 1984), p. 390.

7　Id., *The Philosophical Discourse of Modernity* (Cambridge, 1987), p. 315.

8　Id., *The Theory of Communicative Action*, II (Cambridge, 1987), p. 355.

9　Id., *Between Fact and Norm* (Cambridge, 1996), pp. 105, 56.

10　J. Rawls, *Political Liberalism* (expanded edn, New York, 1996), p. xviii.

11   Habermas, *Between Fact and Norm*, p. 45.
12   Ibid., pp. 46, 26. Compare Habermas, *Theory of Communicative Action*, II, *passim*. In assuming that social reproduction is dependent on normative integration, Habermas (despite the contrast he draws between system and lifeworld) fails to take proper account of the fundamental distinction drawn by David Lockwood between social and system integration: see Lockwood's classic critique of normative functionalism, 'Social Integration and System Integration', reprinted as an Appendix to id., *Solidarity and Schism* (Oxford, 1992), and §6.2 below.
13   Habermas, *Between Fact and Norm*, p. 51. See, on Parsons's evolution, A. Callinicos, *Social Theory* (Cambridge, 1999), pp. 237–45.
14   Habermas, *Between Fact and Norm*, pp. 55, 26.
15   Ibid., p. 4.
16   Ibid., p. 4.
17   Ibid., p. 27.
18   The concept of the force of law has attracted the interest of poststructuralist philosophers: see J. Derrida, *Force de loi* (Paris, 1994), and G. Agamben, *Etat d'exception* (Paris, 2003), ch. 2.
19   Habermas, *Between Fact and Norm*, pp. 27, 30.
20   G. W. F. Hegel, *Elements of the Philosophy of Right* (Cambridge, 1991), §156; p. 197. Compare Habermas, *Between Fact and Norm*, pp. 159–62.
21   Habermas, *Between Fact and Norm*, p. 64.
22   Ibid., p. 457.
23   Habermas, *Theory of Communicative Action*, I, p. 398.
24   Id., *Between Fact and Norm*, p. 99.
25   Callinicos, *Against Postmodernism*, pp. 104–13. See also §5.2 below.
26   Habermas, *Between Fact and Norm*, pp. 445–6.
27   R. Rorty, *Contingency, Irony, Solidarity* (Cambridge, 1989), pp. xvi, 44, 48, 67.
28   Habermas, *Between Fact and Norm*, pp. 62–3.
29   C. S. Peirce, 'Some Consequences of Four Incapacities', in *The Essential Peirce* (2 vols, Bloomington, 1992, 1998), I, p. 52. See also id., 'Pragmatism', ibid., II, p. 419.
30   Habermas, *Between Fact and Norm*, p. 15.
31   Ibid., pp. 20–1.
32   Ibid., p. 155
33   Ibid., p. 14.
34   Rorty, *Contingency, Irony, Solidarity*, ch. 1 (quotations from pp. 5, 7). The fullest discussion of Rorty's views on truth is to be found

in R. Brandom, ed., *Rorty and His Critics* (Oxford, 2000), which includes an exchange between Habermas and Rorty. See also §5.2 below.

35 Habermas, *Between Fact and Norm*, pp. 7, 452–3. Habermas's hostility to giving moral principles any part in the legal system leads him to dismiss Ronald Dworkin's interesting theory of 'law as integrity', which treats judges as offering contestable interpretations of positive law as coherent according to virtues that include, but are not reducible to, justice, as 'monologic', even 'solipsistic' (ibid., ch. 5, quotations from pp. 222, 225) – criticisms that apparently presuppose acceptance of Habermas's theory of communicative action. Compare R. Dworkin, *Law's Empire* (London, 1986).

36 Rawls, *Political Liberalism*, p. 35.

37 Habermas, *Between Fact and Norm*, pp. 17, 66, 460.

38 Ibid., p. 318.

39 Ibid., p. 372, 356, 367. Habermas cites B. Peters, *Die Integration moderner Gesellschaften* (Frankfurt am Main, 1993).

40 Habermas, *Between Fact and Norm*, p. 359, 378.

41 Ibid., p. 175.

42 See, for the British case, G. Monbiot, *Captive State* (London, 2000), and, for broader reflection, E. M. Wood, 'The Uses and Abuses of "Civil Society"', in R. Miliband and L. Panitch, eds, *The Socialist Register 1990* (London, 1990).

43 Habermas, *Between Fact and Norm*, pp. 356, 358. See also ibid., pp. 380–1.

44 Id., *The Structural Transformation of the Public Sphere* (Cambridge, 1989).

45 Id., *Between Fact and Norm*, p. 296.

46 See, for example, Q. Skinner, *Liberty before Liberalism* (Cambridge, 1998).

47 A. Negri, *Le Pouvoir constituant* (Paris, 1997), p. 1.

48 Habermas, *Between Fact and Norm*, pp. 299, 301, 305. See also ibid., p. 486.

49 Ibid., p. 372

50 Ibid., pp. 410, 416.

51 J. Bidet, *Théorie de la modernité* (Paris, 1990), p. 106.

52 Id., *Théorie générale*, pp. 401–26 (quotation from p. 418).

53 Habermas, *Between Fact and Norm*, p. 444. See, on Kosovo, id., 'Bestialität und Humanität', *Die Zeit*, April 1999.

54 P. Anderson, 'Arms and Rights', *New Left Review*, 2nd ser., 31 (2005), p. 31. For critical literature on the Kosovo war, see T. Ali, ed., *Masters of the Universe?* (London, 2000).

55 K. Marx and F. Engels, *Collected Works*, III (London, 1975), p. 332.
56 R. Rorty, 'Universality and Truth', in Brandom, ed., *Rorty and His Critics*, p. 22.
57 J. Habermas, 'Richard Rorty's Pragmatic Turn', in Brandom, ed., *Rorty and His Critics*, p. 46.
58 Rorty, 'Universality and Truth', p. 10.
59 Bidet, *Théorie générale*, p. 136.
60 L. Althusser, *L'Avenir dure longtemps* (expanded edn, Paris, 1994), pp. 523–4. Bidet's most extended discussion of Althusser is 'La Lecture de *Capital* par Althusser', in P. Raymond, ed., *Althusser philosophe* (Paris, 1997).
61 J. Bidet, 'Pour un contractualisme révolutionnaire', in id. and J. Texier, eds, *L'Idée du socialisme a-t-elle un avenir?* (Paris, 1992). See also Bidet, *Théorie de la modernité*, pp. 124–38, *John Rawls et la théorie de la justice* (Paris, 1995), and *Théorie générale*, ch. 7.
62 Bidet, *Théorie générale*, pp. 151, 407. See also the brilliant critical discussion of Habermas in *Théorie de la modernité*, pp. 96–124.
63 Marx, *Capital*, I (Harmondsworth, 1976), pp. 125, 274, 272–3. See also §4.2 below.
64 Bidet, *Théorie de la modernité*, pp. 67, 71–2.
65 Ibid., p. 73. See also ibid., ch. 8.
66 Bidet, *Théorie générale*, pp. 41–2.
67 Id., *Théorie de la modernité*, p. 273. See also id., *Théorie générale*, ch. 4.
68 Id., *Théorie générale*, pp. 36–7, 42, 17–18, 29. See also, on the constituents of the metastructure, ibid., p. 483.
69 Bidet, *Théorie générale*, pp. 120, 127.
70 Ibid., pp. 189, 185.
71 Rawls, *Political Liberalism*, p. 50. The most important attempt to explore systematically the considerations involved in what Rawls calls the reasonable is provided by T. M. Scanlon: see especially *What We Owe to Each Other* (Cambridge, 1998).
72 Bidet, *Théorie de la modernité*, pp. 297–8; *Théorie générale*, p. 171; see also ibid., pp. 149–50.
73 Ibid., p. 51.
74 Ibid., pp. 234–44 (quotation from p. 238).
75 Ibid., pp. 246, 248, 273, 289, 290.
76 Ibid., p. 11.
77 A. Callinicos, 'Socialism and Modern Times', in C. Bertram and A. Chitty, eds, *Has History Ended?* (Aldershot, 1994), and *An*

Anti-Capitalist Manifesto (Cambridge, 2003), esp. ch. 3. See also the detailed account of a democratically planned economy in M. Albert, *Parecon* (London, 2003).

78 See esp. G. Duménil, *Le Concept de loi economique dans le 'Capital'* (Paris, 1978).

79 K. Marx, *Grundrisse* (Harmondsworth, 1973), p. 100.

80 K. Marx, *Theories of Surplus-Value* (3 vols, Moscow, 1963–72), III, p. 74. The most influential version of the historical interpretation was put forward by Engels in an appendix to *Capital*, volume III. For critiques, see, for example, J. Weeks, *Capital and Exploitation* (London, 1981), chs. I and II and Appendix, and C. J. Arthur, *The New Dialectic and Marx's 'Capital'* (Leiden, 2003), ch. 2.

81 Marx, *Capital*, I, p. 274. For more on the implications of market dependence, see R. Brenner, 'The Social Basis of Economic Development', in J. Roemer, ed., *Analytical Marxism* (Cambridge, 1986), and 'The Low Countries in the Transition to Capitalism', in P. Hoppenbrouwers and J. L. Van Zanden, eds, *Peasants into Farmers?* (Turnhout, 2001).

82 For a discussion of some of the epistemological problems posed by Marx's method in *Capital*, see A. Callinicos, 'Against the New Dialectic', *Historical Materialism*, 13.2 (2005).

83 M. Foucault, *The Order of Things* (London, 1970), p. xxii. Bourdieu also espouses a version of the same idea: see §2.2 below.

84 Bidet, *Théorie générale*, pp. 150, 39, 19.

85 E. Balibar, ' "Droits de l'homme" et "droits du citoyen" ', *Actuel Marx*, 8 (1990).

86 Marx, *Capital*, I, p. 152. See also A. Callinicos, *Equality* (Cambridge, 2000), ch. 2.

87 Bidet, *Théorie générale*, p. 38.

88 Ibid., p. 146. Bidet here responds to comments I made on the manuscript of his book: I am grateful to him for the illuminating dialogue that we have had on these issues, either face to face or in correspondence, over the years.

89 See also ibid., pp. 34 n. 1, 224.

90 Ibid., p. 9.

91 Ibid., pp. 177–84. For an alternative interpretation, which conceives the Stalinist societies as a variant of capitalism, see T. Cliff, *State Capitalism in Russia* (London, 1988), and A. Callinicos, *The Revenge of History* (Cambridge, 1991).

92 F. Jameson, *A Singular Modernity* (London, 2002), p. 215. I don't, however, share Jameson's radical scepticism about the very idea of modernity: the best treatments of this topic are, in my view, to be found in Habermas, *The Philosophical Discourse of Modernity*,

Lecture I, and H. Blumenberg, *The Legitimacy of the Modern Age* (Cambridge, MA, 1983).

Chapter 2   Between Relativism and Universalism

1   In *The Critique of Power* (Cambridge, MA, 1991) Axel Honneth thematizes Habermas's mediating role between an early Frankfurt School disabled by, among other things, its refusal to break with many orthodox Marxist positions and Foucault's subjectless genealogy of power.

2   R. Rorty, *Achieving Our Country* (Cambridge, MA, 1998), and 'Back to Class Politics', in id., *Philosophy and Social Hope* (London, 1999).

3   For contemporary responses to this crisis, see A. Callinicos, *Is There a Future for Marxism?* (London, 1982), and P. Anderson, *In the Tracks of Historical Materialism* (London, 1983).

4   J. Derrida, *Spectres of Marx* (New York, 1994), p. 13.

5   D. Bensaïd, 'Spectres et survies', *Rouge*, 21 October 2004. See also Bensaïd's sympathetic discussion of Derrida in *Resistances* (Paris, 2001), part II, ch. 3.

6   B. Cassen, 'On the Attack', *New Left Review*, 2nd ser., 19 (2003).

7   See P. Bourdieu, *Contre-feux* (Paris, 1998), and *Contre-feux 2* (Paris, 2001).

8   L. Boltanski and E. Chiapello, *Le Nouvel Esprit du capitalisme* (Paris, 1999), p. 633. Sebastian Budgen provides a good critical presentation of this book in 'A New "Spirit of Capitalism"', *New Left Review*, 2nd ser., 1 (2000).

9   Boltanski and Chiapello, *Le Nouvel Esprit du capitalisme*, p. 68.

10   M. Weber, *The Protestant Ethic and the Spirit of Capitalism* (London, 1976), p. 181. See A. Callinicos, *Social Theory* (Cambridge, 1999), ch. 7.

11   Boltanski and Chiapello, *Le Nouvel Esprit du capitalisme*, pp. 65, 37, 41.

12   Ibid., pp. 45, 46, 65.

13   L. Boltanski and L. Thévenot, *De la justification* (Paris, 1991), pp. 53–4.

14   Ibid., pp. 27, 59.

15   Ibid., pp. 55–6.

16   Boltanski and Chiapello, *Le Nouvel Esprit du capitalisme*, pp. 63, 64. The original six cities are described in much detail in Boltanski and Thévenot, *De la justification*, chs. II, IV, and VI.

17   Boltanski and Thévenot, *De la justification*, pp. 92, 96, 98, 99.

18 Ibid., p. 100.
19 Ibid., pp. 168, 172, 174, 266.
20 Ibid., pp. 278, 268, 267, 289.
21 Boltanski and Chiapello, *Le Nouvel Esprit du capitalisme*, pp. 37, 582.
22 Ibid., pp. 57, 64, 143, 94.
23 Ibid., pp. 103, 115–16, 123, 397.
24 Ibid., p. 677 n. 49; see generally ibid., pp. 81–5.
25 Ibid., pp. 149, 243, 244.
26 Ibid., pp. 255, 266, 275, 33; see generally chs. III and IV.
27 Ibid., pp. 238, 207, 549, 290.
28 Ibid., pp. 424, 434. See generally ibid., ch. VI.
29 T. Frank, *What's the Matter with Kansas?* (New York, 2004), pp. 108–9. In *The Conquest of Cool* (Chicago, 1997), Frank offers a somewhat similar interpretation of American capitalism to Boltanski's and Chiapello's account of its French counterpart, with the difference that he focuses on the advertising and menswear industries rather than on managerial ideologies, and that, rather than portray a two step-process – first the artistic critique, then its capitalist appropriation – he argues that one of the driving forces of the cultural transformations of the 1960s was the adoption, especially by innovative advertising executives, of an ideology of rebellion by the creative individual against the bureaucratic structures of managerial capitalism.
30 Budgen, 'A New "Spirit of Capitalism"', p. 155.
31 M. Walzer, *Spheres of Justice* (Oxford, 1983), pp. 312, 314.
32 Boltanski and Thévenot, *De la justification*, pp. 432 (emphasis added), 97–8, 103–6.
33 Walzer, *Spheres of Justice*, ch. 2 (quotation from p. 62).
34 Tom Baldwin has pointed out that one way of squaring this difficulty might be the later Rawls's idea of an overlapping consensus of reasonable comprehensive doctrines, all of which, despite the real differences among them, support the same liberal political conception of justice. But there is no hint of such a solution in the books by Boltanski and his collaborators: at most they refer to compromises among cities. Rawls, however, is adamant that an overlapping consensus is not the same as a modus vivendi: the latter's stability derives from 'happenstance and a balance of relative forces', whereas the doctrines involved in an overlapping consensus give *principled* reasons for affirming the same conception of justice, even if these reasons may vary between doctrines: see *Political Liberalism* (expanded edn, New York, 1996), lecture IV (quotation from p. 148).

35 J. Bidet, 'L'Esprit du capitalisme: questions à Luc Boltanski et Eve Chiapello', in J. Lojkine, ed., *Les Sociologies critiques du capitalisme* (Paris, 2002), p. 217.

36 Ibid., p. 221.

37 J. Rawls, *A Theory of Justice* (rev. edn, Oxford, 1999), pp. 14, 54; see also ibid., pp. 273–7. Rawls's first principle of justice, lexically prior to the difference principle, is: 'Everyone is to have an equal right to the most extensive total system of equal basic liberties compatible with a similar system of liberty for all'; ibid., p. 266.

38 Bidet, 'L'Esprit du capitalisme', p. 221.

39 Boltanski and Chiapello, *Le Nouvel Esprit du capitalisme*, pp. 627, 628.

40 Ibid., pp. 76, 77, 437, 171, 173, 438.

41 Ibid., pp. 448, 459.

42 Ibid., p. 464. There is a good discussion of the conceptual issues in E. O. Wright, 'The Class Analysis of Poverty', in id., *Interrogating Inequality* (London, 1994).

43 Boltanski and Chiapello, *Le Nouvel Esprit du capitalisme*, pp. 301ff.

44 A. Harney, 'Going Home: Chinese Migrant Workers Shun Long Factory Hours and Low Pay', *Financial Times*, 3 November 2004.

45 For example, M. Hardt and A. Negri, *Multitude* (New York, 2004), pp. 133–4.

46 Boltanski and Chapiello, *Le Nouvel Esprit du capitalisme*, p. 437.

47 For, among other things, a similar conclusion, see E. Renault, 'Justice et évaluation suivant *Le Nouvel esprit du capitalisme*', *Actuel Marx*, 29 (2001).

48 Boltanski and Thévenot, *De la justification*, pp. 167, 168.

49 Boltanski and Chiapello, *Le Nouvel Esprit du capitalisme*, pp. 89–90, 584–5 (quotation from p. 89); see A. O. Hirschmann, *Exit, Voice, and Loyalty* (Cambridge, 1970).

50 Boltanski and Chiapello, *Le Nouvel Esprit du capitalisme*, pp. 18, 21.

51 For example, C. Harman, *Explaining the Crisis* (London, 1984), R. Brenner, 'The Economics of Global Turbulence', *New Left Review*, 229 (1998), and G. Duménil and D. Lévy, *Capitalism Resurgent* (Cambridge, MA, 2004).

52 Boltanski and Chiapello, *Le Nouvel Esprit du capitalisme*, p. 87.

53 Bidet, 'L'Esprit du capitalisme', p. 233.

54 Boltanski and Chiapello, *Le Nouvel Esprit du capitalisme*, p. 479 (compare pp. 173 and 477–87), 639, 616.

55 It does not follow that it is necessarily wrong to seek to connect justice and functionality: on the contrary, one constraint that any

plausible conception of justice must surely meet is that a society governed by it would be capable of reproducing itself. This is, presumably, one reason for Rawls's preoccupation with 'stability for the right reasons'. But to acknowledge the importance of functionality isn't the same as demanding that a conception of justice must secure the reproduction of a given society, unless it can be shown that that society *deserves* to be reproduced.

56 Bidet, 'L'Esprit du capitalisme', p. 233. For more on these political divergences within the anti-globalization movement, see A. Callinicos, *An Anti-Capitalist Manifesto* (Cambridge, 2003), and 'The Future of the Anti-Capitalist Movement', in H. Dee, *Anti-Capitalism: Where Now?* (London, 2004).

57 J.-P. Sartre, *Critique de la raison dialectique* (Paris, 1960), p. 9.

58 I draw here on A. Callinicos, 'Social Theory Put to the Test of Practice: Pierre Bourdieu and Anthony Giddens', *New Left Review*, 236 (1999), and 'Pierre Bourdieu and the Universal Class', forthcoming in a collection edited by Jim Wolfreys. Two excellent recent surveys of Bourdieu's thought make a point of connecting it to his politics: J. F. Lane, *Pierre Bourdieu: A Critical Introduction* (London, 2000), and J. Wolfreys, 'In Perspective: Pierre Bourdieu', *International Socialism*, new ser., 87 (2000).

59 Bourdieu, *Pascalian Meditations* (Cambridge, 2000), pp. 7, 15, 1.

60 P. Bourdieu, 'Pour un savoir engagé', in id., *Contre-feux 2*, p. 40.

61 G. W. F. Hegel, *Elements of the Philosophy of Right* (Cambridge, 1991), §205, p. 237.

62 Marx and Engels, *Collected Works*, III (London, 1975), pp. 184, 185, 186.

63 Marx later distanced himself from this ultra-Hegelian conception of the proletariat: see M. Löwy, *The Theory of Revolution in the Young Marx* (Leiden, 2003), the contrasting account in S. Kouvelakis, *Philosophy and Revolution* (London, 2003), ch. 5, and §3.3 below.

64 Bourdieu, *Pascalian Meditations*, p. 123.

65 M. Foucault, *Dits et écrits 1954–1988* (2 vols, Paris, 2001), II, pp. 154, 155; id., *Power/Knowledge* (Brighton, 1980), pp. 126, 127.

66 Bourdieu, *Pascalian Meditations*, pp. 93, 124, 52, 65, 73; see generally ibid., ch. 2.

67 Id., *The Rules of Art* (Cambridge, 1996), pp. 130, 129.

68 Ibid., p. 130.

69 Ibid., p. 340.

70 Bourdieu, *Pascalian Meditations*, p. 80.

71 G. Mauger, 'L'Engagement sociologique', *Critique*, 589–90 (1995), p. 8.

72   Bourdieu, *The Rules of Art*, p. 342.

73   P. Bourdieu, *La Domination masculine* (Paris, 1998), p. 123 n. 4.

74   Id., *Distinction* (London, 1984), p. 511. See also id., *Science de la science et réflexivité* (Paris, 2001), pp. 173–84 (section entitled 'Objectiver le sujet d'objectivation').

75   Id., *Pascalian Meditations*, p. 111.

76   Ibid., p. 123.

77   See *Science de la science et réflexivité*, where Bourdieu places himself in 'this French tradition of philosophy of science that has been incarnated by Bachelard, Koyré and Canguilhem' (p. 9), and the warm portrait of Georges Canguilhem in *Esquisse pour un auto-analyse* (Paris, 2004), pp. 40–5.

78   Id., *Science de la science et réflexivité*, p. 136.

79   Id., *Pascalian Meditations*, pp. 112–13.

80   Id., *Science de la science et réflexivité*, pp. 142, 155.

81   Jacques Bouveresse explores the tensions in Bourdieu's conception of scientific objectivity in *Bourdieu, savant et politique* (Marseilles, 2003), ch. V.

82   Bourdieu, *Pascalian Meditations*, pp. 183–4.

83   Ibid., p. 173.

84   Ibid., p. 234. See also on the Don Quixote effect, for example, ibid., p. 160, and P. Bourdieu, *The Logic of Practice* (Cambridge, 1990), p. 62.

Chapter 3   Touching the Void

1   F. Braudel, *The Mediterranean and the Mediterranean World in the Age of Philip II* (2 vols, London, 1978), I, p. 21.

2   M. Foucault, *L'Ordre du discours* (Paris, 1971), pp. 56, 57–8.

3   Ibid., pp. 59–60. This conception of events reflects the influence of the theory of meaning advanced in G. Deleuze, *Logique du sens* (Paris, 1969).

4   M. Foucault (1971) 'Nietzsche, la geneaologie, l'histoire', *Dits et ecrits 1954–1988* (2 vols, Paris, 2001), I, p. 1011; P. Rabinow, ed., *The Foucault Reader* (Harmondsworth, 1986), p. 83.

5   J. Derrida, *Spectres of Marx* (New York, 1994), p. 75; see generally ibid., chs. 1 and 2. Daniel Bensaïd exploits Derrida's idea of contretemps to help evoke a non-determinist version of historical materialism: *Marx for Our Times* (London, 2002), ch. 1.

6   W. Benjamin, *Illuminations* (London, 1970), pp. 259, 265, 266. See, among many discussions of this text, R. Wolin, *Walter Benjamin: An Aesthetic of Redemption* (New York, 1982), M.

Löwy, 'Revolution against "Progress"', *New Left Review*, 151 (1985), L. Niethammer, *Posthistoire* (London, 1992), ch. 6, and A. Callinicos, *Making History* (rev. edn, Leiden, 2004), ch. 5. For Derrida on Messianism, see especially his reply to Marxist critics of *Spectres of Marx*, 'Marx & Sons', in M. Sprinker, ed., *Ghostly Demarcations* (London, 1999).

7   J. Derrida, *Politics of Friendship* (London, 1997), p. 107 n. 4.

8   G. Balakrishnan, *The Enemy: An Intellectual Portrait of Carl Schmitt* (London, 2000), pp. 261, 113, 45–6.

9   C. Schmitt, *Political Theology* (Cambridge, MA, 1985), pp. 5, 6, 13, 37.

10 Quoted in Balakrishnan, *The Enemy*, p. 49; see generally ibid., chs. 2 and 3, and G. Agamben, *Etat d'exception* (Paris, 2003), ch. 2.

11 G. Agamben, *Homo Sacer* (Stanford, CA, 1998), pp. 15, 18.

12 Benjamin, *Illuminations*, p. 259. Agamben offers an account of what he describes as 'the debate between Walter Benjamin and Carl Schmitt on the state of exception' in *Etat d'exception*, ch. 4 (quotation from p. 89).

13 Derrida, *Politics of Friendship*, p. 127.

14 Id., *Force de loi* (Paris, 1994), p. 58.

15 Agamben, *Etat d'exception*, pp. 18, 145–6. Agamben offers an admirable 'Short History of the State of Emergency', ibid., pp. 26–41.

16 Schmitt, *Political Theology*, p. 15. The concept of 'bare life' is important for Agamben, but the key influences here are Heidegger and Foucault: see *Homo Sacer*, *passim*.

17 Balakrishnan, *The Enemy*, p. 76.

18 Agamben, *Homo Sacer*, p. 25. Badiou himself invokes the idea of the state of exception in *Le Siècle* (Paris, 2005), p. 226.

19 S. Žižek, *The Ticklish Subject* (London, 1999), p. 135.

20 P. Hallward, *Badiou: A Subject to Truth* (Minneapolis, 2003). Badiou's latest book, *Le Siècle*, offers a relatively accessible presentation of the main themes of his thought in the context of a critical vindication of the 'Short Twentieth Century' against *fin-de-siècle* liberal triumphalism.

21 A. Badiou, 'Le (Re)commencement du matérialisme dialectique', *Critique*, 240 (1967), and *Le Concept de modèle* (Paris, 1969). In 'La Politique dans ses limites, ou les paradoxes d'Alain Badiou', *Actuel Marx*, 28 (2000), Stathis Kouvelakis seeks, among other things, to situate Badiou ' "between Sartre and Althusser" ' (p. 47).

22 A. Badiou, 'Kampuchea vaincra!', *Le Monde*, 17 January 1979.

23 P. Anderson, *In the Tracks of Historical Materialism* (London, 1983), p. 32.

24 A. Badiou, *Théorie du sujet* (Paris, 1982), p. 318. For Badiou's more recent critical reflections on Maoism, see *Le Siècle*, pp. 92–7.

25 *Réponse à John Lewis* (Paris, 1973) is probably the text that Althusser published himself where these tensions are most visible; the posthumously published *Sur la reproduction* (Paris, 1995) is perhaps his most sustainedly Maoist text. For more on these ambiguities, see A. Callinicos, *Is There a Future for Marxism?* (London, 1982), ch. 6, which is unusual (though not unique: see P. Anderson, *Arguments in English Marxism*, London, 1980) in seeking to resolve them by moving in an 'objectivist' direction.

26 Badiou, *Théorie du sujet*, pp. 294, 296, 40, 25. See id., *Le Siècle*, pp. 92–3, on the Chinese philosophical debate of 1965 about the relationship between the One and the Two.

27 Id., *Théorie du sujet*, pp. 29, 148, 160.

28 Ibid., pp. 204, 205, 148. See also §3.3 below for more on this treatment of working class and proletariat.

29 See T. Cliff, 'Trotsky on Substitutionism', in id., *Selected Writings* (3 vols, London, 2001–3), I, and N. Harris, *The Mandate of Heaven* (London, 1978).

30 Badiou, *Théorie du sujet*, pp. 59, 56, 62. See L. Althusser, *Politics and History* (London, 1972), p. 166.

31 Hallward, *Badiou*, pp. 36, xxv.

32 Badiou, *Théorie du sujet*, p. 106.

33 Id., *Saint Paul* (Paris, 1997), p. 8.

34 Hallward, *Badiou*, p. 198.

35 Badiou, *Théorie du sujet*, pp. 48, 242. Set theory first makes its appearance in *Théorie du sujet* when Badiou formulates the idea of the subject as exceptional (pp. 108–9); see also especially ibid., pp. 281–90. Hallward has a good discussion of Lacan's influence on Badiou: *Badiou*, pp. 11–15. Probably the most accessible discussion of the later Lacan is provided by Žižek in *The Sublime Object of Ideology* (London, 1989).

36 Badiou quoted in Hallward, *Badiou*, p. 226; id., *L'Etre et l'événement*, p. 7.

37 Badiou, *L'Etre et l'événement*, pp. 15, 144–5, 143–4. See also ibid., p. 16.

38 Ibid., p. 144.

39 Ibid., pp. 212, 32, 33.

40 Hallward, *Badiou*, p. 57.

41 Badiou, *L'Etre et l'événement*, pp. 31, 32.

42 Ibid., p. 32.

43 Ibid., pp. 44, 66.

44 Hallward, *Badiou*, p. 100.

45 Badiou, *L'Etre et l'événement*, pp. 69, 32.
46 Ibid., pp. 95, 99–100, 101.
47 Ibid., p. 109.
48 Ibid., p. 109. Though Badiou's use of the term 'metastructure' precedes that by Bidet (see §1.2 above), the same word expresses quite different concepts in the two philosophers' writing.
49 Ibid., pp. 111, 114, 115.
50 Hallward, *Badiou*, p. 96.
51 Badiou, *L'Etre et l'événement*, pp. 146, 193–4.
52 Hallward, *Badiou*, p. 114.
53 Badiou, *L'Etre et l'événement*, p. 195.
54 Ibid., pp. 200, 201, 202.
55 Ibid., pp. 204, 363, 361.
56 Ibid., pp. 223, 429. Badiou argues that there are four kinds of generic procedures – love, art, science, and politics: see Hallward, *Badiou*, part III.
57 Badiou, *L'Etre et l'événement*, p. 430.
58 Hallward, *Badiou*, pp. 122, 114.
59 Badiou, *Le Siècle*, pp. 144, 251.
60 Badiou, *L'Etre et l'événement*, pp. 233, 257.
61 Badiou, *Théorie du sujet*, pp. 143–4; here, however, Badiou identifies the Christian event with the Incarnation, whereas his later view is that '*Paul's thought dissolves the Incarnation into the Resurrection*': *Saint Paul*, p. 78.
62 Badiou, *Saint Paul*, pp. 2, 40, 5, 47, 116.
63 Badiou actually dismisses 1989–91 as 'exemplary of the fact that a sudden and complete change in the situation does not at all signify that the grace of an event has been bestowed on it' – *D'un désastre obscur* (Paris, 1998), p. 12. This is presumably a consequence of his requirement that events partake of the universal, which I criticize below.
64 Benjamin, *Illuminations*, p. 264.
65 Hallward, *Badiou*, pp. 75, 76.
66 Galileo Galilei, 'The Assayer', in S. Drake, ed., *Discoveries and Opinions of Galileo* (New York, 1957), pp. 237–8. On Galileo's Platonism, see A. Koyré, *Etudes galiléenes* (Paris, 1966).
67 Badiou, *Le Siècle*, pp. 83, 85.
68 Hallward, *Badiou*, p. 406 n. 4. See also Kouvelakis, 'La Politique dans ses limites', p. 47.
69 D. Bensaïd, *Resistances* (Paris, 2001), p. 160; see generally ibid., part II, ch. 2.
70 Žižek, *The Ticklish Subject*, p. 142.
71 Badiou, *Saint Paul*, pp. 6, 81.

72 Ibid., pp. 85, 89.
73 St Augustine, *Concerning the City of God against the Pagans* (Harmondsworth, 1984), XIV, 26, pp. 591–2.
74 Rom. 11: 33.
75 Augustine, *City of God*, XX, 2, pp. 897, 898.
76 Badiou, *L'Etre et l'événement*, p. 265.
77 Hallward, *Badiou*, p. 273; see ibid., ch. 13, for an excellent critique of Badiou's exclusion of relationality. It would be interesting to confront Badiou's emphasis on purification, for example, in his treatment of Modern art in *Le Siècle*, with Fredric Jameson's critique of the role played by purity in what he calls the 'ideology of late modernism' that developed after the Second World War: see *A Singular Modernity* (London, 2002), pp. 161–96.
78 Badiou, *L'Etre et l'événement*, pp. 125, 126–7.
79 Ibid., p. 127.
80 Hallward, *Badiou*, p. 223.
81 This is true even of very sophisticated Maoist texts such as Charles Bettelheim's *Class Struggles in the USSR* (2 vols, New York, 1977, 1978).
82 See, for example, 'Ethics as the dissipation of the paradoxes of party spirit', in Badiou, *Théorie du sujet*, pp. 325–32.
83 Id., *D'un désastre obscure*, p. 7.
84 Id, *Théorie du sujet*, p. 341.
85 Id., *L'Ethique* (Paris, 1993), p. 65.
86 Hallward, *Badiou*, p. 251; see A. Badiou, 'Eight Theses on the Universal', in id., *Theoretical Writings* (ed. R. Brassier and A. Toscano, London, 2004).
87 Badiou, *L'Etre et l'événement*, p. 447.
88 Hallward, *Badiou*, p. 228.
89 Bensaïd, *Resistances*, pp. 160–1.
90 T. Eagleton, *Sweet Violence* (Oxford, 2003), p. 240; see Badiou, *Le Siècle*, pp. 85–9, for *White on White*. Badiou has on a number of occasions acknowledged that his metaphysics requires modification, in part at least to take into account the criticisms made by Hallward and others: for example, 'Preface to the English Edition', *Ethics* (London, 2001), pp. lvi–lviii. But, to judge by the previews so far published of *Logiques du monde*, the promised sequel to *L'Etre et l'événement*, these changes do not rescue Badiou from the difficulties outlined above. *Logiques du monde* develops a 'logic of appearance' that is distinct from the mathematics of Being and that includes relations. The following extract indicates the relatively limited character of this concession, as well as the deep continuities in Badiou's thought: 'when a truth shows itself, when

being seems to displace itself before our very eyes, it is always despite appearance, in a local collapse of the consistency of appearance and therefore in a temporary cancellation of logic. For what comes to the surface at that point, displacing or revoking the logic of place is being itself, in its redoubtable and creative inconsistency, that is, in the void, which is the placelessness of every place.' A. Badiou, 'Being and Appearance', in *Theoretical Writings*, p. 175.

91 Žižek's growing distance from Laclau is registered in the three-way debate between them and Judith Butler in *Contingency, Hegemony, Universality* (London, 2000). I offer a much fuller assessment than is appropriate here of Žižek's Marxism in my review of this book and of *The Ticklish Subject* in *Historical Materialism*, 8 (2001).

92 Žižek, *Organs without Bodies: Deleuze and Consequences* (London, 2004).

93 Id., *The Ticklish Subject*, pp. 154, 162–3.

94 Quoted, ibid., pp. 29–30. For another rendering of this passage, see L. Rauch, ed., *Hegel and the Human Spirit* (Detroit, 1983), p. 87.

95 Žižek, *The Ticklish Subject*, p. 36.

96 J. Lacan, *The Four Fundamental Concepts of Psychoanalysis* (London, 1977), p. 205. See Žižek, *The Sublime Object of Ideology*, ch. 4, for a discussion of Lacan's evolving views on the death drive.

97 Žižek, *The Ticklish Subject*, p. 54.

98 T. Eagleton, 'Enjoy!', *London Review of Books*, 17 November 1997, p. 7. Eagleton's more recent study of tragedy, *Sweet Violence*, expounds a version of Marxism that, in the importance it accords to the Real, is close to Žižek .

99 Žižek, *The Sublime Object of Ideology*, p. 162.

100 S. Žižek, 'Class Struggle or Postmodernism? Yes, please!', in Butler et al., *Contingency, Hegemony, Universality*, pp. 120, 121.

101 E. Laclau and C. Mouffe, *Hegemony and Socialist Strategy* (London, 1985), p. 125. See also E. Laclau, 'Metaphor and Social Antagonisms', in C. Nelson and L. Grossberg, eds, *Marxism and the Interpretation of Culture* (London, 1988).

102 S. Žižek, 'The Spectre of Ideology', in E. Wright and E. Wright, eds, *The Žižek Reader* (Oxford, 1999), p. 75.

103 Badiou, *Théorie du sujet*, p. 145. 'There is no sexual relationship' is a proposition of Lacan's: see Žižek 's essay of that name, reprinted in *The Žižek Reader*.

104 S. Žižek, 'Over the Rainbow', *London Review of Books*, 4 November 2004.

105 Id., 'The Spectre of Ideology', p. 74.
106 S. Žižek, 'Georg Lukács as the Philosopher of Leninism', Postface to G. Lukács, *A Defence of History and Class Consciousness* (London, 2000), p. 169.
107 S. Kouvelakis, *Philosophy and Revolution* (London, 2003), pp. 330, 333. See also ibid., pp. 83ff. (Heine's conception of communism as an event evoking 'the *antagonism* of bourgeois society').
108 Badiou, *L'Etre et l'événement*, p. 368. Compare Žižek, *The Ticklish Subject*, pp. 226–7.
109 K. Marx and F. Engels, *Collected Works*, XI (London, 1979), p. 133. Relevant studies include H. Draper, *Karl Marx's Theory of Revolution* (4 vols, New York, 1977–90), and A. Gilbert, *Marx's Politics* (Oxford, 1981). Kouvelakis may be led towards Badiou and Žižek by his concern to think the specificity of the political in Marx's thought in a non-reductive way: 'Rather than an Achilles heel, or the sign of a lacuna, politics is, in my opinion, Marx's *strong point*, the point where his work is at its most open and innovative'; *Philosophy and Revolution*, p. 351; see also §7.1 below. But the problem with Badiou's ontology is that it makes the relationship between the social and political simply unthinkable.
110 Badiou, *Théorie du sujet*, p. 89.

Chapter 4   The Generosity of Being

1 A. Badiou, *Deleuze* (Minneapolis, 1999), p. 96. The English translation renders Bernanos's words somewhat differently: 'Does it matter? Grace is everywhere' *The Diary of a Country Priest* (London, 1937), p. 253. See the discussion of Badiou and Deleuze in P. Hallward, *Badiou: A Subject to Truth* (Minneapolis, 2003), pp. 174–80.
2 G. Greene, *The Lawless Roads* (Harmondsworth, 1947), p. 138.
3 J. Derrida, 'Marx & Sons', in M. Sprinker, ed., *Ghostly Demarcations* (London, 1999), p. 269.
4 M. Hardt and A. Negri, *Empire* (Cambridge, MA, 2000), p. 62.
5 Ibid., pp. 91–2.
6 Ibid., pp. 387, 388, 389, 391. See generally ibid., chapters 4.1, 'Virtualities', and 4.2, 'Generation and Corruption'.
7 For a good critical history of *operaismo*, see S. Wright, *Storming Heaven* (London, 2002).
8 In this chapter I develop aspects of the critique of both *Empire* and Negri's earlier thought first advanced in my article 'Toni Negri in Perspective', *International Socialism*, 92 (2001), which discusses

Empire in much more detail than I do here. There are two good collections of critical responses to *Empire*: G. Balakrishnan, ed., *Debating 'Empire'* (London, 2003), and P. A. Passavant and J. Dean, eds, *Empire's New Clothes* (New York, 2004).

9   A. Negri, *Marx Beyond Marx* (South Hadley, MA, 1984), pp. 4, 18, 23. See also ibid., p. 138: 'At the heart of this relationship, the capitalist relation is immediately a relation of power.'

10   Ibid., pp. 35, 24.

11   Ibid., pp. 14, 154.

12   Ibid., p. 9.

13   Quoted in Wright, *Storming Heaven*, p. 28. David Harvey has written eloquently about reading *Capital* as a shared, generational experience: *Spaces of Hope* (Edinburgh, 2000), ch. 1.

14   Negri, *Marx Beyond Marx*, p. 91.

15   Ibid., pp. 100–1.

16   Ibid., p. 101.

17   Ibid., p. 102.

18   A. Negri, 'Marx on Cycle and Crisis', in id., *Revolution Retrieved* (London, 1988), pp. 66, 72.

19   Id., 'Archaeology and Project: The Mass Worker and the Social Worker', ibid., pp. 224, 225.

20   Id., *Marx Beyond Marx*, p. 27. See also ibid., pp. 187ff.

21   Ibid., p. 188.

22   A. Negri, (1968) 'Keynes and the Capitalist Theory of the State post-1929', in id., *Revolution Retrieved*.

23   Negri, *Marx Beyond Marx*, p. 27. See, for example, N. I. Bukharin, *Economics of the Transformation Period* (New York, 1971), and C. Castoriadis, 'Modern Capitalism and Revolution', in id., *Political and Social Writings* (2 vols, Minneapolis, 1988), II.

24   Negri, *Marx Beyond Marx*, p. 172.

25   See especially ibid., Lessons 7–9.

26   Ibid., p. 121.

27   K. Marx, *Grundrisse* (Harmondsworth, 1973), pp. 459–60.

28   E. P. Thompson, *The Poverty of Theory and Other Essays* (London, 1978), p. 253.

29   See Marx, *Grundrisse*, pp. 239–376, and, for critical commentary, for example, J. Mepham, 'From the *Grundrisse* to *Capital*', in id. and D.-H. Ruben, eds, *Issues in Marxist Philosophy* (3 vols, Brighton, 1979), I. J. Bidet, *Que faire du 'Capital'?* (Paris, 1985), ch. VI, and id., *Théorie de la modernité* (Paris, 1990), pp. 67–73.

30   Bidet, *Que faire du 'Capital'?*, pp. 124, 161; see generally ibid., ch. VII. For two other important studies of the progressive recast-

ing of Marx's economic concepts and of the critical role in this process of the *Economic Manuscript of 1861–3*, see V. S. Vygodsky, *The Story of a Great Discovery* (Tunbridge Wells, 1974), esp. chs. 5–7, and E. Dussel, *Towards an Unknown Marx* (London, 2001).

31 Negri, *Marx Beyond Marx*, pp. 57, 123, 186.

32 In pursuing this theme I have benefited from reading Daniel Bensaïd's critique of *Marx Beyond Marx*, 'A la recherche du sujet perdu (Negri corrige Marx)', in id., *Le Discordance de temps* (Paris, 1995).

33 Marx, *Grundrisse*, pp. 449, 414. The distinction between capital in general and many capitals is one of the main themes of Roman Rosdolsky's classic commentary on the *Grundrisse*, *The Making of Marx's 'Capital'* (London, 1977). See also C. Arthur, 'Capital, Competition, and Many Capitals', in M. Campbell and G. Reuten, eds, *The Culmination of Capital* (Basingstoke, 2002).

34 R. Brenner, 'The Economics of Global Turbulence', *New Left Review*, 229 (1998), p. 23.

35 The interpretation of this chapter in its successive versions raise many issues that I cannot discuss here, but that I first addressed in my doctoral thesis, 'The Logic of *Capital*' (Oxford University, 1978). I have also greatly benefited from Bidet's discussions of the market and competition in Marx's thought in *Que faire du 'Capital'?* and *Théorie de la modernité* (though, for my reservations about the latter, see §1.2 above).

36 Marx, *Capital*, I (Harmondsworth, 1976), p. 139.

37 It is important to see that, by the stage of *Capital*, the commodification of labour-power is not treated as somehow implicit in the very concept of a market economy: see Bidet's discussion, summarized and criticized in §1.2 above. This is an example of how, in *Capital*, Marx proceeds by what Althusser calls 'the position of concepts', the progressive introduction (rather than the deduction) of new theoretical determinations that permit the elaboration of more concrete levels of analysis: see Althusser's preface to G. Duménil, *Le Concept de loi economique dans 'Le Capital'* (Paris, 1978).

38 Marx, *Capital*, I, p. 899. See E. M. Wood, 'The Separation of the Economic and Political in Capitalism', *New Left Review*, 127 (1981).

39 K. Marx, *A Contribution to the Critique of Political Economy* (London, 1971), p. 86. See Rosdolsky, *The Making of Marx's 'Capital'*, ch. 4, and Vygotsky, *The Story of A Great Discovery*, ch. 3.

40   Marx, *Capital*, I, p. 181 n. 4.
41   Marx, *Grundrisse*, p. 657.
42   Ibid., p. 414.
43   Bidet, *Que faire du 'Capital'?*, p. 135. The ambiguity of Marx's treatment of competition in the *Grundrisse* is perhaps partly a consequence of a similar ambiguity in one of the main influences on that text, Hegel's account of essence and appearance in *The Science of Logic*, where appearance is an externalization of essence, which might seem to reduce it to merely epiphenomenal status, but at the same time essence is nothing but the relationship among appearances. As Charles Taylor puts it, for Hegel, 'the more essential reality is externalized, the more the relatedness of reality is developed and the more inwardness it has': *Hegel* (Cambridge, 1975), p. 278.
44   Marx, *Capital*, I, pp. 433–6.
45   Marx, *Capital*, III (Harmondsworth, 1981), p. 300. See, on the role of the struggle for surplus-profits in the TRPF, ibid., pp. 373–4, and, on the law of value more generally, p. 1020.
46   See A. Callinicos, 'Periodizing Capitalism and Analysing Imperialism', in R. Albritton et al., *Phases of Capitalist Development* (Basingstoke, 2001).
47   See, for example, the detailed evidence of the impact of international competition on costs, prices, and profits especially in the manufacturing sectors of the US, Japanese, and German economies assembled by Robert Brenner in 'The Economics of Global Turbulence' and *The Boom and the Bubble* (London, 2002).
48   See esp. P. Gowan, *The Global Gamble* (London, 1999).
49   See C. Harman, 'The State and Capitalism Today', *International Socialism*, 2nd ser., 51 (1991), and 'Globalization: A Critique of a New Orthodoxy', ibid., 2nd ser., 73 (1996).
50   Hardt and Negri, *Empire*, pp. xii, 190, 314–15.
51   K. Marx and F. Engels, *The Communist Manifesto* (London, 1998), p. 37; Hardt and Negri, *Empire*, pp. 304, 321, 323 (italics in original).
52   T. Negri, 'Ruptures dans l'empire, puissance de l'exode', 27 October 2001, interview in *Multitudes*, 7 (online version), multitudes-infos@samizdat.net. See also M. Hardt and A. Negri, *Multitude* (New York, 2004), p. 177. John Holloway notes Negri's functionalism: *Change the World Without Taking Power* (London, 2002), pp. 171–2.
53   Marx, *Grundrisse*, p. 449. Under (2) Marx does go on to assign 'capital in general . . . a *real* existence', namely as money capital, an idea that is developed in *Capital*, volume III, part 5, where the

circuit of money capital is interpreted as, among other things, where '[t]he capital relationship assumes its most superficial and fetishized form' as 'self-valorizing value, money breeding money', *Capital*, III, pp. 515–16.

54 A. Callinicos, 'Marxism and Global Governance', in D. Held and A. McGrew, eds, *Governing Globalization* (Cambridge, 2002), id., *The New Mandarins of American Power* (Cambridge, 2003), ch. 5, and E. M. Wood, 'Global Capital, National States', in M. Rupert and H. Smith, eds, *Historical Materialism and Globalization* (London, 2002).

55 See C. Harman, *The Fire Last Time* (London, 1988), and Boltanski's and Chapiello's account of this process in France, discussed in §2.1 above.

56 Negri, 'Archaeology and Project', p. 209. How Negri's hyper-politicized understanding of capitalism helped to legitimate some disastrous political misjudgements on his part in Italy during the late 1970s is explored in A. Callinicos, 'Antonio Negri and the Temptation of Ontology', in T. S. Murphy and A.-K. Mustapha, eds, *The Philosophy of Antonio Negri 2: Revolution in Theory* (London, 2006).

57 See Hardt and Negri, *Empire*, p. 409.

58 A Negri et al., (1993) 'Do You Remember Revolution?', in id., *Revolution Retrieved*, p. 242. Negri does more directly confront the reality of defeat (though primarily as a personal experience) in A. Negri and A. Dufourmantelle, *Negri on Negri* (New York, 2004), pp. 39–57.

59 Hardt and Negri, *Empire*, p. 268: see generally ibid., ch. 3.3.

60 A. Negri, 'Capitalist Domination and Working-Class Sabotage', available at www.geocities.com/cordobakaf/negri_sabotage.html, p. 10.

61 A. Callinicos, *Making History* (2nd edn, Leiden, 2004).

62 Negri, *Marx Beyond Marx*, p. 56.

63 Id., *Le Pouvoir constituant* (Paris, 1997), p. 40, and ibid., n. 1.

64 Ibid., pp. 428, 49.

65 Ibid., p. 438.

66 Ibid., pp. 435, 296; A. Negri, 'La Multitude, nouveau sujet révolutionnaire', *Politis*, 28 October 2004, www.politis.fr. See id., *Le Pouvoir constituant*, p. 345ff., for a more detailed discussion of Marx's treatment of cooperation in *Capital*.

67 A. Badiou, *Deleuze*, p. 15. For a discussion of the differences between Deleuze's and Foucault's conceptions of power and resistance, see A. Callinicos, *Against Postmodernism* (Cambridge, 1989), pp. 80–7.

68 I briefly discuss some of the analogies between the two texts in 'Toni Negri in Perspective', pp. 47–8. There are other, arguably more productive Marxist appropriations of Deleuze, perhaps most notably by Jean-Jacques Lecercle – see, for example, *Une philosophie marxiste de langage* (Paris, 2004).

69 Daniel Bensaïd has written a fine critique of this book (and Paolo Virno's *The Grammar of the Multitude*): 'Multitudes ventriloques', www.multitudes.samizdat.net.

70 Hardt and Negri, *Multitude*, pp. 100, 106, 102, xiv.

71 Ibid., p. 223. Negri and Dufourmantelle, *Negri on Negri*, p. 112.

72 Hardt and Negri, *Multitude*, p. 108.

73 P. Taylor et al., 'Work Organization, Control and the Experience of Work in Call Centres', *Work, Employment and Society*, 16 (2002), p. 148. For a critique of Hardt's and Negri's conception of immaterial labour, see J.-M. Harribey, 'Le Cognitivisme, nouvelle société ou impasse théorique et politique?', *Actuel Marx*, 36 (2004). Discussion of these issues is not helped by the confusion evident in the following remark: 'If . . . in capitalist society labour is the source of all wealth, then abstract labour must be the source of value in general', Hardt and Negri, *Multitude*, pp. 144–5. Marx rejects the antecedent of this sentence, because it confuses use-value (wealth) with value (abstract social labour). Thus in the 'Critique of the Gotha Programme' he insists that '[l]abour is *not the source* of all wealth', arguing that to assert the contrary is to attribute '*supernatural creative power* to labour' by ignoring the role of nature in the production of use-values: K. Marx and F. Engels, *Collected Works*, XXIV (London, 1989), p. 81. For a critique of the same confusion in *Marx Beyond Marx*, see J. Bidet, *Théorie générale* (Paris, 1999), pp. 460–3.

74 Hardt and Negri, *Multitude*, pp. xvi, xv, 148.

75 P. Virno, *The Grammar of the Multitude* (New York, 2004), p. 103.

76 Holloway, *Change the World Without Taking Power*, p. 40; see also ibid., pp. 40–1 and 167–75. Hardt and Negri do at points register this: for example, *Multitude*, p. 333.

77 Hardt and Negri, *Multitude*, p. 145.

78 C. Harman, 'The Workers of the World', *International Socialism*, 2nd ser., 96 (2002).

79 F. Zakaria, *The Future of Democracy* (New York, 2004). See also Callinicos, *The New Mandarins of American Power*, pp. 23–34.

80 Hardt and Negri, *Multitude*, p. 350.

81 E. Laclau, 'Can Immanence Explain Social Struggles?', in Passavant and Dean, eds, *Empire's New Clothes*.

82 Hardt and Negri, *Empire*, pp. 76, 70, 62. Also: 'I absolutely reject all transcendence', Negri and Dufourmantelle, *Negri on Negri*, p. 158.

83 Hardt and Negri, *Multitude*, p. 337.

84 G. Deleuze and F. Guattari, *Mille plateaux* (Paris, 1980), p. 633; see esp. ibid., ch. 6.

85 G. Deleuze, *Spinoza et le problème d'expression* (Paris, 1968), p. 157. '*God is the immanent, not the transitive, cause of all things*', B. Spinoza, *Ethics* (Harmondsworth, 1996), prop. 18, p. 16. Spinoza is, of course, a very important reference point for Negri: see, especially, *The Savage Anomaly* (Minneapolis, 1991).

86 Laclau, 'Can Immanence Explain Social Struggles?', pp. 23, 24, 26. For more on Laclau's concept of articulation, see §6.2 below.

87 D. Bensaïd, 'Plèbes, classes, multitudes', in id., *Un monde à changer* (Paris, 2003), p. 81.

88 For a brilliantly dialectical exploration of these issues in a military context and from a neo-conservative perspective, see E. Luttwak, *Strategy* (rev. edn, Cambridge, MA, 2001), and, for an equally fine Marxist treatment, D. Bensaïd, 'La Politique comme art stratégique', in id., *Un monde à changer*.

89 Hardt and Negri, *Empire*, pp. 326, 336; see also the section entitled 'A Smooth World', pp. 332–6. The economic analysis implied by such assertions has been powerfully criticized by Giovanni Arrighi: see 'Lineages of Empire', *Historical Materialism*, 10: 3 (2002). Hardt and Negri at least partially retreat from this analysis and acknowledge persisting unevenness in *Multitude*, e.g., p. xii.

90 Hardt and Negri, *Multitude*, pp. 87, 88, 336. The authors' failure to acknowledge the actuality of US imperialism is forcefully criticized by A. Boron, '*Empire*' *and Imperialism* (London, 2005).

91 Negri and Dufourmantelle, *Negri on Negri*, p. 69.

92 Hardt and Negri, *Multitude*, p. 341. See also, e.g., ibid., p. 333.

93 *Financial Times*, 30 November 2004.

94 Holloway, *Change the World Without Taking Power*, pp. 205, 208, 209. For more on these strategic problems, see A. Callinicos, *An Anti-Capitalist Manifesto* (Cambridge, 2003), esp. chs. 2 and 3.

95 Hardt and Negri, *Multitude*, pp. 356, 358.

Chapter 5   A Critical Realist Ontology

1 G. Deleuze, *Spinoza et le problème d'expression* (Paris, 1968), p. 157.

2 M. Hardt and A. Negri, *Empire* (Cambridge, MA, 2000), p. 413.
3 Bhaskar's lapse into spiritualism is announced in *From East to West* (London, 2000). Andrew Collier has written an outstandingly good introduction to Bhaskar's philosophy: *Critical Realism* (London, 1994). I offer critical assessments of Bhaskar's work in 'Le Réalisme critique et au delà', in J. Bidet and E. Kouvelakis, eds, *Dictionnaire Marx contemporain* (Paris, 2001), and in R. Bhaskar and A. Callinicos, 'Marxism and Critical Realism: A Debate', *Journal of Critical Realism*, 1.2 (2003).
4 M. Devitt, *Realism and Truth* (Oxford, 1984), pp. 14, 15–16, 22. The adjective 'objectively' doesn't seem to add anything here: 'To say that an object has an objective existence . . . is to say that its existence and nature is in no way dependent on our epistemic capacities', ibid., p. 13.
5 R. Bhaskar, *The Possibility of Naturalism* (Brighton, 1979), and M. Archer, *Realist Social Theory* (Cambridge, 1995).
6 W. V. Quine, 'On What There Is', in id., *From a Logical Point of View* (New York, 1963).
7 R. Bhaskar, *A Realist Theory of Science* (2nd edn, Hassocks, 1978), p. 39.
8 See ibid., chs. 1 and 2, and, for a critique of Bhaskar's transcendental argument, Callinicos, 'Le Réalisme critique et au-delà', pp. 402–4.
9 D. Bensaïd, *Marx for Our Times* (London, 2003), p. 83.
10 See Bourdieu's splendid *The Political Ontology of Martin Heidegger* (Cambridge, 1991).
11 Bhaskar, *A Realist Theory of Science*, p. 51.
12 R. Harré and E. H. Madden, *Causal Powers* (Oxford, 1975), pp. 5ff. This book, co-authored by Bhaskar's doctoral supervisor, is an important supplement to his writings. See R. Bhaskar, *Dialectic* (London, 1993), pp. 225–6, where he credits Harré with developing 'a *structural*, theoretical, vertical or *existential* realism', and describes his own contribution as 'the development of a "horizontal" *causal*, *transfactual* or depth dynamic nomic realism'.
13 Bhaskar, *A Realist Theory of Science*, p. 98.
14 Ibid., p. 35.
15 Collier, *Critical Realism*, p. 45.
16 Bhaskar, *The Possibility of Naturalism*.
17 Collier, *Critical Realism*, pp. 7–8.
18 Bhaskar, *A Realist Theory of Science*, p. 64.
19 P. Hallward, *Badiou: A Subject to Truth* (Minneapolis, 2003), p. 177. See, on the univocity of Being, G. Deleuze, *Différence et*

répétition (Paris, 1968), pp. 52–61, and A. Badiou, *Deleuze* (Minneapolis, 1999), ch. 2.

20   Deleuze, *Différence et répétition*, p. 53.
21   Id., *Spinoza et le problème d'expression*, p. 166; see, on the crucial notion of real (or formal) but non-numerical distinction, ibid., ch. 1.
22   Badiou, *Deleuze*, p. 25.
23   Deleuze, *Différence et repetition*, pp. 270, 272–3.
24   Ibid., pp. 270–1; see Badiou, *Deleuze*, ch. 4.
25   This way of putting it needs to be qualified to the extent that Deleuze has his own theory of events as meanings that are incorporeal surface effects of physical states of things (*états des choses*): see *Logique du sens* (Paris, 1969). But this distinction needs to be mapped onto that between the actual and the virtual. Thus: 'In general, a state of things doesn't actualize a chaotic virtual without taking from it a *potential* that distributes itself in the system of coordinates', G. Deleuze and F. Guattari, *Qu'est-ce que la philosophie?* (Paris, 1991), p. 116.
26   A. Badiou, *L'Etre et l'événement* (Paris, 1988), p. 363.
27   Id., *Deleuze*, p. 50.
28   Bhaskar, *A Realist Theory of Science*, p. 99.
29   For example, S. Kripke, 'Naming and Necessity', in D. Davidson and G. Harman, eds, *Semantics of Natural Languages* (Dordrecht, 1972), and S. P. Schwartz, ed., *Naming, Necessity, and Natural Kinds* (Ithaca, NY, 1977).
30   B. Greene, *The Elegant Universe* (London, 1999).
31   The Bhaskarian real is plainly also different from the Lacanian Real: for more about this, see my review of S. Žižek, *The Ticklish Subject* (London, 1999), and J. Butler, E. Laclau, and S. Žižek, *Contingency, Hegemony, Universality* (London, 2000), in *Historical Materialism*, 8 (2001).
32   Deleuze and Guattari, *Qu'est-ce-que la philosophie?*
33   Bhaskar, *A Realist Theory of Science*, p. 44; see also ibid., pp. 169ff.
34   Collier, *Critical Realism*, pp. 46, 47, 50.
35   Ibid., pp. 110–11. See also J. H. Holland, *Emergence* (Oxford, 1998).
36   Deleuze, *Différence et repetition*, p. 55.
37   G. Deleuze and F. Guattari, *Mille plateaux* (Paris, 1980), p. 73.
38   P. Bourdieu, *Science de la science et réflexivité* (Paris, 2001), p. 127.
39   Bhaskar, *A Realist Theory of Science*, p. 21.

40   Deleuze, *Spinoza et le problème d'expression*, ch. XI.

41   See, on the difference between physicalism and realism, Devitt, *Realism and Truth*, pp. 23–4.

42   One question that, as far as I know, Bhaskar does not directly address is whether the stratification of the real must be thought of as terminating in some ultimate level. Harré and Madden argue that 'Parmenidean individuals' whose nature is unchanging and identical to their powers are the 'ultimate entities' posited by the natural sciences and suggest that physical fields and the singularities that occur in them are the best candidates for this role: *Causal Powers*, ch. 9.

43   R. Rorty, 'Is Truth a Goal of Inquiry? Davidson vs. Wright', *Philosophical Quarterly*, 45 (1995), p. 282.

44   J. Habermas, 'Richard Rorty's Pragmatic Turn', in R. B. Brandom, ed., *Rorty and His Critics* (Oxford, 2000), pp. 44, 46.

45   A. Giddens, 'Reason without Revolution?', in R. J. Bernstein, ed., *Habermas and Modernity* (Cambridge, 1985), p. 115, and A. Callinicos, *Making History* (2nd edn, Leiden, 2004), §3.4, pp. 119–29.

46   Devitt, *Realism and Truth*, pp. 27–8.

47   A. Badiou, *Théorie du sujet* (Paris, 1982), p. 140. See the interesting discussion of Deleuze's views on truth in id., *Deleuze*, ch. 5.

48   A. Tarski, 'The Concept of Truth in Formalized Languages', in id., *Logic, Mathematics, Metamathematics* (Oxford, 1969).

49   Rorty, 'Is Truth a Goal of Inquiry?', p. 282. See also id., 'Pragmatism, Davidson, and Truth', in E. LePore, ed., *Truth and Interpretation* (Oxford, 1986).

50   Bhaskar, *A Realist Theory of Science*, p. 249. See Collier, *Critical Realism*, pp. 239–42, for a good critique of Bhaskar's rejection of the correspondence theory. Bhaskar later developed a hopelessly confused 'alethic' conception of truth: see, for example, *Dialectic*, pp. 217–20, 319.

51   D. Davidson, 'On the Very Idea of a Conceptual Scheme', in id., *Inquiries into Truth and Interpretation* (Oxford, 1984). John McDowell has a very challenging and probing discussion of Davidson in *Mind and World* (expanded edn, Cambridge, MA, 1996), pp. 129–61.

52   D. Davidson, 'The Structure and Content of Truth', *Journal of Philosophy*, LXXXVII (1990), p. 325.

53   R. Rorty, 'Universality and Truth', in Brandom, ed., *Rorty and His Critics*, p. 16. It is important to see here that 'agreement' does not denote a Habermasian ideal consensus but rather what Wittgenstein calls 'agreement . . . in judgements': *Philosophical*

Investigations (Oxford, 1968), I, §242. Rorty also argues that 'human beings usually divide up into mutually suspicious (*not* mutually unintelligible) communities of justification' ('Universality and Truth', p. 15), but this goes beyond anything Davidson says, and indeed is contradicted by his insistence (registered in Rorty's parenthetical qualification) that the speech of any human being can in principle be understood by any other by virtue of their common nature in a shared world.

54 Davidson, 'The Structure and Content of Truth', p. 303. This text was written in response to Rorty's 'Pragmatism, Davidson, and Truth'; for a critical discussion, see A. Callinicos, *Theories and Narratives* (Cambridge, 1995), pp. 81–2.

55 D. Davidson, 'Truth Rehabilitated', in Brandom, ed., *Rorty and His Critics*, pp. 66, 73. Incidentally, in this essay, Davidson writes: 'We know many things, and will learn more; what we will never know for certain is which of the things we believe are true', ibid., p. 67. But this view – which is entailed by realism when conjoined with the correspondence theory of truth – is precisely what, according to realist critics of Davidson who interpret his Principle of Charity (according to which we must, when interpreting another, ascribe to her largely true beliefs) as anti-realist, he cannot hold: for examples of these (to my mind bizarre) criticisms of Davidson, see Devitt, *Realism and Truth*, ch. 10, and D. Papineau, *Reality and Representation* (Oxford, 1990). In my view, it is less Davidson who is inconsistent here than his critics who are mistaken.

56 P. F. Strawson, 'Truth', in id., *Logico-Linguistic Papers* (London, 1971).

57 Devitt, *Realism and Truth*, pp. 107, 62.

58 Note that I am seeking here to dissociate realism from the issue of whether or not truth is the goal of inquiry. Rorty and Davidson agree that it isn't while disagreeing over truth, while Crispin Wright argues that it is when seeking to defend a version of realism: Rorty, 'Is Truth the Goal of Inquiry?', Davidson, 'Truth Rehabilitated', and C. J. G. Wright, *Truth and Objectivity* (Cambridge, MA, 1992). It seems better to say that, when we seek knowledge, arriving at true beliefs is what counts as success.

59 Collier, *Critical Realism*, p. 239.

60 I. Lakatos, *Philosophical Papers* (2 vols, Cambridge, 1978), I. Lakatos and P. Feyerabend, *For and Against Method* (Chicago, 1999), and J. Kadvany, *Imre Lakatos and the Guises of Reason* (Durham, NC, 2001).

61 Bhaskar, *The Possibility of Naturalism*, p. 3.

62 See esp. D. Davidson, *Essays on Actions and Events* (Oxford, 1980).

63 It would be wrong to see the concepts of stratification and emergence as implying a general ban on reductive explanations. In some cases the latter may succeed. Moreover, for working scientists the cash-value of the concept of emergence seems to be that it allows them to focus on the step-changes through which a qualitatively new pattern arises that is irreducible to the phenomena on which it supervenes, rather than that it mandates peaceful coexistence among different theories: see Holland, *Emergence*. But certainly the moral of conceiving nature as stratified is that the reduction of one level to another is not the default position for scientific inquiry.

64 See, for example, the following exchanges: P. Binns, 'What are the Tasks of Marxism in Philosophy?', *International Socialism*, 2nd ser., 17 (1982), A. Callinicos, 'Marxism and Philosophy: A Reply to Peter Binns', ibid., 2nd ser., 19 (1983), and C. Harman, 'Philosophy and Revolution', ibid., 2nd ser., 21 (1983). The best study of *Materialism and Empirio-Criticism* is D. Lecourt, *Une crise et son enjeu* (Paris, 1973).

65 See also Collier, *Critical Realism*, pp. 15–16, for a good explanation of why '[d]epth realism . . . is . . . transformative and potentially emancipatory'.

66 K. Marx, *Capital*, III (Harmondsworth, 1981), p. 956.

67 For an example of a fairly mainstream critique of the Washington Consensus, see J. Stiglitz, *Globalization and its Discontents* (London, 2002).

68 See A. Callinicos, *Equality* (Cambridge, 2000), ch. 4, the review of this book by Harry Brighouse and Erik Olin Wright in *Historical Materialism*, 10 (2002), and my reply, 'Egalitarianism and Anti-Capitalism', ibid., 11.1 (2003).

Chapter 6   Structure and Contradiction

1 David Lockwood offers a path-breaking critique of normative functionalism in 'Social Integration and System Integration', appendix to id., *Solidarity and Schism* (Oxford, 1992); Althusser contests the charge of functionalism in 'Note sur les AIE', in *Sur la reproduction* (Paris, 1995); Charles Taylor accuses Foucault of functionalism in 'Foucault on Freedom and Truth', in D. C. Hoy, ed., *Foucault* (Oxford, 1986).

2 J. Derrida, 'Structure, Sign, and Play in the Discourse of the Human Sciences', in id., *Writing and Difference* (London, 1978). Perry Anderson critically assesses poststructuralism in the context

of the structure/agency debate in *In the Tracks of Historical Materialism* (London, 1983).

3   A. Giddens, *Central Problems in Social Theory* (London, 1979) and *The Constitution of Society* (Cambridge, 1984), R. Bhaskar, *The Possibility of Naturalism* (Brighton, 1979), and A. Callinicos, *Making History* (2nd edn, Leiden, 2004).

4   E. Laclau and C. Mouffe, *Hegemony and Socialist Strategy* (London, 1985), p. 110.

5   Of course poststructuralists, given their tendency to deny any coherence or originating power to the subject, might be tempted to respond by dissociating the discursive from the mental, but we could respond by restating realism as the claim that the social exists independently of both the mental and the discursive.

6   K. R. Popper, *The Open Society and its Enemies* (2 vols, London, 1973), II, ch. 14.

7   G. A. Cohen, 'Introduction to the 2000 Edition', *Karl Marx's Theory of History* (2nd edn, Oxford, 2000), p. xxiii; see also J. Elster, *Making Sense of Marx* (Cambridge, 1985), J. Roemer, ed., *Analytical Marxism* (Cambridge, 1986), and my discussion of analytical Marxism in *Making History*, esp. pp. xxiv–xxvii, 85–102, and in 'G. A. Cohen and the Critique of Political Economy', forthcoming in *Science and Society*.

8   M. Archer, *Realist Social Theory* (Cambridge, 1995), pp. 9–10.

9   Ibid., pp. 3–4, 66.

10 Ibid., pp. 121, 122, 124, 125; see, generally, ibid., ch. 4. I criticize Giddens's insufficiently emphatic conception of structure in 'Anthony Giddens: A Contemporary Critique', *Theory and Society*, 14 (1985).

11 Archer, *Realist Social Theory*, pp. 73, 70. See ibid., ch. 5, on Bhaskar, and also A. Collier, *Critical Realism* (London, 1994), ch. 8, which makes some analogous criticisms of Bhaskar for overstating the differences between the social and the physical sciences.

12 Archer, *Realist Social Theory*, part II.

13 D. Davidson, *Inquiries into Truth and Interpretation* (Oxford, 1984), p. 137; compare R. Grandy, 'Reference, Meaning, and Belief', *Journal of Philosophy*, LXX (1973). See, for much more discussion of these matters, Callinicos, *Making History*, chs. 1 and 3. Archer endorses the Principle of Humanity: *Realist Social Theory*, p. 281.

14 Archer, *Realist Social Theory*, pp. 106, 177.

15 F. de Saussure, *Course in General Linguistics* (New York, 1966), p. 120.

16 P. Corcuff, 'L'Egalité entre Marx et Rawls', *ContreTemps*, 1 (2001), pp. 148–9.

17 P. Bourdieu, *The Rules of Art* (Cambridge, 1996).

18 See A. Callinicos, *Social Theory* (Cambridge, 1999), pp. 287–95.

19 W. H. Sewell Jr., 'A Theory of Structure: Duality, Agency, and Transformation', *American Journal of Sociology*, 98 (1992) (quotations from pp. 8–9).

20 Id., 'Historical Events as Transformations of Structures: Inventing Revolution at the Bastille', *Theory and Society*, 25 (1996), pp. 843, 879 n. 4.

21 Giddens, *Central Problems in Social Theory*, pp. 69–70.

22 See, for example, D.-H. Ruben, *The Metaphysics of the Social World* (London, 1985), and A. Levine et al., 'Marxism and Methodological Individualism', *New Left Review*, 162 (1987).

23 Callinicos, *Making History*, esp. 'Introduction to the Second Edition', chs. 1 and 2, and Conclusion.

24 Heikki Patomäki offers a critical realist account of financial markets in *Democratizing Globalization* (London, 2001).

25 Callinicos, *Making History*, ch. 4.

26 Id., 'Plumbing the Depths: Marxism and the Holocaust', *Yale Journal of Criticism*, 14 (2001).

27 Lockwood, 'Social Integration and System Integration', pp. 400, 405.

28 Archer, *Realist Social Theory*, p. 69; see also ibid., ch. 7.

29 Cohen, *Karl Marx's Theory of History*, p. 62.

30 Ibid., p. 111. Cohen, however, excludes the material relations of production from the productive forces: see Callinicos, *Making History*, pp. 43–6, and 'G. A. Cohen and the Critique of Political Economy'.

31 The best discussions of these issues will be found in M. Rosen, *The Hegelian Dialectic and its Criticism* (Cambridge, 1982), and J. Rees, *The Algebra of Revolution* (London, 1998). Žižek offers an ingenious but implausible Lacanian reading of Hegel that seeks to explain away the Absolute and the teleological structure of the dialectic: see, for example, *The Ticklish Subject* (London, 1999), ch. 2, and Laclau's highly effective critique in 'Identity and Hegemony', in J. Butler et al., *Contingency, Hegemony, Universality* (London, 2000), pp. 59–64.

32 R. Bhaskar, *Dialectic* (London, 1993), p. 62.

33 G. W. F. Hegel, *Logic* (Oxford, 1975), §120 Zusatz; p. 174.

34 Bhaskar, *Dialectic*, pp. 73, 62. In such discussions 'materialism' covers both realism – in particular, the thesis that the real exists independently of the mental – and Marx's substantive theory of history.

35 L. Colletti, 'Marxism and the Dialectic', *New Left Review*, 93 (1975). See also id., *Marxism and Hegel* (London, 1973).

36   E. Laclau, 'Metaphor and Social Antagonisms', in G. Nelson and L. Grossberg, eds., *Marxism and the Interpretation of Culture* (Basingstoke, 1988), pp. 255–6.

37   Id., 'Identity and Hegemony', p. 70.

38   Laclau and Mouffe, *Hegemony and Socialist Strategy*, p. 113.

39   Laclau, 'Metaphor and Social Antagonisms', pp. 254–5.

40   Laclau and Mouffe, *Hegemony and Socialist Strategy*, p. 113.

41   Laclau, 'Identity and Hegemony', pp. 58, 72, 79.

42   Bhaskar, *Dialectic*, pp. 4–5, 49, 48. For critical assessments of this book, see A. Callinicos, 'Le Réalisme critique et au-delà', in J. Bidet and E. Kouvelakis, *Dictionnaire Marx contemporain* (Paris, 2001), and S. Craven, 'The Pulse of Freedom? Bhaskar's *Dialectic* and Marxism', *Historical Materialism*, 10 (2002).

43   Bhaskar, *Dialectic*, p. 58.

44   Callinicos, *Making History*, p. 56.

45   R. Harré and E. Madden, *Causal Powers* (Oxford, 1975).

46   See, for example, T. Smith, *The Logic of Marx's 'Capital'* (Albany, NY, 1990), C. J. Arthur, *The New Dialectic and Marx's 'Capital'* (Leiden, 2002), and – in criticism – A. Callinicos, 'Against the New Dialectic', *Historical Materialism*, 13.2 (2005).

47   This is an enormously controversial subject: see esp. Cohen, *Karl Marx's Theory of History*, and Callinicos, *Making History*, 'Introduction to the Second Edition' and ch. 2.

48   Marx, *Capital*, III (Harmondsworth, 1981), p. 319. The TRPF is, once again, a highly controversial subject: see M. C. Howard and J. E. King, *A History of Marxist Economics* (2 vols, London, 1989, 1992), esp. II. The present state of the discussion is well represented in the debate provoked by Robert Brenner's analysis of post-war capitalism: see *Historical Materialism*, 4 and 5 (1999). For a state-of-the-art survey of theoretical issues in Marxist political economy, see A. Saad-Filho, *The Value of Marx* (London, 2002).

49   For treatments of profitability crisis as a cyclical phenomenon consequent on the interaction of tendencies and counter-tendencies, see B. Fine and L. Harris, *Rereading 'Capital'* (London, 1979), and G. Reuten, ' "*Zirkel Vicieux*" or Trend Cycle? The Course of the Profit Rate in Marx's *Capital* III', *History of Political Economy*, 36 (2004).

50   Marx, *Capital*, I (Harmondsworth, 1976), ch. 23.

51   R. Brenner, 'The Social Basis of Economic Development', in Roemer, ed., *Analytical Marxism*.

52   K. Marx, *Grundrisse* (Harmondsworth, 1973), pp. 100, 101.

53   Rees, *The Algebra of Revolution*, p. 7; see esp. ibid., ch. 2.

54 Laclau, 'Metaphor and Social Antagonisms', p. 254.

55 Laclau and Mouffe, *Hegemony and Socialist Strategy*, p. 88 n. 1. See also ibid., pp. 105, 113.

56 Incidentally, Michael Mann's argument that social theory should think societies as open networks rather than closed totalities in no way threatens the Marxist conception of totality discussed here: see *The Sources of Social Power*, I (Cambridge, 1986), ch. 1. This argument is directed in particular against the idea that societies must be conceived as having clearly delimited spatial boundaries (typically co-extensive with nation-states). But one can grant this and still maintain that societies have structural properties that are ordered in the kind of way outlined in this section. To believe that the spatially unbounded character of societies counts against the Marxist conception of totality is to confuse two different levels of determination.

57 K. Marx, *Theories of Surplus-Value* (3 vols, Moscow, 1963–72), II, p. 500.

58 Ibid., III, p. 88. See the discussion of these and related passages in Rees, *The Algebra of Revolution*, pp. 99–107.

59 See A. W. Wood, *Hegel's Ethical Thought* (Cambridge, 1990), A. Callinicos, *Social Theory* (Cambridge, 1999), ch. 2, and S. Kouvelakis, *Philosophy and Revolution* (London, 2003), ch. 1.

60 Letter to Engels, 30 April 1868, in K. Marx and F. Engels, *Selected Correspondence* (Moscow, 1965), p. 208.

61 J. Holloway, *Change the World without Taking Power* (London, 2002), p. 1.

62 See A. Callinicos, 'Sympathy for the Devil? John Holloway's Mephistophelean Marxism', *Capital and Class*, 85 (2005), J. Holloway and A. Callinicos, 'Can We Change the World without Taking Power?', *International Socialism*, 2nd ser., 106 (2005), and D. Bensaïd, 'Le Pouvoir et la révolution', in id., *Un monde à changer* (Paris, 2003).

63 Laclau and Mouffe, *Hegemony and Socialist Strategy*, chs. 1 and 2.

64 D. Bensaïd, *Marx for Our Times* (London, 2002), p. 23. For much more on these topics see, in addition to Bensaïd's brilliant 'La Politique comme art stratégique', in id., *Un monde à changer*, Callinicos, *Making History*, chs. 4 and 5, and id., *Theories and Narratives* (Cambridge, 1995), chs. 3 and 4.

65 I. Kant, *The Critique of Judgement* (Oxford, 1973), p. 5.

66 See, for example, S. H. Holtzmann and C. M. Leich, eds, *Wittgenstein: To Follow a Rule* (London, 1981), and S. Kripke, *Wittgenstein on Rules and Private Language* (Oxford, 1982).

67 L. Colletti, 'A Political and Philosophical Interview', *New Left Review*, 86 (1974), p. 16.

68 J. Roemer, '"Rational Choice" Marxism', in id., ed., *Analytical Marxism*, p. 191.

69 Bhaskar, *Dialectic*, pp. 150–2.

70 T. Pinkard, *Hegel's Phenomenology* (Cambridge, 1994).

71 G. W. F. Hegel, *Philosophy of Nature* (Oxford, 1970), §247 Zusatz; p. 14.

72 F. Engels, *Dialectics of Nature* (Moscow, 1972), pp. 24, 27. See generally P. McGarr, 'Engels and Natural Science', *International Socialism*, 2.65 (1994).

73 Bensaïd, *Marx for Our Times*, p. 288.

74 Engels, *Dialectics of Nature*, p. 63.

75 For contrasting treatments of the negation of the negation, see L. Althusser, 'Marx's Relation to Hegel', in id., *Politics and History* (London, 1972), Bhaskar, *Dialectic*, p. 152, Rees, *The Algebra of Revolution*, pp. 103–4, and Arthur, *The New Dialectic and Marx's 'Capital'*, ch. 6.

76 See D. Lecourt, *Proletarian Science?* (London, 1977).

77 P. Pomper, ed., *Trotsky's Notebooks 1933–1935* (New York, 1986), pp. 88, 89. See Rees, *The Algebra of Revolution*, ch. 6.

78 Pomper, ed., *Trotsky's Philosophical Notebooks 1933–1935*, p. 92.

79 For example, R. Dawkins, *The Blind Watchmaker* (London, 1991), D. Dennett, *Darwin's Dangerous Idea* (London, 1995), N. Eldredge, *Reinventing Darwin* (London, 1995), S. J. Gould, *The Structure of Evolutionary Theory* (Cambridge, MA, 2002), R. Levins and R. Lewontin, *The Dialectical Biologist* (Cambridge, MA, 1985), S. Rose, *Lifelines* (London, 1995), E. Sober, *The Nature of Selection* (Chicago, 1993).

80 B. Greene, *The Elegant Universe* (London, 2000), ch. 14.

81 For example, I. Prirogine and I. Stengers, *Order Out of Chaos* (London, 1984), P. McGarr, 'Order Out of Chaos', *International Socialism*, 2.48 (1990), and S. Kauffman, *At Home in the Universe* (London, 1996). Bensaïd compares Marx's method in *Capital* to chaos theory: *Marx for Our Times*, ch. 10.

82 Prirogine and Stengers, *Order Out of Chaos*, p. 252.

83 J. H. Holland, *Emergence* (Oxford, 1998), pp. 225–9.

84 Bhaskar, *Dialectic*, p. 98. I am indebted to Phil Gasper for the formulation of multiple dialectics of nature.

85 R. Dawkins, *River Out of Eden* (London, 1996), p. 155.

86 Kauffman, *At Home in the Universe*, pp. 304, 217.

Chapter 7   Justice and Universality

1 For two interesting discussions of these and related difficulties, see R. Geuss, *The Idea of a Critical Theory* (Cambridge, 1981), and E. Renault, *Marx et l'idée de critique* (Paris, 1995).

2 Steven Lukes presents the problem lucidly in *Marxism and Morality* (Oxford, 1986). Terry Eagleton offers a powerful vindication of morality in *After Theory* (London, 2003), esp. chs. 5 and 6.

3 F. Jameson, *Postmodernism, or, The Cultural Logic of Late Capitalism* (London, 1991), p. 46.

4 S. Kouvelakis, *Philosophy and Revolution* (London, 2003), pp. 23, 18.

5 For example, G. Comninel, *Rethinking the French Revolution* (London, 1987); compare E. J. Hobsbawm, *Echoes of the Marseillaise* (London, 1989), and A. Callinicos and P. McGarr, *Marxism and the Great French Revolution* (London, 1993).

6 Kouvelakis, *Philosophy and Revolution*, p. 18.

7 Derrida's reflections on law and justice are, among other things, an exploration of the ambiguities of this vocabulary: *Force de loi* (Paris, 1994).

8 Kouvelakis has discussed Badiou, in 'La Politique dans ses limites, ou les paradoxes de Alain Badiou', *Actuel Marx*, 28 (2000), from a sympathetic but critical perspective that has strong affinities with the approach taken by Žižek (see §3.3 above).

9 N. Geras, 'The Controversy about Marx and Justice', *New Left Review*, 100 (1985).

10 K. Marx, *Capital*, III (Harmondsworth, 1981), p. 911.

11 See, for example, G. A. Cohen, *Self-Ownership, Freedom, and Equality* (Cambridge, 1995), and *If You're an Egalitarian, How Come You're So Rich* (Cambridge, MA, 2000).

12 A. Callinicos, 'Having Your Cake and Eating It', *Historical Materialism*, 9 (2001).

13 D. Bensaïd, *Marx for Our Times* (London, 2002), p. 158; see generally ibid., ch. 5. Bensaïd does, however, qualify his dismissal of justice: 'The collapse of the bureaucratically managed economies and the questions involved in the ecological crisis oblige us to conceptualize the transition to socialism (including its juridical dimension) in more precise terms than Marx. When principle and practice are no longer at loggerheads, a critical theory of justice could be a precious contribution in this context. For the "narrow horizon of bourgeois right" can be positively transcended only at the end of a protracted process' (ibid., p. 155). But this seems to confine the relevance of justice (conflated, as Kouvelakis does, with

the juridical) to the transition to what Marx in the 'Critique of the Gotha Programme' calls 'the higher stage of communist society': the confusions about justice in this text are discussed in A. Callinicos, *Equality* (Cambridge, 2000), pp. 81–2.

14 Callinicos, *Equality*, esp. ch. 4.

15 B. A. O. Williams, *Ethics and the Limits of Philosophy* (London, 1985).

16 M. Walzer, *Spheres of Justice* (Oxford, 1983), and M. Sandel, *Liberalism and the Limits of Justice* (Cambridge, 1982).

17 B. Barry, *Culture and Equality* (Cambridge, 2001), p. 331 n. 27.

18 See A. Callinicos, *Against the Third Way* (Cambridge, 2001), ch. 3, and P. Anderson, 'Arms and Rights', *New Left Review*, 2nd ser., 31 (2005).

19 K. Marx, *Theories of Surplus-Value* (3 vols, Moscow, 1963–72), II, p. 174.

20 G. A. Cohen, 'On the Currency of Egalitarian Justice', *Ethics*, 99 (1989). See, for surveys of these debates, J. Roemer, *Theories of Distributive Justice* (Cambridge, MA, 1996), and Callinicos, *Equality*, pp. 52–64.

21 A. K. Sen, 'Equality of What?', in id., *Choice, Welfare and Measurement* (Oxford, 1982), and *Inequality Reexamined* (Oxford, 1992).

22 R. Dworkin, *Sovereign Virtue* (Cambridge, MA, 2000), ch. 1.

23 Ibid., ch. 2.

24 E. S. Anderson, 'What is the Point of Equality?', *Ethics*, 109 (1999).

25 Dworkin, *Sovereign Virtue*, p. 287.

26 For example, A. K. Sen, *Development as Freedom* (Oxford, 1999).

27 Ibid., p. 75.

28 G. A. Cohen, 'Equality of What? On Welfare, Goods, and Capabilities', in M. Nussbaum and A. K. Sen, eds, *The Quality of Life* (Oxford, 1993), p. 28. See also id., 'On the Currency of Egalitarian Justice'.

29 Roemer, *Theories of Distributive Justice*, pp. 249, 309, and Callinicos, *Equality*, pp. 62–4, and, on adaptive preferences, J. Elster, *Sour Grapes* (Cambridge, 1983).

30 For example, R. Arneson, 'Equality and Equal Opportunity for Welfare', *Philosophical Studies*, 56 (1989).

31 J. Griffin, *Well-Being* (Oxford, 1986), pp. 56, 62, 70; see generally ibid., ch. IV.

32 L. Doyal and I. Gough, *A Theory of Human Need* (Basingstoke, 1991).

33 Griffin, *Well-Being*, pp. 46, 53, 54.

34 Ibid., pp. 372 n. 26, 11, 30, 105. See also ibid., pp. 29–30, 137, 155, on the inadequacy of the dualisms of subjective and objective, desire and understanding.

35 Ibid., pp. 122, 137, 156–7, 208, 210, 239.

36 I. Kant, *Groundwork of the Metaphysics of Morals*, in id., *Practical Philosophy* (Cambridge, 1996), p. 80. For Rawls's criticisms of utilitarianism see, for example, *A Theory of Justice* (rev. edn, Oxford, 1999), pp. 19–24, 160–8, and, for Griffin's discussion of these matters, *Well-Being*, chs IX and X.

37 Nietzsche's importance as a critic of moral discourse is, of course, one of the main themes of Alasdair MacIntyre's *After Virtue* (London, 1981).

38 Griffin, *Well-Being*, p. 38.

39 J. Raz, *The Morality of Freedom* (Oxford, 1986), pp. 289, 318, 370. See ibid., pp. 140–2, on 'the reason-dependent character of desire'. It is worth comparing both Griffin and Raz on the relationship between reasons and desires with T. M. Scanlon's brilliant treatment of this topic in *What We Owe to Each Other* (Cambridge, MA, 1998), ch. 1.

40 Griffin, *Well-Being*, pp. 89, 90; see generally ibid., chs V, VI, VII, and X.

41 Raz, *The Morality of Freedom*, p. 346; see generally ibid., ch. 13.

42 Raz, *The Morality of Freedom*, p. 240; see generally ibid., ch. 9.

43 See, on these issues, T. M. Scanlon, 'The Diversity of Objections to Inequality', D. Parfit, 'Equality or Priority?', and L. Temkin, 'Equality, Priority, and the Levelling Down Objection', all reprinted in M. Clayton and A. Williams, eds, *The Ideal of Equality* (Basingstoke, 2000).

44 J. Waldron, 'Two Essays on Basic Equality', consulted at www.law.nyu.edu, 30 April 2001, pp. 3, 21.

45 See, for example, D. Miller, *Principles of Social Justice* (Cambridge, 1999), ch. 7.

46 Waldron, 'Two Essays on Basic Equality', p. 71. Waldron develops the idea of a range property in ibid., pp. 62–8; compare Rawls, *A Theory of Justice*, pp. 444–5.

47 Rawls, *A Theory of Justice*, pp. 442, 443.

48 Waldron, 'Two Essays on Basic Equality', p. 74.

49 Raz, *The Morality of Freedom*, p. 228.

50 Quoted in Waldron, 'Two Essays on Basic Equality', pp. 8, 9. I am grateful to Chris Bertram for drawing to my attention to this passage, and to the paper by Waldron in which it is quoted.

51 '100,000 Excess Civilian Deaths After Iraq Invasion', *The Lancet*, 29 October 2004.

52 M. Hastings, *Overlord* (London, 1984), p. 50.
53 T. W. Pogge, *World Poverty and Human Rights* (Cambridge, 2002), pp. 97–8. Mike Davis puts mass killing by famine in the longer term context of the impact of liberal capitalism on non-European societies in his masterpiece *Late Victorian Holocausts* (London, 2001).
54 United Nations Development Programme, *Human Development Report 1999* (New York, 1999), p. 3. Pogge and Sanjay Reddy are highly critical of the World Bank's methodology, which has been used to produce estimates suggesting a steep decline in global poverty and inequality: see, for example, (2003) 'Unknown: The Extent, Distribution, and Trajectory of Global Income Poverty', www.columbia.edu.
55 Pogge, *World Poverty and Human Rights*, p. 2.
56 T. W. Pogge, 'Priorities of Global Justice', in id., ed., *Global Justice* (Oxford, 2001), p. 13.
57 US Department of Defense, News Release, 7 February 2005, www.dod.mil.
58 Pogge, 'Priorities of Global Justice', p. 14.
59 Ibid., p. 19. Pogge offers some institutional reforms aimed at limiting these privileges in *World Poverty and Human Rights*, ch. 6.
60 See the discussion of inequalities in the North in Callinicos, *Equality*, pp. 3–12.
61 Pogge, *World Poverty and Human Rights*, pp. 132, 144.
62 See, for example, Griffin, *Well-Being*, p. 333 n. 19.
63 See Barry, *Culture and Equality*, pp. 32, 37–8, and id., *Why Social Justice Matters* (Cambridge, 2005), ch. 2.
64 See also A. Callinicos, *Making History* (2nd edn, Leiden, 2004).
65 M. Mann, *The Sources of Social Power* (2 vols, Cambridge, 1986, 1993).
66 J. Bidet, *John Rawls et la théorie de la justice* (Paris, 1995), esp. ch. V.
67 J. Rawls, *The Law of Peoples* (Cambridge, MA, 1999), p. 117; see generally ibid., pp. 105–20.
68 Rawls, *A Theory of Justice*, p. 89. Pogge also accuses Rawls of double standards: *World Poverty and Human Rights*, ch. 4.
69 B. Barry, 'Statism and Nationalism: A Cosmopolitan Critique', in I. Shapiro and L. Brilmayer, eds, *Global Justice: Nomos XLI* (New York, 1999), p. 36. Charles Beitz offers a classical statement of the case for cosmopolitan principles of justice in *Political Theory and International Relations* (rev. edn, Princeton, NJ, 1999). See also the essays collected in Pogge, ed., *Global Justice*, and in the Nomos volume cited above.

70 G. Arrighi, 'The African Crisis', *New Left Review*, 2nd ser., 15 (2002), quotation from pp. 35–6. Compare this analysis with Sen's approach to poverty in *Development as Freedom*, which, for all its subtlety, veers dangerously close to the Washington Consensus view.

Chapter 8   Conclusion

1 There is a good discussion of the idea of immanent critique in M. Rosen, *Hegel's Dialectic and its Criticism* (Cambridge, 1982), ch. 1, which shows the dependence of the claim that such critique produces positive results on Hegel's speculative conception of determinate negation.

2 P. K. Feyerabend, *Science in a Free Society* (London, 1978), p. 34.

3 R. G. Collingwood's account in *An Essay on Metaphysics* (Oxford, 1940) of how metaphysics makes explicit the 'absolute presuppositions' of the sciences is still in many ways compelling, despite the relativist gloss he puts on the process. The complexities of the Copernican revolution are brilliantly conveyed in H. Blumenberg, *The Genesis of the Copernican World* (Cambridge, MA, 1987).

4 M. C. Howard and J. E. King, *A History of Marxist Economics* (2 vols, London, 1989, 1992), esp. I.

5 D. Harvey, *The New Imperialism* (Oxford, 2003), pp. 26, 30. Harvey's most important earlier works are *The Limits to Capital* (Oxford, 1982) and *The Condition of Postmodernity* (Oxford, 1989). Arrighi's *chef d'œuvre* is *The Long Twentieth Century* (London, 1994). I consider Harvey's overall contribution to Marxism in 'David Harvey and the Classics', in N. Castree and D. Gregory, eds, *David Harvey: Critical Perspectives* (Oxford, 2006).

6 For my own interpretation, starting from theoretical premises very similar to Harvey's, see *The New Mandarins of American Power* (Cambridge, 2003).

7 Important discussions of this enterprise include J. Rancière, 'Le Concept de critique et la critique de l'économie politique dès les *Manuscrits* de 1844 au *Capital*', in L. Althusser et al., *Lire le Capital* (4 vols, Paris, 1973), E. Renault, *Marx et l'idée de critique* (Paris, 1995), and H.-G. Backhaus, 'Some Aspects of Marx's Concept of Critique in the Context of his Economic-Philosophical Theory', in W. Bonefeld and K. Psychopedis, eds, *Human Dignity* (Aldershot, 2005).

8 Reinhart Koselleck goes further, arguing that the Enlightenment critique of Absolutism was the source of the crisis of modern society: *Critique and Crisis* (Oxford, 1988).

9   S. Žižek, *The Ticklish Subject* (London, 1999), p. 137.
10 G. Lukács, *History and Class Consciousness* (London, 1971), p. 168.
11 Ibid., pp. 172, 149.
12 A. Callinicos, *Making History* (2nd edn, Leiden, 2004), pp. 152–6.
13 Lukács, *History and Class Consciousness*, pp. 121–2, 149. For an important critique of Lukács's ultra-Hegelianism, see G. Stedman-Jones, 'The Marxism of the Early Lukács', *New Left Review*, 70 (1971).
14 A. Callinicos, *Social Theory* (Cambridge, 1999), p. 208.
15 P. Bourdieu, *Pascalian Meditations* (Cambridge, 2000), p. 99.
16 F. Jameson, *The Political Unconscious* (London, 1981), pp. 52–3. On this basis Jameson seeks to reconcile Lukács and Althusser, arguing that 'Althusserian structure, like all Marxisms, necessarily insists on the interrelatedness of all elements in a social formation; only it relates them by way of their structural *difference* and distance from one another . . . Difference is then here understood as a relational concept, rather than as the mere inert inventory of unrelated diversity' (p. 41).
17 See, for example, G. Guttiérrez, *A Theology of Liberation* (London, 1974), esp. ch. 13, and M. Löwy, *The War of Gods* (London, 1996).
18 E. Dussel, *Towards an Unknown Marx* (London, 2001), esp. chs 1 and 14 and appendix 2 (quotation from p. 8).
19 K. Marx and F. Engels, *Collected Works*, XXX (Moscow, 1988), pp. 170–1; see also Marx, *Grundrisse* (Harmondsworth, 1973), pp. 295–6.
20 This incorporation, however, takes highly complex forms: see, for example, M. Davis, 'Planet of Slums', *New Left Review*, 2nd ser., 26 (2004). Despite embracing the language of poverty recommended by Dussel, Hardt and Negri make the same point as I do in the text: *Multitude* (New York, 2004), pp. 152–3.
21 Žižek, *The Ticklish Subject*, pp. 198–9.
22 The best statement of this view remains Nicos Poulantzas's last book, *State, Power, Socialism* (London, 1978), though it is best read in conjunction with Chris Harman's magisterial 'The State and Capitalism Today', *International Socialism*, 2nd ser., 51 (1991). Two useful attempts to situate the Marxist theory of the state today are B. Jessop, *The Future of the Capitalist State* (Cambridge, 2002), and M. Rupert and H. Smith, eds, *Historical Materialism and Globalization* (London, 2002).
23 Žižek, *The Ticklish Subject*, pp. 189, 190. Žižek presumably has in mind Engels's remark that under communism 'the government

of persons is replaced by the administration of things'; K. Marx and F. Engels, *Collected Works*, XXIV (London, 1989), p. 321.

24 Ibid., p. 519. See the critical discussion of this passage in J. Elster, *Making Sense of Marx* (Cambridge, 1985), pp. 456–8.

25 J. Rawls, *A Theory of Justice* (rev. edn, Oxford, 1999), pp. 109–12.

26 See A. Callinicos, *The Revenge of History* (Cambridge, 1991), pp. 118–33.

27 Žižek, *The Ticklish Subject*, p. 241 n. 20.

28 V. I. Lenin, *Collected Works*, XXXII (Moscow, 1964), p. 32.

29 D. Bensaïd, *Une lente impatience* (Paris, 2004), p. 121; see generally ibid., ch. 7, and id., 'La Politique comme art stratégique', in id., *Un monde à changer* (Paris, 2003).

30 For discussions of democratic economic structures and their guiding principles, see M. Albert, *Parecon* (London, 2003), and A. Callinicos, *An Anti-Capitalist Manifesto* (Cambridge, 2003), ch. 3.

31 Hardt and Negri, *Multitude*, p. xiv.

32 Gopal Balakrishnan invokes Machiavelli in a way that at least partially coincides with the approach taken here: 'Future Unknown', *New Left Review*, 2nd ser., 32 (2005).

Index